Modeling Enterprise Architecture with TOGAF®

Modeling Enterprise Architecture with TOGAF®
A Practical Guide Using UML and BPMN

Philippe Desfray – Gilbert Raymond

AMSTERDAM • BOSTON • HEIDELBERG • LONDON
NEW YORK • OXFORD • PARIS • SAN DIEGO
SAN FRANCISCO • SINGAPORE • SYDNEY • TOKYO

Morgan Kaufmann is an imprint of Elsevier

Acquiring Editor: Andrea Dierna
Editorial Project Manager: Kaitlin Herbert
Project Manager: Malathi Samayan
Designer: Mark Rogers

Morgan Kaufmann is an imprint of Elsevier
225 Wyman Street, Waltham, MA 02451, USA

Notices

Knowledge and best practice in this field are constantly changing. As new research and experience broaden our understanding, changes in research methods or professional practices, may become necessary. Practitioners and researchers must always rely on their own experience and knowledge in evaluating and using any information or methods described here in. In using such information or methods they should be mindful of their own safety and the safety of others, including parties for whom they have a professional responsibility.

To the fullest extent of the law, neither the Publisher nor the authors, contributors, or editors, assume any liability for any injury and/or damage to persons or property as a matter of products liability, negligence or otherwise, or from any use or operation of any methods, products, instructions, or ideas contained in the material herein.

Library of Congress Cataloging-in-Publication Data
Desfray, Philippe.
    Modeling enterprise architecture with TOGAF : a practical guide using UML and BPMN / Philippe Desfray, Gilbert Raymond.
        pages cm
    Includes bibliographical references and index.
    ISBN 978-0-12-419984-2 (paperback)
1. Computer network architectures–Computer simulation. 2. Workflow–Management–Computer simulation. 3. UML (Computer science) I. Raymond, Gilbert. II. Title. III. Title: Modeling enterprise architecture with The Open Group Architecture Framework.
    TK5105.52.D47 2014
    658.4′0380285–dc23

                                                                                2014003631

British Library Cataloguing-in-Publication Data
A catalogue record for this book is available from the British Library

ISBN: 978-0-12-419984-2

Printed and bound in the United States of America
14 15 16   13 12 11 10 9 8 7 6 5 4 3 2 1

For information on all MK publications
visit our website at www.mkp.com or www.elsevierdirect.com

Working together
to grow libraries in
developing countries

www.elsevier.com • www.bookaid.org

Contents

Preface

AIM OF THIS BOOK

Today TOGAF[a] is widely recognized as a standard for enterprise architecture. The TOGAF framework focuses on the architecture transformation method in all its dimensions (business, organization, and information system).

Since enterprise architecture often uses representations and models, both valuable instruments in elaboration and communication, the aim of this book is to provide a hands-on practitioner's view of TOGAF and, notably, of the models used during transformation work.

We chose to build these models using the most widely used standards, such as UML and BPMN. Specific UML extensions (a UML profile dedicated to TOGAF) are provided in this book to further explain all necessary concepts. We have also aligned this modeling technique with ArchiMate,[b] which is explained in a dedicated appendix to this book.

This book does not replace the TOGAF reference specification.[c] Read as an initiation into or an accompaniment to the standard, it presents both the foundations of the TOGAF framework and tangible enterprise architecture elements.

We hope that this book will be a useful tool in your TOGAF-based enterprise transformation projects.

TOGAF is not the only enterprise architecture framework. Zachman, DODAF, MODAF, NAF, EAF, and even ITIL for certain aspects, all broach the subject of enterprise architecture in their own way. The number of frameworks available is probably explained by the complexity of the subject, as well as the diversity of situations encountered within different enterprises. As a consequence, TOGAF should not be considered as the "miracle cure," but rather as a proposal capable of bringing together a number of practices around its architecture development method (ADM).

The inevitably generic nature of TOGAF can sometimes be disconcerting. However, TOGAF is generally intended to be customized in order to instantiate the method for a particular use.

WHO IS THIS BOOK FOR?

From a general standpoint, this book is for anyone interested in enterprise architecture, from enterprise analysts and architects to project managers and business owners, from business managers and CIOs to students and consultants.

No prior knowledge of TOGAF is necessary before reading this book. Wherever possible, we have provided links to the corresponding chapters in the TOGAF documentation. Interested readers can refer to these chapters for more detailed information on certain points, or to consult related sections of the

---

[a]TOGAF® Version 9.1. USA: ©2009–2012 The Open Group. TOGAF is a registered trademark of The Open Group in the United States and other countries.
[b]ArchiMate (Version 2.0) is a registered trademark of The Open Group in the United States and other countries.
[c]TOGAF Version 9.1—The Open Group, http://www.opengroup.org/togaf/.

TOGAF documentation. References to UML and BPMN are relatively limited, and should be readily understandable to all readers who have already worked with the models.

This book is structured into two main parts:

- Part 1 (Chapters 1–4) describes the TOGAF standard and its structure, from the architecture transformation method through to governance.
- Part 2 (Chapters 5–11) presents practices and examples of enterprise architecture modeling. An example is provided for each TOGAF view, in the context of a case study.

Chapter 12 revisits three major themes of enterprise architecture: service-oriented architecture (SOA), business processes, and information. Chapter 13 presents two hands-on testimonials. Chapters 14 and 15 present ArchiMate and the EAP profile.

Additional elements online

The examples in this book were developed using the Modelio modeling tool, which provides the following useful features to support TOGAF modeling:

- UML and BPMN support
- Support of the "UML profile" extension mechanism
- Catalog and matrix generation
- Support of goal analysis and requirement analysis
- Traceability management

An open-source version of the Modelio tool can be downloaded from www.modelio.org. This version enables users to access the model database containing the examples presented in this book.

The model examples provided in Chapters 6–11 can be downloaded from www.togaf-modeling.org/togaf-en-pratique/.

ACKNOWLEDGMENTS

We would like to take this opportunity to thank Yves Caseau, Alain Delfin, Marc Garagnon, Tony Marchand, Pierre Moyen, Jim Amsden, and Joan Le Bris, as well as SOFTEAM's entire consulting team, for their contributions and experience-based input.

Foreword

Enterprise architecture is the principal formal tool available to general managers working on the continuous transformations that are necessary to their business. We live in a world characterized by its complexity—the richness of interactions and the speed of perpetual change. Consequently, the evolution of system architecture has been twofold. First, we switched from information system architecture to enterprise architecture to reflect the complex relationships between the information system and its stakeholders. Second, we abandoned the static vision of architecture, which describes a target by means of a "blueprint" that must be rigorously built for a more dynamic view, focusing on the continuous enrichment of the "situational potential" of the company and its information system. The ongoing transformation is based on a double alignment: that of all stakeholders around common objectives and capabilities and that of the potential of the "system" on the "opportunities" of the business environment, designated as "strategic alignment."

Enterprise architecture remains a difficult art that requires the support of methods like TOGAF from The Open Group. Enterprise architecture is primarily an act of communication between senior management, business management, and IT specialists. It therefore needs a common language and a consensus on words and their meanings. Enterprise architecture is a collective practice that aims to find compromise between divergent views and that requires each party to cooperate for the common good. For this reason, an external repository is required as an exogenous justification of the steps and the effort required of each participant. According to TOGAF, architecture is not just a matter for IT specialists but rather a subject that concerns all roles within a company. Because this is a complex proposal, it must follow a method, and this is precisely what TOGAF offers and what this book deals with. Enterprise architecture is a difficult subject, and we should use other people's work and enjoy their "best practices," which is exactly how TOGAF has been built over the years, from the 1990s onward.

TOGAF is the result of very large-scale group work, and is a "treasure chest" that requires a guide and a manual. The book you have in your hands is the key to this chest, and is designed to enable you to enjoy these treasures without getting lost. TOGAF has been developed openly, and the main TOGAF documents are available online. However, these documents are extremely rich (the result of group work) and somewhat intimidating because of the inevitable complexity of the metamodel that structures the approach. Nonetheless, this architecture approach metamodel is the very cornerstone of enterprise architecture, and this book presents it in a very clear and progressive way. The boxes you will find throughout the book explain concepts and definitions using practical knowledge resulting from the extensive experience of the authors.

System architecture is not learned by reading a book, but rather through hands-on experience. However, the use of a method that follows the approach of the TOGAF framework will enable better capitalization and most importantly easier communication with other architects. It is interesting to understand the genesis of TOGAF: committee work consists of bringing together best practices, and filtering them according to how their relevance is perceived by each member of the work group. This still results in a very rich volume of material, which is not necessarily "coherent" precisely because it is too rich and does not have the consistency of an approach proposed by a small group of people. TOGAF provides a *checklist* to ensure that the enterprise architecture approach that you are using will not end up in a dead end, a *toolkit* whose aim is not to implement all best practices but rather to import those that consolidate the weaknesses of your own practices, and a *standard*. The use of a standard is essential if we are to share, compare, and learn from other companies.

This book will be a tremendous time-saver for those who want to become familiar with TOGAF, by clearly indicating the strengths of the method and by providing the more personal view of the authors as a backdrop, enabling TOGAF to be situated in the context of the main IS architecture trends around business objects, services, and processes. One of the most important points is the compatibility between TOGAF and the iterative process, which produces architecture through successive refinements. Constraints linked to complexity and agility have led to the diversification of development methods, which include more and more "agile methods" based on rapid iterations. This possibility of iteratively declining TOGAF is essential, since enterprise architecture is a "fractal" approach, spanning everything from the overall vision of the company to the "simple" information system component development project. The concept of the "solution concept diagram" proposed by TOGAF, which is very well explained in this book, is an iterative and fractal approach to the design of subsystems, starting with a simple and comprehensive vision that can be shared with future clients and users. This is exactly what could be called "agile architecture."

Yves Caseau
Deputy Director General, Bougues Telecom, Technologies,
Services and Innovation
Member of the Academy of Technologies

TOGAF®: General Presentation

CHAPTER OUTLINE

This chapter presents the foundations, positioning, and principles of TOGAF and introduces some dedicated vocabulary, as well as the structure and key concepts of the framework. It also discusses the architecture development method (ADM) as an enterprise architecture transformation approach integrating different facets (business, system, technical) into its process and the place of the organization.

1.1 WHAT IS TOGAF?

1.1.1 Positioning and history

TOGAF[1] has long been recognized as a major reference in the field of enterprise architecture. It is successful because it meets a real need: the need for a common framework that will facilitate the capitalization and mutualization of architectural practices throughout a community. More specifically,

---

[1]The Open Group Architecture Framework; www.opengroup.org/togaf.

TOGAF is positioned as a generic method, which groups together a set of techniques focusing on the transformation of enterprise architecture.

Developed by The Open Group (TOG) international consortium, the current version of TOGAF (version 9.1, December 2011) is the result of work carried out over several years by dozens of companies. Released in 1995, the first version of TOGAF was based on TAFIM,[2] itself developed by the DOD.[3] Initially built as a technical framework, TOGAF then evolved, resulting in version 8 ("Enterprise Edition") in 2003, whose content focused more on the enterprise and the business. Version 9 continued and built on this orientation. In 2008 a certification program was put in place, and today more than 20,000 people around the world are TOGAF-certified.

> It should be noted that TOGAF can be applied to all types of architecture, including architecture based on enterprise resource planning systems. One example of this is SAP, who provide their own architecture framework[4] (EAF) as an adaptation of TOGAF.

The sheer size of the TOGAF reference document (nearly 750 pages) should not overshadow the orientation of the project, which focuses on the enterprise architecture transformation approach. This approach, described by the ADM, constitutes the heart of the reference document.

1.1.2 "A" for Enterprise Architecture

The "A" of TOGAF implies "Enterprise Architecture" in all its forms and is not limited to information systems (ISs). Admittedly, the goal remains the implementation of operational software systems, but to achieve this goal, a wider view is required, covering strategic, business, and organizational aspects. Moreover, the alignment of "business" and "technology" is a major concern for business managers and chief information officers (CIOs), who are constantly looking for IS agility. Architecture therefore covers requirements and strategies as well as business processes and technical applications and infrastructures and strives for optimal articulation between these different facets. It should be pointed out here that the term *enterprise* is not limited to its legal sense, but rather designates any organization linked by a common set of goals.[5]

In this context, TOGAF provides a pragmatic view of enterprise architecture, while highlighting the central role of organization. Any architectural transformation requires close collaboration between the different people involved in the enterprise architecture. Governance, stakeholder management, and an architecture-dedicated team implementation are among the many subjects dealt with by TOGAF.

This collaboration is based on an organized process. It is the role of the ADM to provide a structure for the progress of architectural transformation projects. Communication plays a vital role here. At each

---

[2]Technical Architecture Framework for Information Management.
[3]US Department of Defense.
[4]SAP Enterprise Architecture Framework.
[5]TOGAF defines *enterprise* as any collection of organizations that has a common set of goals. For example, an enterprise could be a government agency, a whole corporation, a division of a corporation, a single department, or a chain of geographically distant organizations linked together by common ownership.

stage of transformation work, a common understanding of the goals and the target must constantly be sought. The media used (documents, models, etc.) must be clearly defined and adapted to the different participants.

Beyond the implementation of architecture projects, capitalization and reuse are constantly present goals. Consequently, the task of setting up an architecture repository is central to TOGAF. This repository can include all sorts of elements, such as examples, norms, models, rules, or guidelines. Fed by the different work carried out, the repository guarantees centralization and homogeneous distribution throughout the enterprise.

> It should be noted that TOGAF does not recommend any particular style of architecture, let alone any specific technical infrastructure. Definition references are provided for these subjects, such as EAI, SOA, or BPM, accompanied by guides and best practices. This choice is justified by the sheer diversity of situations encountered and by the generic nature of the proposed framework.

1.1.3 "F" for framework

A framework groups together a collection of means and procedures dedicated to a particular field of activity. When used as a reference and a tool, a framework is most often presented as being complete and consistent for the field in question. TOGAF does not go against this definition. It provides a language, an approach, and a set of recommendations covering all facets of enterprise architecture, from organization and strategy, to business and technology, to planning and change management.

At first glance, this diversity can be disconcerting, due to its generic and pragmatic nature. However, this approach reveals the maturity of the project, which does not try to impose a universal, finished solution, preferring instead to provide a toolbox that can be used by all participants in enterprise architecture, from senior management, CIOs, and business managers to IS architects and project managers.

Naturally, the genericity of the TOGAF framework means that each company adapts it to its own context, for example, by adapting the framework, identifying the specific stakeholders, and so on. TOGAF allows for a phase dedicated to setting up and adapting the framework. We look at this subject in Section 1.4.

> Some readers will search the TOGAF document in vain for a formal proposal like those that can be found in language standards such as UML or BPMN. The management of enterprise architecture or ISs cannot easily be tied down to the constraints linked to the use of a specific metamodel.[6] In this case, pragmatism is the key.

Does TOGAF have the answer to everything? It goes without saying that a novice will not be transformed into an enterprise architecture expert just by reading the reference document. As with everything, experience remains invaluable, but in view of the complexity of the subject, an organized framework and recognized method constitute an essential asset.

---

[6]TOGAF provides a limited metamodel, presented as a widely customizable reference framework.

1.1.4 The TOGAF document

In concrete terms, TOGAF is presented in the form of a single reference document[7] and a dedicated web site.[8]

This document is broken down into seven parts:

I.   Introduction
II.   ADM (Architecture Development Method)
III. ADM Guidelines
IV.   Architecture Content
V.   Enterprise Continuum and Tools
VI.   Reference Models
VII. Architecture Capability Framework

Figure 1.1 presents an overview of the breakdown of the different parts of TOGAF: Method, Best practices, Components, Repository, and Governance.

The ADM (*part II*, "Architecture Development Method") is the main entry point to the TOGAF reference document, with its crop circle diagram (or TOGAF wheel), which describes the different phases of the method.

Part III discusses guidelines and best practices linked to the ADM, from security and gap analysis to stakeholder management. It should be noted that in general TOGAF does not provide "standard solutions" but rather a series of practices "that work," accompanied by more or less detailed examples.

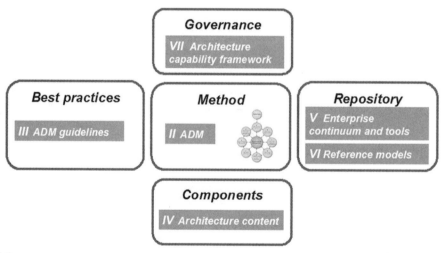

FIGURE 1.1

TOGAF: general structure. (For color version of this figure, the reader is referred to the online version of this chapter.)

---

[7]The TOGAF9 reference document is available on The Open Group web site.
[8]www.opengroup.org/togaf.

Part IV (architecture content) is dedicated to the tangible elements used in development work: deliverables, catalogs, matrices, diagrams, or the "building blocks" that constitute the architecture.

Parts V and VI focus on the enterprise architecture repository, and its partitioning, typology, and tools.

Part VII ("Architecture Capability Framework") deals with architecture governance, including repository management.

We look at the different parts of the TOGAF document in the following chapters:

- Chapter 2: The ADM and Guides for the ADM (parts II and III)
- Chapter 3: Architecture Content (part IV)
- Chapter 4: Repository and Governance (parts V, VI, and VII)

1.2 TOGAF: KEY POINTS

1.2.1 ADM and the TOGAF crop circle diagram

The ADM crop circle diagram presents the structure of the method with its phases and transitions (Figure 1.2), and is the first striking image encountered when broaching TOGAF.

In classic fashion, the phases define the high-level work stages, which consume and provide products (deliverables). Each of the eight phases contributes to achieving determined strategic objectives, from the overall vision of the architecture (phase A) to the maintenance of the deployed architecture (phase H).

This sequence, called the *ADM cycle*, takes place in the context of an architecture project managed by the enterprise's executive management. The work carried out is supervised by the architecture board, in partnership with all the business and IS stakeholders.

As you can see, the proposed path is a cycle, which finishes by looping back on itself. Admittedly, this is merely a schematic representation that only partially represents reality. However, it does successfully express the continuous nature of enterprise architecture work, which responds to the constant demands of businesses.

> How long does an ADM cycle last? Naturally, there is no one categorical answer to this question. Anywhere between 6 months and 2 years seems reasonable. Beyond this, it is undoubtedly preferable to break a subject down into several subprojects.

The central position occupied by requirements management in the diagram is testament to the pivotal role it plays within the ADM cycle. Strictly speaking, requirements management is more a permanent activity than a phase. However, the term "phase" is used to designate it in order to harmonize vocabulary. The same is true for the preliminary phase, which groups cross-organizational activities such as the definition of context, methods and tools for enterprise architecture, and the start of an ADM cycle.

Fundamentally, the aim of an ADM cycle is to successfully complete a transformation project, whose aim is to enable the enterprise to respond to a set of business goals.

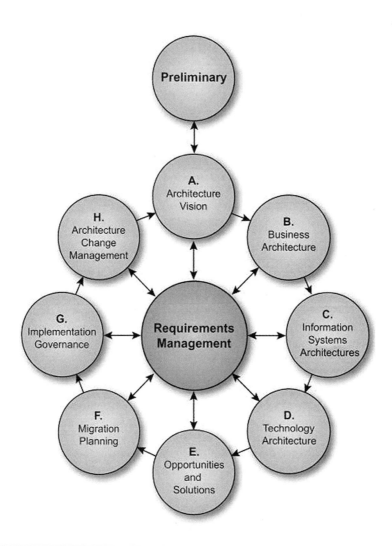

FIGURE 1.2

The "TOGAF crop circle diagram" with the ADM phases—TOGAF9. (For color version of this figure, the reader is referred to the online version of this chapter.)

Source: © 2008 The Open Group.

1.2.2 Architecture transformation
From baseline architecture to target architecture

As we have just seen, enterprise architecture transformation is at the heart of the subject matter dealt with by TOGAF, which discusses the following questions in detail:

- Which routes to follow?
- How to organize oneself?

FIGURE 1.3

From baseline architecture to target architecture. (For color version of this figure, the reader is referred to the online version of this chapter.)

- How to communicate?
- What are the main risks and how can they be reduced?

In this way, TOGAF distinguishes itself from other Zachman[9]-type frameworks, which primarily propose a typical architecture structure, and concentrate far less on the actual transformation approach. However, TOGAF provides its own content framework, with its specific terminology and structure (Figure 1.3).

But let's get back to the heart of the matter: Which approach should be adopted to make our enterprise architecture evolve? This can be summed up in four points:

- Knowing where we are coming from
- Determining where we want to go
- Choosing the best path to get there
- Successfully completing the transformation

Knowledge of the baseline architecture is not always clearly established. Consequently, a more or less detailed "reappraisal" of what already exists is often necessary. All the more so when we consider that the transformation roadmap depends on the gap analysis between these two states, and on the impact that this transformation has within the enterprise.

Determining the destination, that is to say the target architecture, depends above all on business goals, but also on a series of technical, organizational, and budgetary factors.

Finally, the means used to conduct the transformation must be chosen. What is the timeframe? How can we guarantee that certain critical parts will continue to function? How can we best prepare participants confronted with changes in their activities?

Transforming architecture

Any person who has been confronted with the exercise will say the same thing: making enterprise architecture evolve is a delicate and complex activity. Successfully completing transformation means fully understanding all the constraints that apply to this type of operation.

First off, any evolution of enterprise architecture requires that a large number of highly dependent elements be coordinated. Consequently, the involvement of the different stakeholders is a determining factor in the success of the operation, especially when we consider that this evolution often has significant consequences on the enterprise itself, its activities, and its employees.

---

[9]http://zachman.com/about-the-zachman-framework.

Furthermore, the conditions that start an architecture project are diverse, ranging from the introduction of new services or products or the renovation of a part of the system, to internal restructuring or company mergers or buyouts and acquisitions, and so on. This means that the reference framework must have a certain degree of flexibility, since too much rigidity would run the risk of "jamming" the machine.

The scope covered by the transformation also has an influence on the variety of situations encountered. In most cases, we are not building a complete system "from scratch." On the contrary, developments generally concern specific parts of the system, linked to business goals.

Enterprises behave like living organisms, constantly reacting to external requests. Like a shop that advertises "business as usual during renovation," the enterprise never suspends its activities, since continuity of service must be guaranteed.

To sum up, the road to follow is not "preordained." However, the framework can help accelerate and guide change initiative, although the combination of parameters that must be taken into account means that it will always need to be adapted to a particular context.

Transition architectures and increments (states)

How do you move from existing (baseline) architecture to target architecture? The answer to this question, provided in the form of a path (or migration architecture), is a key element of TOGAF, founded on the following principles:

- If it is to succeed, this path must take into account all the facets of the enterprise, and the effects resulting from all changes.
- The path includes intermediate states, described by the transition architecture.
- These intermediate states must bring real, measurable added value.
- Gap analysis between the target architecture and the baseline architecture is a determining element in the choice of path.

Operationally speaking, this path results in a series of implementation projects of various different types: software development or evolution, data migration, training, and business reorganization. The successful coordination of these different projects goes a long way to determining the success or failure of the operation (Figure 1.4).

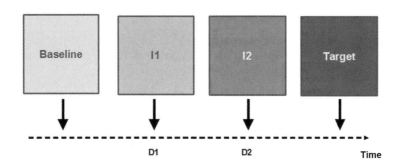

FIGURE 1.4

Transition architecture. (For color version of this figure, the reader is referred to the online version of this chapter.)

The number of states varies according to the domain, scope, time horizon, and level of details as well as the difficulties encountered. A direct transition (with no intermediate states) to the target architecture is possible where the gap between the baseline architecture and the target architecture is limited. Progress through states reduces resistance to change, and reduces risk by making adjustments easier.

The description of this migration path is one of the major TOGAF[10] deliverables, notably for developing the operational project schedule.

For example, a company selling mobile phones and contracts decides to add a "triple-play box" to its product range. The roadmap for this would be made up of the following four states:

State 1: Evolution of the product repository, with migration of the database, and of the applications destined for staff in charge of managing this product repository.
State 2: Consideration of the supplier logistics chain. Training in new products provided to staff.
State 3: Evolution of the client web site. Marketing study. Restructuring of the departments concerned.
State 4: Integration and production.

Gap analysis

In order to choose the appropriate path between two states, the gap between these two states must be analyzed. The same is true when transitioning from a baseline architecture to a target architecture.

The principles of gap analysis are relatively simple. The comparison of baseline architecture and target architecture results in answers to the following questions:

- Which elements are new (organizations, applications, infrastructures)?
- Which elements have been deleted?
- Which elements have been modified?
- Which elements remain unchanged?

However, these results must be considered alongside the business goals of the transformation, in order to check their pertinence. Is the deletion of such and such an element appropriate? Have we forgotten to add such and such an element?

Chapter 27 of TOGAF (*Gap Analysis*) proposes the use of a baseline/target matrix, which highlights differences and makes them easier to analyze.

One advantage of this tool is that it proposes a systematic approach, which helps avoid "flaws." During the different phases of the ADM, the aim is to identify elements that have potentially been overlooked, but that play an important role in measuring the gap between baseline and target architectures, and that will be significant to the change operations that are to be carried out. Beyond aspects linked to IT systems, this gap measures the distance that must be covered if the enterprise is to be *capable* of meeting new business goals: for example, employee skills, modifications to organizational structures, or the availability of technical means.

---

[10]Particularly the "migration and deployment plan" deliverable.

Impact evaluation

An enterprise is often a complex organization with multiple branches. Consequently, the modification of one part of its architecture may potentially affect other components situated outside the scope of the implemented changes.

First, the impact can be technical: any modification of a software component can potentially have repercussions on all the components that use it.

Second, the changes made can also indirectly affect certain business aspects. For example, increasing the number of products available will probably have an impact on how other products are presented.

Finally, the restructuring of an enterprise's organization, even partial, can have repercussions on the way the enterprise functions, through the relationships that exist between different departments and their members.

We will see that during architecture development phases, gap analysis and impact assessment go hand in hand, each influencing the other in terms of architecture choices and transition management. Even though this development initially focuses on its scope, it must take into account the enterprise in its entirety.

The concept of capability

Capability designates the ability of an organization to provide a given product or service. Capability manifests itself through a series of factors that contribute to the realization of these products or services at the required level of quality. These factors can vary widely in type: for example, personnel training, availability of an expert in a field, surface area of premises, power of IT servers, and so on.

The notion of capability is also widely used in other frameworks. ITIL defines it as being "The ability of an organization, person, process, application, IT service or other configuration item to carry out an activity."[11] It is also naturally found in the acronym CMMI (*capability maturity model*).

The fact that this term appears nearly 500 times in the TOGAF document is testament to just how essential it is to consider a business function as a whole, far beyond a strictly "IT system" view. The enterprise must be able to satisfy its clients, and in order to do this, it must be fully operational. Even the most perfect application can only function in an environment that is able to use it. A badly informed user, a badly adapted procedure, or unmotivated management will inevitably prevent the realization of the defined goal.

More generally, the goal of an ADM cycle is to improve or put in place new business capabilities. This goal is present during each phase, so as to coordinate the different dimensions of the architecture (business, system, and technology) in order to converge on the final solution. This goal also applies to each step of the path, as we saw earlier.

In TOGAF, two chapters are specifically dedicated to this:

- Chapter 32, "Capability-Based Planning," a technique for planning the transition from baseline architecture to target architecture based on capabilities.
- Part VII of the TOGAF document, "Architecture Capability Framework," deals with the organization and governance of enterprise architecture. We discuss this point further in Chapter 4.2. Here, the term "capability" designates all the organization elements that have to be implemented in order to guarantee efficient management of enterprise architecture.

---

[11]ITIL® glossary and abbreviations; www.itil-officialsite.com/InternationalActivities/ITILGlossaries.aspx.

1.2.3 Architecture in TOGAF
Architecture and description of architecture

We have already spoken at length about architecture and transformation, but it is useful at this point to refresh our memories regarding the term "architecture" and its content. In its introduction,[12] TOGAF gives two definitions of the term "architecture":

1. "A formal description of a system, or a detailed plan of the system at component level, to guide its implementation."
2. "The structure of components, their inter-relationships, and the principles and guidelines governing their design and evolution over time."

The first definition considers the term "architecture" as a synonym of "system description." For the second, "architecture" designates the structure and principles of the system, independent of its description.

This double definition may seem surprising, but it does reflect a very real situation. Software systems are, by nature, opaque, so much so that their structure is only visible through representations. Factories, ships, or engines all have a physical structure, which is more or less visible. However, it is impossible to "lift the hood" of an IT system, whose architecture only exists through its representation. This is also the case for business elements such as processes, organization, or strategy, which can only be communicated through descriptions or models. The proliferation of schemas, diagrams, and tables within enterprises is testament to this reality.

In this context, communication on architecture plays a determining role. Just like the blueprints of a building, communication is a vital tool for those working on the different tasks involved: development, evaluation, exchange, and construction. In this book, we have chosen to focus particularly on this point, through the use of concrete examples (Chapters 6–11).

Domains and phases

What are some of the main subject areas in enterprise architecture? TOGAF proposes a high-level breakdown into four large domains:

- *Business architecture*, which covers strategy, goals, business processes, functions, and organization.
- *Data architecture*, dedicated to the organization and management of information.
- *Application architecture*, which presents applications, software components, and their interactions.
- *Technology architecture*, which describes the techniques and components deployed, as well as networks and the physical infrastructure upon which the applications and data sources run.

This breakdown is unsurprising and fairly similar to other proposals on the same subject, although each has its own particularities and vocabulary.[13] Chapter 3 takes a more detailed look at the contents and structure of TOGAF architecture.

---

[12]TOGAF9, Chap. 3.9.
[13]For example, the RM-ODP model breaks the model down into Enterprise, Information, Computational, Engineering, and Technology (www.rm-odp.net).

The first part of the ADM approach is structured using the same typology, with one main difference: only three phases are dedicated to the elaboration of the architecture: business (phase B), IS (phase C), and technology (phase D). The IS architecture phase has two subphases (data and application), which correspond to the two aforementioned domains. From here on, we either use the term "IS architecture" or else directly refer to "data architecture" and "application architecture." Figure 1.5 summarizes the two structures (by domain and by phase) used in TOGAF.

We see in Chapter 3.2.4 that this equivalence between architecture domains and ADM phases, while pertinent at first glance, is not strictly valid in detail.

Architecture repository

Naturally, enterprises need to conserve, diffuse, and reuse the EA information that constitutes one of their key assets. This is the role of the architecture repository, which includes descriptions from each of the four domains, as well as a whole host of knowledge, guiding principles, and techniques linked to enterprise architecture. Far from being a static source of information, the repository is constantly evolving throughout architecture transformations, thereby participating in know-how capitalization. It also provides an overview of the architecture, which facilitates decision making at a strategic level.

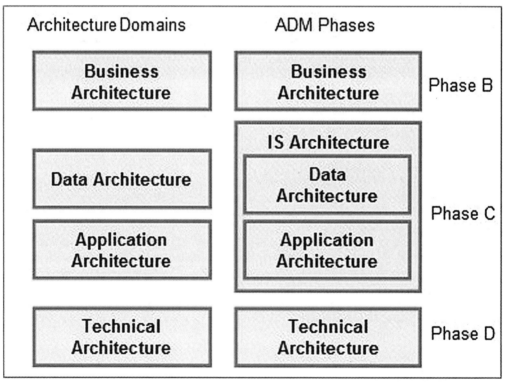

FIGURE 1.5

Architecture breakdowns.

Architecture and solution

For TOGAF readers, one item of vocabulary still has to be explained. TOGAF often refers to solution architecture. Here, the term "architecture" designates a description, and more precisely a logical view, as opposed to the "solution," which represents a technical reality. This distinction can be clearly seen in the terms "Architecture Building Block" and "Solution Building Block" (respectively ABB and SBB). The logical specification of an element is an ABB, while its physical equivalent is a SBB. These two types of element are present in the architecture repository, which enables either the documentation or the physical component to be reused, according to the context.

1.2.4 **Goals, constraints, and requirements**

To successfully carry out a transformation operation, we must be perfectly clear about the results we hope to obtain. This statement may seem trivial, but it is worth bearing in mind.

In this domain, TOGAF distinguishes a series of elements that participate in a more structured formalization:

- Strategic objectives, or *goals*, which describe general orientations.
- Operational objectives, or *objectives*, which formalize these goals in terms of measurable results at a given date.
- *Drivers*, which often motivate decisions regarding architectural change, such as changes in conjecture or the need to adapt to technical evolutions. These are the "why," which justify and orient goals.
- *Requirements*, which specify exactly what will be concretely implemented to reach these goals.
- *Constraints*, which are external elements that influence the system, sometimes restraining its capacities.

> A constraint is imposed by the outside world, and cannot be reduced or removed. For example, a software system delivery lead-time is not a constraint but rather an objective, since it is the enterprise which has fixed this lead-time to meet a need. However, an administrative circular (for example, in the field of tax) or international regulations (Solvency, Bale, ...) are constraints that must be respected, and which impose a set of rules which must be respected, independently of the enterprise's own goals.

How are these elements integrated into an architectural project? Let's immediately remove any ambiguity: the role of an enterprise architect is not to define objectives (strategic or operational) for an organization. However, he/she will formalize them within a structured context, and will use this formalization to better link decisions and architectural elements. Despite its imperfection, this kind of "traceability" between system components and desired results is extremely useful, since it helps reduce the risk of "technological" dispersion by constantly focusing on the business vision of the architecture and facilitates high-level impact analysis.

1.2.5 **Stakeholders and the human factor**

We know that the organizational aspect is one of the most delicate points in this type of operation. Like any enterprise process, architecture transformation involves a combination of activities involving different participants, each one of them a "stakeholder" in the operation he or she undertakes.

TOGAF deals with this question through the following themes:

- Stakeholder management
- Transformation Readiness Assessment
- Efficiency of communication through the concept of viewpoints

Managing stakeholders

First, it is essential to clearly define each stakeholder as early as possible during the ADM cycle. This identification mainly uses a pragmatic approach in order to avoid simply reusing existing organizational structures, which only partially represent the reality of the activities and responsibilities that will be put in motion. Leaving a key participant by the wayside would significantly affect the quality of the results. Consequently, in order to determine with whom and in what form work will be carried out, a series of key questions must be answered on the subject:

- Who defines goals?
- Who gains and who loses from this change?
- Who controls the transformation process?
- Who designs new systems?
- Who will make the decisions?
- Who procures IT systems and who decides what to buy?
- Who controls resources?
- Who has or controls the necessary specialist skills?
- Who influences the project?

From these questions, TOGAF recommends that the position of each stakeholder be clarified, notably his or her degree of involvement. Figure 1.6 presents these different degrees.

Each stakeholder will be positioned using these degrees of involvement, which determine the relationships to develop and the level of involvement in architecture project steering committees. Naturally, key players play a determining role and must be on the front line in all areas of decision making.

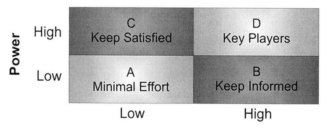

FIGURE 1.6

Degrees of stakeholder involvement—TOGAF9. (For color version of this figure, the reader is referred to the online version of this chapter.)

Source: © 2008, The Open Group.

This qualification is cross-referenced with the role played in the context of the current project:

- The executive management, who defines strategic goals
- The client, who is responsible for the allocated budget, with regard to the expected goals
- The user, who directly interacts with the system in the course of his or her activities
- The provider, who delivers the component elements of the architecture, notably its software components
- The sponsor, who drives and guides the work
- The enterprise architect, who turns business goals into reality within the structure of the system

Transformation Readiness Assessment

Is the organization ready for the envisaged change? This question may seem incongruous, but how many projects have finished unsuccessfully because this dimension was not taken into account? In just a few years, "change management" has become a discipline in its own right, producing a large number of articles and seminars.

Chapter 30 of TOGAF[14] is entirely dedicated to this question, which is widely discussed in the description of the ADM phases. The identification of change resistance risks and the definition of actions to take to limit these risks are essential tasks that must be carried out before embarking upon a transformation project. This is particularly important for an operation covering a broad scope and resulting in significant restructuring.

While it is not possible to provide turnkey solutions on such a subject, it is possible to use certain techniques that will help reduce this type of risk:

- A clear presentation of the impacts of changes made, notably on an organizational level
- A concrete view of the expected business benefits, in the form of "business cases"
- An objective assessment of the enterprise's IT, business, and financial aptitudes, with no overestimation of its real capacities
- An executive management team recognized as being able to defend the project in the long term
- High-quality communication, which aims to promote a common understanding of the stakes and the solutions to implement

Views and viewpoints

If a message is to be successfully understood, the most important aspect to consider is that its content and form must be tailored to the intended recipient.

For this, TOGAF uses the concept of *viewpoints*. A viewpoint designates the most appropriate perspective for a given participant, and is materialized by a certain number of *views* of the architecture, in the form of diagrams, documents, or other elements. For example, executive management will be more interested in a high-level description, while communication with operational staff will require much more detailed representations.

This is a critical point, one that will condition the quality of communication and that will be encountered during each phase of the ADM cycle. Consequently, it is imperative that views and viewpoints be defined for each stakeholder before beginning work on the four architecture domains (business, data,

---

[14]TOGAF9 30, Business Transformation Readiness Assessment.

application, and technology). We discuss this question in detail in Chapters 7–10, with examples taken from TOGAF views.

1.2.6 Architecture strategy, governance, and principles
A strategic view of enterprise architecture

We have just seen that implementing transformation constitutes the main theme of TOGAF. We have also seen that architecture transformation is driven according to business goals defined for a specific scope.

However, a wider, more long-term perspective is also necessary. It is clearly up to the enterprise's executive management to define general goals and develop the strategy. These translate into decisions concerning architecture, notably in terms of evolutions to the IS.

In a framework such as TOGAF, this aspect is found in the form of links between business strategy elements and system components. The formalization of "drivers," "strategic goals," or "business requirements" is included in the business architecture part of TOGAF. This formalization of the "why" contributes to a common understanding of business fundamentals, and clarifies the role of each component in a wider perspective.

Moreover, architecture choices will affect the system for years to come. The system must meet today's requirements, but must also be able to adapt to tomorrow's needs. Ensuring overall consistency on the functional and technical levels is therefore vitally important for those in charge of enterprise architecture.

Governance

In a complex organization, this strategic view cannot be taken for granted. Consequently, to slow down the centrifugal forces and retain a certain level of overall consistency, it is essential that an appropriate organization be established. This organization, which is centralized by nature, uses a cross-organizational mode of governance that handles architecture in terms of the enterprise, its strategic choices, its principles, and its action plan.

This organization, called the "architecture board," is responsible for the following goals: to guarantee that common rules are respected, and to ensure that implementation projects are supported. In its capacity as a steering and control committee, the architecture board also takes care of managing the architecture repository. We go into more detail on this point in Chapter 4.

Architecture principles

Architecture principles provide invaluable help in this strategic view of the architecture. They establish a set of rules and recommendations, which encourage the harmonization of choices and practices.

TOGAF recommends that these architecture principles be established as early as possible, as a unifying element for future projects. Architecture principles are a kind of table of statutes, which must respect the following properties:

- Stability: Principles are stable by nature. They are only rarely modified compared with the frequency of developments.
- General scope: A principle applies to the entire enterprise, and does not depend on the transformation carried out.
- Comprehensibility: A principle is interpreted clearly by all stakeholders.
- Coherence: With regard to the set of principles. Two principles cannot be contradictory.

Every time a transformation project is begun, each participant must be able to consider these principles as a guide, and use them as a basis for his or her choices.

TOGAF provides an example of a relatively detailed catalog of architecture principles,[15] which includes around 20 principles organized into four families similar to the four architecture domains: business, data, application, and technology.

Rules on relatively diverse aspects are found in this catalog, such as:

- The systematic involvement of users in architectural choices
- The harmonization of application design
- Continuity of service
- The respect of intellectual property protection rules
- The sharing of information
- Data quality levels
- The harmonization of vocabulary
- Security
- Independence with regard to technical platforms
- Ease of use
- The respect of deadlines
- The respect of standards

The reader can refer to the TOGAF document for a more detailed description. Each principle is described in a standard way: the name of the principle, its statement and rationale, and its implications.

This catalog is a relatively broad basis upon which each enterprise can establish its own set of architecture principles. It goes without saying that the wide range of enterprise histories, businesses, and priorities makes individually adapted formulation essential.

It should also be noted that there is no point in having too big a catalog. It is always preferable to work on a limited number (a few dozen) of widely accepted principles, rather than a multitude of badly assimilated rules.

In practice, the catalog of architecture principles is often built based on existing elements, from several sources or spread across different organizations. Where this is the case, the main task is to compile and consolidate information based on the aforementioned characteristics.

1.3 SUMMARY

By way of a partial conclusion, let's recall the foundations of the TOGAF project:

- Business goals. Architecture is above all based on an enterprise's business goals. Constantly present at every stage of work, they act as the main driving force for change.
- The "human factor." Enterprise architecture is implemented by staff members, teams, and organizations. The quality of the results obtained depends greatly on the commitment of all participants.

---

[15]TOGAF9, Chap. 23.6.

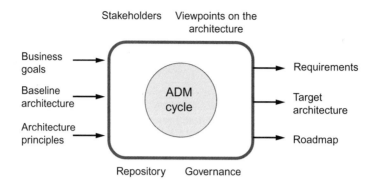

FIGURE 1.7

Summarized view of the architecture transformation approach.

- Communication. The main aim of enterprise architecture is the facilitation of communication between participants. This means that architecture formalization and communication must be mastered, at all decision-making levels.
- Capitalization and reuse. Beyond the context of methodological frameworks (of which TOGAF is an example), accumulated experience is an irreplaceable asset. Sharing through a common repository constitutes one of the key elements in this regard.
- The use of standards. As a long-term activity, enterprise architecture is built on a solid and durable base. In this way, TOGAF takes responsibility for a series of acquisitions recognized by the community.
- Governance. Solid and efficient governance, which drives transformation work and maintains overall architectural consistency.

Figure 1.7 presents a summarized view of the approach and its main components. As a "machine" used to transform enterprise architecture, the ADM cycle is based on business goals, the initial state, and the principles that govern the entire architecture. This operation draws on elements from the repository, and is driven by dedicated governance. Each stakeholder is linked to a viewpoint that describes the architecture through a series of adapted views. Requirements guide the choice of solutions for the target architecture. The implementation plan defines the transition path, organization, implementation, and monitoring of the new architecture.

1.4 USING TOGAF
1.4.1 Adapting the framework

As we have already seen, TOGAF is not intended to be used as is, as one would use a recipe in cookery, where each step is faithfully followed to produce a final result.[16] On the contrary, TOGAF is presented as the foundation upon which an organization builds its own architecture framework. Adapting TOGAF

---

[16]As those who have already tried this will confirm, the end result sometimes bears little or no resemblance to what would be served by a real chef in a restaurant! Skill includes knowledge, know-how, and the famous "knack" acquired through years of experience.

is therefore one of the first activities to carry out, one that will guide all future operations. This adaptation is an integral part of TOGAF, which provides the necessary practices and principles.

Adaptation takes place on two levels:

- The definition of the general framework, used in each cycle of the ADM
- The adjustment for each cycle, according to its particularities

This adaptation is carried out during the preliminary phase. It is essential to remember that enterprise architecture transformation is not a unique project, but rather a permanent activity consisting of specific architecture projects for each ADM cycle, providing feedback that enables the overall framework to be adjusted.

Adaptation can take place on several levels:

- Vocabulary, the basic architecture entities
- Deliverable templates
- Architecture principles
- Architecture elements: catalogs, matrices, diagrams
- The phases of the ADM and their possible iterations
- Architecture governance
- The first view of the architecture repository

This includes adapting to what you are trying to accomplish with the EA:

- Manage your portfolio of applications
- Address new business influencers
- Address new competition, the introduction of a new disruptive technology, and so on.

These examples illustrate how flexibly the entire ADM cycle can be used, and show how fully it plays its role of generic blueprint. However, it is important to explain and justify the iterations chosen through a detailed plan before embarking upon the whole cycle in order to avoid improvisation during the work itself.

> Best practice: Avoid defining your architecture framework "above ground." Use a concrete example based on real evolution before embarking on your first TOGAF ADM cycle.

Furthermore, this flexibility in no way weakens the value of the TOGAF framework, which provides both a "compass" and content. These will both be vital during the implementation of architecture evolution, which remains a complex activity that is difficult to control.

1.4.2 TOGAF: One framework among many?

TOGAF is not defined in an isolated manner. On the contrary, the joint use of other frameworks is recommended, since each brings added value to its sphere of operation. "In all cases, it is expected that the architect will adapt and build on the TOGAF framework in order to define a tailored method that is integrated into the processes and organization structures of the enterprise. This architecture tailoring may include adopting elements from other architecture frameworks, or integrating TOGAF methods with other standard frameworks, such as ITIL, CMMI, COBIT, PRINCE2, PMBOK, and MSP."[17]

TOGAF and DODAF

DODAF (Department of Defense Architecture Framework)[18] provides an architecture management and representation framework. The concept of the viewpoint, also found in TOGAF, plays a central role, linked to governance and stakeholder management.

DODAF viewpoints are structured as follows:

- All Viewpoint (AV)
- Capability Viewpoint (CV)
- Data and Information Viewpoint (DIV)
- Operational Viewpoint (OV)
- Project Viewpoint (PV)
- Services Viewpoint (SvcV)
- Standards Viewpoint (StdV)
- Systems Viewpoint (SV)

As in TOGAF, each viewpoint is broken down into a collection of views, each designed to represent a part of the architecture. For example, the operational viewpoint includes the following views:

- OV-1 High Level Operational Concept Graphic
- OV-2 Operational Node Connectivity Description
- OV-3 Operational Information Exchange Matrix
- OV-4 Organizational Relationships Chart
- OV-5 Operational Activity Model
- OV-6a Operational Rules Model
- OV-6b Operational State Transition Description
- OV-6c Operational Event-Trace Description
- OV-7 Logical Data Model

A fairly similar approach can be found in the MODAF[19] framework, notably with regard to the use of viewpoints and views.

Despite the fact that these frameworks (DODAF and MODAF) are established in a governmental context, and more specifically in the field of defense, they can be used in other contexts. Where necessary, the definition of viewpoints and views can be used to adapt them to the TOGAF framework.

TOGAF and ITIL

ITIL is a framework dedicated to managing ISs. ITIL has been popular since the mid-2000s, notably after the release of version 3 in 2007.[20]

---

[17]TOGAF9, Chap. 2.10.
[18]http://cio-nii.defense.gov/sites/dodaf20/index.html.
[19]www.mod.uk/DefenceInternet/AboutDefence/CorporatePublications/InformationManagement/MODAF.
[20]www.itil-officialsite.com.

The main ITIL concept, the service center, clarifies the position of the IS within the enterprise as a provider at the service of its clients, be they internal or external. It establishes a set of recommendations and best practices that aim to control system quality, in terms of reliability, response to needs, and risk reduction.

ITIL deals with all aspects linked to the management of the IT system infrastructure through the description of its processes: service deployment, operation, support, security, and lifecycle.

- Incident Management
- Problem Management
- Change Management
- Release Management
- Configuration Management

Highly quality oriented, ITIL greatly inspired the ISO 20000 norm, as well as the enterprise certification program. For readers wishing to learn more, there are a number of works on the subject.[21]

What is the relationship between ITIL and TOGAF? Since version V3, ITIL has been structured into five "volumes," focused on the notion of service:

- Service strategy
- Service design
- Service transition
- Service operation
- Continual service improvement

This structure makes certain overlaps with TOGAF[22] appear: service strategy with the preliminary phase and phase A; service design with phases C and D; service transition with phases E and F; service operation and improvement with phases G and H.

At first glance, this correspondence can be interpreted as a similarity between the two frameworks. In this case, should we choose between the two approaches and forbid their simultaneous use?

Beyond these formal similarities, the fundamental difference between the two frameworks is first and foremost a question of perspective. ITIL has been developed as a tool dedicated to IT services used to manage IT systems. TOGAF is clearly oriented toward a business view of architecture and the transformation method.

It is clear what the subjects dealt with during phases G and H of TOGAF, which concern the use and maintenance of IT system components, are also widely present in the ITIL community. However, the development of architecture and its impact on the business and the organization, subjects at the very heart of the TOGAF project, are less prevalent in ITIL "culture."

It should be noted that neither ITIL nor TOGAF is presented as "turnkey" solutions, but rather as reference frameworks. Consequently, the right attitude for enterprises must probably include a healthy dose of pragmatism, taking the best from both approaches.

---

[21]For example, Foundations of IT Service Management with ITIL 2011, Brady Orand, Julie Villarreal, CreateSpace Independent Publishing Platform.
[22]TOGAF9 and ITIL V3, Two Frameworks Whitepaper, Tom van Sante and Jeroen Ermers, September 2009.

TOGAF and CMMI

The CMMI[23] is a repository of best practices organized into levels of maturity. It is both a certification framework and a set of processes destined to improve the quality of development projects.

Dissemination of the maturity-level structure is real, and CMMI certification is a guarantee of quality often requested of enterprises. Moreover, this method of evaluating an organization or a system has been used in several different contexts. TOGAF dedicates an entire chapter to this (Chapter 51), and proposes an enterprise architecture maturity evaluation model, which uses the CMMI's five maturity levels. This model is a result of the "Enterprise Architecture Capability Maturity Model" from the DoC (US Department of Commerce), and is presented below.

Enterprise architecture process maturity levels (Copyright TOGAF 9.1)

   Level 0: None. No enterprise architecture program. No enterprise architecture to speak of.

   Level 1: Initial. Informal enterprise architecture process underway.

1. Processes are *ad hoc* and localized. Some enterprise architecture processes are defined. There is no unified architecture process across technologies or business processes. Success depends on individual efforts.
2. Enterprise architecture processes, documentation, and standards are established by a variety of *ad hoc* means and are localized or informal.
3. Minimal or implicit linkage to business strategies or business drivers.
4. Limited management team awareness or involvement in the architecture process.
5. Limited operating unit acceptance of the enterprise architecture process.
6. The latest version of the operating unit's enterprise architecture documentation is on the web. Little communication exists about the enterprise architecture process and possible process improvements.
7. IT security considerations are *ad hoc* and localized.
8. No explicit governance of architectural standards.
9. Little or no involvement of strategic planning and acquisition personnel in the enterprise architecture process. Little or no adherence to existing standards.

   Level 2: Under Development. Enterprise architecture process is under development.

1. Basic enterprise architecture process is documented based on OMB Circular A-130 and Department of Commerce Enterprise Architecture Guidance. The architecture process has developed clear roles and responsibilities.
2. IT vision, principles, business linkages, baseline, and target architecture are identified. Architecture standards exist, but not necessarily linked to target architecture. Technical reference model (TRM) and Standards Profile framework established.
3. Explicit linkage to business strategies.
4. Management awareness of architecture effort.
5. Responsibilities are assigned and work is underway.
6. The DoC and operating unit enterprise architecture web pages are updated periodically and are used to document architecture deliverables.
7. IT security architecture has defined clear roles and responsibilities.
8. Governance of a few architectural standards and some adherence to existing Standards Profile.
9. Little or no formal governance of IT investment and acquisition strategy. Operating unit demonstrates some adherence to existing Standards Profile.

---

[23]http://www.sei.cmu.edu/cmmi/.

Level 3: Defined. Defined enterprise architecture including detailed written procedures and TRM.

1. The architecture is well defined and communicated to IT staff and business management with operating unit IT responsibilities. The process is largely followed.
2. Gap analysis and migration plan are completed. Fully developed TRM and Standards Profile. IT goals and methods are identified.
3. Enterprise architecture is integrated with capital planning and investment control.
4. Senior management team aware of and supportive of the enterprise-wide architecture process. Management actively supports architectural standards.
5. Most elements of operating unit show acceptance of or are actively participating in the enterprise architecture process.
6. Architecture documents updated regularly on DoC enterprise architecture web page.
7. IT security architecture Standards Profile is fully developed and is integrated with enterprise architecture.
8. Explicit documented governance of majority of IT investments.
9. IT acquisition strategy exists and includes compliance measures to IT enterprise architecture. Cost benefits are considered in identifying projects.

Level 4: Managed. Managed and measured enterprise architecture process.

1. Enterprise architecture process is part of the culture. Quality metrics associated with the architecture process are captured.
2. Enterprise architecture documentation is updated on a regular cycle to reflect the updated enterprise architecture. Business, data, application, and technology architectures defined by appropriate *de jure* and *de facto* standards.
3. Capital planning and investment control are adjusted based on the feedback received and lessons learned from updated enterprise architecture. Periodic reexamination of business drivers.
4. Senior management team directly involved in the architecture review process.
5. The entire operating unit accepts and actively participates in the enterprise architecture process.
6. Architecture documents are updated regularly, and frequently reviewed for latest architecture developments/standards.
7. Performance metrics associated with IT security architecture are captured.
8. Explicit governance of all IT investments. Formal processes for managing variances feed back into enterprise architecture.
9. All planned IT acquisitions and purchases are guided and governed by the enterprise architecture.

Level 5: Optimizing. Continuous improvement of enterprise architecture process.

1. Concerted efforts to optimize and continuously improve architecture process.
2. A standards and waivers process is used to improve architecture development process.
3. Architecture process metrics are used to optimize and drive business linkages. Business involved in the continuous process improvements of enterprise architecture.
4. Senior management involvement in optimizing process improvements in architecture development and governance.
5. Feedback on architecture process from all operating unit elements is used to drive architecture process improvements.
6. Architecture documents are used by every decision-maker in the organization for every IT-related business decision.
7. Feedback from IT security architecture metrics is used to drive architecture process improvements.
8. Explicit governance of all IT investments. A standards and waivers process is used to make governance-process improvements.
9. No unplanned IT investment or acquisition activity.

1.5 FUNDAMENTAL CONCEPTS

The following fundamental concepts were introduced in this chapter:

- Enterprise architecture framework: Coherent set of methods, practices, models, and guides dedicated to enterprise architecture.
- Architecture transformation: Set of actions that consist of making architecture evolve from an initial state to a final state.
- Impact assessment: Assessment of the impact of an architecture transformation project. Impact can be multifaceted (business, organization, IS, etc.).
- Gap analysis: Assessment of the differences between two architectures (baseline and target).
- Capability: The ability of an organization to provide a given product or service.
- Architecture principles: Set of stable rules and recommendations concerning the architecture in its entirety.

The ADM Method

2

CHAPTER OUTLINE

The ADM method constitutes the heart of the TOGAF document, as an enterprise architecture transformation method. This chapter describes how it functions and explains the different phases involved and the relationships between them. It also covers the iterative approach of the method, which should be understood as a guide that can be adapted according to the reality of a given situation. This chapter also looks at best practices associated with the ADM method, which are described in part III of the TOGAF document. The ADM method itself is described in part II.

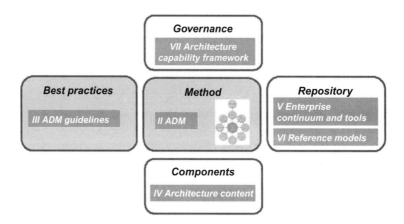

2.1 THE ADM CYCLE

2.1.1 The breakdown into phases

The ADM method defines eight sequential phases (A to H) and two other special phases: the preliminary phase and the requirements management phase. Figure 2.1 shows the most frequently referenced TOGAF diagram, which summarizes this approach through a high-level four-part breakdown: business, information technology (IT), planning, and change.

The sequence of phases A to H is broken down as follows:

- Phase A: Vision
- Phase B: Business architecture
- Phase C: Information system architecture
- Phase D: Technology architecture
- Phase E: Opportunities and solutions
- Phase F: Migration planning
- Phase G: Implementation governance
- Phase H: Architecture change management

All phases are described in a similar way:

- The objectives, which define the expected results
- The approach, which provides a guide and recommended strategy
- The input and output, which specify what each phase consumes or modifies
- The different steps, in the form of a breakdown of the work to be carried out

Even though the progression of phases is described in a strictly sequential manner (from A to H), this sequence can be reviewed and adapted according to the context, notably in the form of iterations within the ADM cycle (see Section 2.3). More generally, the "crop circle" diagram should be considered as a

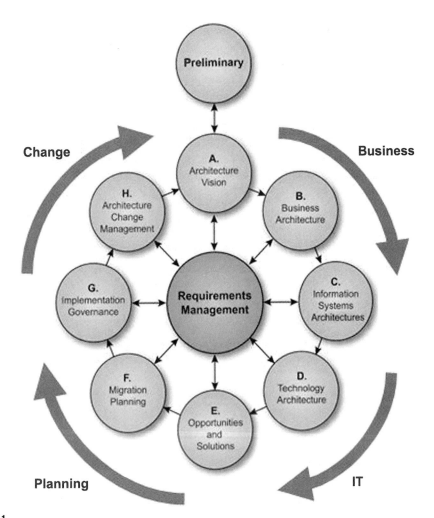

FIGURE 2.1

Architecture development method (ADM)—TOGAF9. (For color version of this figure, the reader is referred to the online version of this chapter.)

Source: © *2008 The Open Group.*

reference structure rather than an immutable progression, especially since it remains possible, and even preferable, to question or adjust at any time a part of the results obtained earlier. The identification of new constraints or the reformulation or addition of details to requirements can cause certain new aspects to appear, aspects that were not sufficiently exploited during earlier phases. As an example, the main output document of phase A, "architecture vision," is only definitively validated during phase F. However, high-quality elaboration implies convergent progression, which does not call into question the principles and foundations defined at the outset.

2.1.2 **The typical path**

Figure 2.2 presents an overview of the progression of an ADM cycle, from the preliminary phase right through to phase H. This typical path is guided by one major goal: the need to obtain the expected result by mastering each step of the process. This goal requires rigorous preparation, a description of the target with regard to what already exists for all facets (business, information system, and technology), precise evaluation of the gaps and risks determining the choice of trajectory, and finally evaluation of the results and careful management of any adjustments made.

> It should be noted that the actual realization of changes falls outside the scope covered by enterprise architecture. Phases G and H are dedicated to implementation governance, notably through the control and follow-up of implementation projects. These implementation projects remain the responsibility of the usual enterprise entities, managed by project managers. The fundamental role of the team in charge of enterprise architecture consists of guaranteeing the conformity of deployed elements with regard to the architecture principles defined for all impacted units.

TOGAF describes each step of each phase in detail. This does not mean that the realization of each of these steps is systematic. Some results are already available, either because they are produced by other entities or because they are linked to more general activities. For example, if architecture principles are recorded as results from phase A, they can simply be checked where they already exist. The main thing here is that the presence and conformity of each result must be checked, just like a checklist associated with each phase.

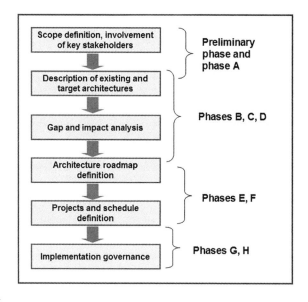

FIGURE 2.2

Typical path of an ADM cycle.

2.2 THE PHASES OF THE ADM

2.2.1 The preliminary phase

The goal of this phase is to prepare the enterprise for the realization of the architecture work:

- The organization and governance of the architecture
- General principles
- Methods
- Tools
- The architecture repository
- The start of the ADM cycle

These elements directly concern the adaptation of the architecture framework, in other words TOGAF.

In this way, the preliminary phase is not part of an ADM cycle but can be considered at any time during the ADM cycle as part of the evolution of the EA practice, especially in the context of using maturity models as a means of identifying opportunities for transition initiatives. Preliminary phase activities are essentially cross-organizational, linked to the general governance of the enterprise architecture, and their aim is to enable the enterprise to master the management and transformation of its architecture. However, it is during the preliminary phase that the start of a particular ADM cycle is decided upon and prepared for. This is detailed in the "Request for Architecture Work" document, which contains all the elements that form the basis of an enterprise architecture change project (sponsors, strategic goals, constraints, the budget framework, and the strategic plan). This document constitutes a contractual reference guide for the progress of the entire TOGAF cycle itself, from phase A onward.

Finally, TOGAF provides a good summary of this phase in the form of where, what, why, who, and how.[1]

2.2.2 Phase A (vision)

Phase A is the first phase of the ADM cycle, triggered by the validation of the "Request for Architecture Work" document. Phase A has two main goals:

- First, phase A further develops and enriches elements resulting from the preliminary phase, such as architecture principles, key indicators, and the organization or planning of elaboration work.
- Second, phase A prepares subsequent phases by providing a general representation of the baseline and target architectures. At this stage, these remain high-level representations, whose goal is to highlight structuring points and typical solutions.

Communication plays a key role during this phase. All stakeholders must have the same understanding, in order to obtain consensus on orientations and expected results. Other points are also dealt with, such as the identification of fundamental requirements, their links to strategic goals, or risk management. The "Architecture vision" document constitutes the main output of this phase.

---

[1]TOGAF9, chapter 6.2: This preliminary phase is about defining "where, what, why, who, and how we do architecture" in the enterprise concerned.

To sum up, at the end of phase A we have a common vision of:

- Organization: the stakeholders, their roles, their respective involvement
- Orientation: a consensus on the principles, goals, major requirements, and constraints
- The scope covered, the most impacted parts
- The roadmap: the ADM cycle development plan, the resources, and the budget allocated
- A macroscopic vision of baseline architecture and target architecture
- Major risks and associated risk reduction actions

In other words, we know where we're going, how we're getting there, and with whom.

Note that at this stage the perspective is horizontal, and covers all architecture domains (business, information system, and technology), unlike the following three phases, which operate vertically, focusing on one particular domain.

2.2.3 Phases B, C, and D (Elaboration of Business, Information System, and Technology Architectures)

Most of the content of the following three phases—B (Business), C (Information System), and D (Technology)—consists in detailing the target and baseline architecture, measuring the gap between the two, and evaluating the impact of change on all facets of the enterprise. The combination of these elements is used to draft the roadmap for transition. This first draft of the roadmap is elaborated progressively throughout phases B, C, and D, and serves as the foundation for phases E and F, which are in charge of defining the transformation plan (Figure 2.3).

Each phase begins with the definition of the views that will be used to materialize the baseline and target architectures. Remember that the goal of these views is to adapt the representations of the architecture to each stakeholder's viewpoint.

Architecture descriptions are consigned to the architecture definition document (central document). This document is enriched during each phase, before being finalized and validated prior to the start of migration work. Concretely, each phase will complete the chapter(s) that concerns it, so that the document spans all architecture domains.

Of course, as well as depending on each situation, the choice of target architecture also integrates recurrent questions. Consequently, TOGAF recommends that the repository be reviewed before each decision in order to reuse the experience accumulated during earlier work wherever possible. This repository review is noted as a "checklist" action at the start of each phase, so as to conform to the norms in place within the enterprise and to promote general harmonization.

Impact assessment should be considered in a cross-organizational way, for two reasons. First, because each phase evaluates its impact beyond its own scope. During phase B, for example, the impact of evolutions on technical elements is also assessed. If, for example, the executive management team

FIGURE 2.3

Main activities common to phases B, C, and D.

decides to remove a product range, it is easy to work out the consequences of this decision on the corresponding database. Second, because the sheer number of relationships within an enterprise can lead to all sorts of unexpected side effects on entities outside the initial scope.

During these three phases, another essential result is expected, namely the definition of requirements. We go into this point in more detail in the chapter dedicated to the requirements management phase (Section 2.2.6). Generally speaking, the aim here is to clearly specify what will be implemented in the target architecture. These requirements are recorded in the "Architecture Requirements Specification" document, which is delivered by each of the three phases. Special attention must be paid to so-called "nonfunctional" requirements, which determine the conditions and limitations surrounding the delivery of services. These limitations have a significant influence on solutions, their feasibility, and their cost, which can draw into question certain choices made earlier.

Phase B (business architecture)

The structural similarity of phases B, C, and D should not detract from the determining role of phase B, since it is the business that drives the architecture in all its forms. The formalization of business elements (requirements, processes, entities) is the prelude to all valid logical or technical constructions.

This is all the more true when we consider that the goal of phase B is also to demonstrate the pertinence of the work being carried out. Goals are established during the earlier phases, but it is only when business architecture elements are precisely developed that the target solution can be installed and its consequences observed. For example, the description of modifications carried out on a business process shows the real-life result of these modifications on tasks run by operators, new services to provide, or modifications applied to exchanged information.

In terms of architecture descriptions, phase B mainly concentrates on the following elements:

- Business motivation elements (drivers, goals, objectives)
- Organizational units
- Business functions and services
- Business processes
- Business roles and actors
- Business entities

Business entities describe key business concepts and provide the essential entry point to phase C (in the Data Architecture subphase). Business processes are often the key to understanding an enterprise's real activity, and by extension its architecture.[2]

Phase C (information systems architecture)

Information system architecture is a kind of bridge between the business view and its physical translation. It defines software components (applications and data) that support the automation or realization of business capabilities and functions, without integrating technological realities (this point is discussed in the Phase D part).

Remember that phase C (information system architecture) is itself composed of two subphases: data architecture and application architecture.

---

[2]We look at these two points in detail in Chapter 12.

These two facets (data and application) are reunited in a single phase because of their proximity in the construction of information system architecture. One of the expected results consists in allocating each data group to one application component, which will handle its management, becoming, as it were, the owner of the data group in question.

Phase D (technology architecture)

Unsurprisingly, the role of phase D is to establish the technological and physical correspondence of the elements developed during the previous phases. In particular, technology architecture defines the platforms and execution environments on which the applications run and the data sources are hosted for use.

So what are the links between application architecture and technology architecture? A first approach consists in considering them as two separate elements, so as to avoid any technical "intrusion" into the work of the application architect. The opposite approach would lead us to consider application architecture as a simple reformulation of the technical reality.

A position that is too dogmatic will lead to a dead end: What is the point of developing a "virtual" application architecture with no link to the reality of the deployed applications? Common sense (and purse strings) calls for more realism. Even though it must remain logical, application architecture (including its service-oriented architecture (SOA) formulation) is not completely separate from its physical translation. The most important thing here is the identification of the role of each application or component, independent of its technical implementation: the fundamental structure is similar and the viewpoint is different, just like a logical service interface, which is not fundamentally modified by its implementation in Java or via a web service.

Bearing in mind these two perspectives, a question comes to mind: Should we start by describing the technical architecture or the application architecture? This point is linked to the iterations of the ADM cycle, which will be more generally dealt with in Section 2.3. Remember that the ADM cycle is a generic framework, which does not forbid intrusions into earlier or later phases (the TOGAF document is strewn with suggestions of this type). In practice, no preestablished choices exist: this is the famous choice between "top down" and "bottom up," which always finishes with a compromise. The deployment of external tools imposes a type of architecture that can sometimes have a significant impact on application architecture solutions. In other contexts, architecture will be more oriented by architectural principles, for example to obtain a more progressive structure.

However, let's get back to the result of phase D: the technological architecture, in other words, a coherent set of software components, infrastructures, and technical platforms. These elements can come from external providers or be produced directly by teams within the enterprise. Moreover, the choice between deploying tools that are available in the marketplace or tools resulting from specific developments is a recurrent theme for an enterprise architect. Here too, the repository (see Section 4.1) will assist in this type of choice by making available a set of common norms, patterns, tools, and practices, which will help harmonize solutions within the enterprise.

2.2.4 Phases E and F (opportunities and solutions, migration planning)

At this point of the ADM cycle, the operational realization of architecture transformation truly begins: projects are set up, schedules defined, resources identified, and operational monitoring put in place. The previous phases have provided the target, an overall roadmap, and now their concrete implementation has to be defined.

Phases E and F look at the scheduling and organization of the implementation of new architecture. Emphasis is placed on building the migration path, which must bring true business benefit to each step.

During phase E, the results of the elaboration phases (B, C, and D) are consolidated: architectures, requirements, and gaps. This consolidation constitutes the raw material used to define transition architectures, while bearing in mind the enterprise's capability for change (for example, new applications to develop and evolutions of existing applications, according to the coverage of the business functions). Technical and organization feasibility, compromises between requirements and costs, and integration constraints are also studied.

Phase F precisely establishes migration scheduling, as well as the constitution of implementation projects and their organization, goals, and costs.

2.2.5 Phases G and H (implementation governance, architecture change management)

Phase G establishes the definitive version of architecture contracts with implementation projects, including recommendations from the architecture board. These signed contracts constitute the basis for conformity reviews of implementation projects.

Phase H handles the management of the deployed architecture: change management, including the evaluation of change requests that impact the architecture. It should be noted that certain evolution requests can lead to new ADM cycles.

2.2.6 Requirements management

What is a requirement?

TOGAF provides the following definition: "A quantitative statement of a business need that must be met by a particular architecture or work package."

In concrete terms, a set of requirements determines what must actually be implemented, and conversely, what is not retained. Based on given business goals, concrete requirements generally translate how different factors, be they technical, budgetary or organizational, are to be taken into account.

It must be emphasized here that TOGAF advocates a dynamic view of requirements, which are not frozen at the beginning of a cycle but rather can evolve over the course of the project. This is a very important point, since experience has shown that there is often a difference between the initial requirements defined by the business actors and the actual reality of implementation within information systems. Consequently, it is through constant comparison that a solution is developed, in order to take into account all kinds of constraints as early as possible.

Functional requirements and nonfunctional requirements

Based on goals, which are defined in general terms, requirements are usually described in the form of short, precise statements. For example, if the goal is "to provide clients with a mode for ordering online, to replace the current telephone ordering mode," then requirements of the following type will be found: "The client must be able to order a product online at all times."

In actual fact, this requirement contains two requirements of different types:

- A functional requirement: "The client must be able to order a product online."
- A nonfunctional requirement: "It must be possible to place an order at all times."

This distinction between the functional and the nonfunctional is widely recognized today. The functional handles the "what," while the nonfunctional deals with the conditions under which the service is provided. These conditions concern performance, security, availability, reliability, and so on and are the object of detailed listings.[3]

The impact of nonfunctional requirements on architecture is particularly important. For example, for one functional requirement, a high-level reliability requirement will result in the implementation of appropriate means (duplication, dedicated infrastructure, etc.), which will have a significant influence on the architecture of the future system. As a consequence, the way in which nonfunctional requirements are expressed must be particularly well thought out, and above all quantitatively specified wherever possible. In the previous example, the initial formulation proves to be both too vague and too radical. In this case, it would be better to formulate the requirement as follows: "The product ordering system will be unavailable for a maximum of one hour per month" (obviously as far as this corresponds to the actual reality).

Who writes requirements? The most accurate answer to this question is "pretty much everyone." Even if it seems at first glance that responsibility for this task lies primarily with the business side, the previous example illustrates that this activity requires specific skills. While it is true that business needs must not be driven by technical considerations, it is the role of the architect to clarify the formulation of requirements, based on his knowledge of the underlying consequences.

A typical approach is to request an "expert" reformulation of requirements. In this way, we can ensure that requirements make sense to "experts" (in other words, to people specialized in domains above the current domain), that they are taken into account, and that they are feasible according to a reformulation that is accepted by several parties.

The following is an example of a functional requirement formulated during the preliminary phase: "Every client has an account which can be accessed by the account manager."

A business analyst then reformulates this requirement as follows: "An account manager has access to all his clients' accounts. He does not have access to accounts which do not belong to his clients. When a client has no designated account manager, "cross-organizational" account managers have access to the account, and temporarily play the role of account manager. Conflicts (absence of an account, account manager rights, and so on) are managed by the system administrator in co-ordination with the sales manager."

Here, the business analyst has reformulated the requirement, notably by taking into account concepts and information that were not defined during the preliminary phase. The concepts of "administrator" and "cross-organizational account manager" and information on rights were only defined during phase B, thereby allowing the requirement to be reformulated more precisely.

Centralized requirements management

Appearing as it does in the center of the crop circle diagram, requirements management occupies a special place in the ADM cycle. It applies to all phases of the ADM, yet is considered to be independent of each. This choice is explained by the fact that requirements management, as we have just seen, requires particular know-how, independent of the domain in question. Moreover, requirements are not defined according to the type of architecture, since they express a view that is external to the system,

---

[3]See ISO 9126.

and constitute an inseparable whole. Thus, all requirements are analyzed together, using dedicated tools and techniques.

Requirements management is an activity involving the rationalization, hierarchical organization, and monitoring of a set of requirements grouped together within a dedicated repository. This repository is not frozen, and can evolve during the different phases, each of which can add, further define, or invalidate certain requirements.

Figure 2.4 illustrates the overall functioning. Each phase of the ADM produces or modifies requirements, which are then collected, qualified, and organized into a hierarchy by requirements management. These requirements then serve as input for other ADM phases, during which they are analyzed and their impact on architecture determined. This permanent roundtrip encourages an objective view of requirements (for example, removal of repetition), as well as facilitating homogeneous formulation and maintaining overall consistency.

Phase A provides an initial list of requirements, most of which are not described in detail. During phases B, C, and D, certain requirements will be specified, while others will be added according to the type of architecture in question (business, system, or technical). Business requirements are obviously central. Developed during phase B, these requirements are implemented from a system and technical standpoint during phases C and D.

Phase E reviews and consolidates the set of requirements, with particular focus on requirements linked to interoperability. Functional requirements are allocated to the different transition states.

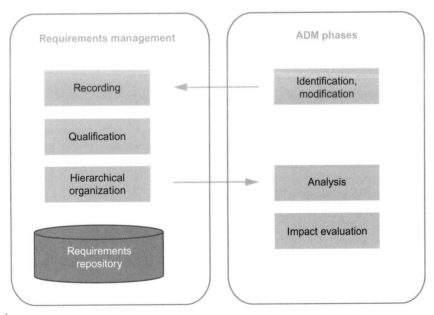

FIGURE 2.4

Dialog between requirements management and ADM phases. (For color version of this figure, the reader is referred to the online version of this chapter.)

Phase G establishes requirements related to scheduling and divides responsibility for requirements between the different implementation projects.

Requirements are consigned to the "Architecture Requirements Specification" deliverable, which provides a view of the state of the requirements repository at a given point of the ADM cycle.

Requirements management techniques

Requirements management is a domain in its own right, and has been the subject of several published works resulting from the fields of software development or business analysis (Volere,[4] BABOK[5]) and systems engineering (SysML[6]).

The scope of enterprise architecture is appreciably different. However, tried and tested techniques can be used and adapted. An enterprise architect is not responsible for writing application specifications documents. However, the formulation of the main requirements, which concretely translate goals, does orient architecture choices.

Probably the most useful technique is that of the "requirement list," which consists of breaking down requirements into basic statements, each of which has a set of properties. These properties help organize requirements according to numerous criteria, and make it easier to objectively analyze them. We have already used a statement of this type with the example "The client must be able to order the product online."

Each basic requirement facilitates the identification and maintenance of links to other architecture elements (goals, processes, application components, etc.). This structured set in a tooled repository constitutes a precious decision-making aid. Several examples of this type are available in Section 7.4.

Business scenarios

Business scenarios derive the characteristics of architecture directly from the high-level requirements of the business. They are used to help identify and understand business needs, and thereby to derive the business requirements that architecture development has to address.

A business scenario describes:

- A business process, application, or set of applications that can be enabled by the architecture
- The business and technology environment
- The people and computing components (called "actors") who execute the scenario
- The desired outcome of correct execution

A good business scenario is representative of a significant business need or problem and enables vendors to understand the value that a developed solution brings to the customer organization.

A business scenario is essentially a complete description of a business problem, both in business and in architectural terms, which enables individual requirements to be viewed in relation to one another in

---

[4]www.volere.co.uk/template.htm.
[5]www.iiba.org/imis15/IIBA/Home/IIBA_Website/home.aspx.
[6]www.sysml.org.

the context of the overall problem. Business scenarios also play an important role in gaining the buy-in of these key personnel members to the overall project and its end-product: the enterprise architecture.

Business scenarios exist to elucidate requirements, show feasibility, and show how the new architecture will enable goals and requirements to be properly supported.

Business scenarios can be prototypes, but can also be descriptions that show, for example, that a new component combined with the existing application will facilitate the essential parts of a business process.

2.3 ITERATIONS

2.3.1 Iteration cycles

TOGAF strongly recommends the iterative approach and provides a set of best practices and advice on this subject.[7] For example, TOGAF proposes four iteration cycles, based on a grouping of phases:

- Architecture capability iteration, which groups the preliminary phase and the vision phase (phase A).
- Architecture development iteration in the business, system and technological fields, during phases B, C, and D, respectively.
- Transition planning iteration, made up of phases E and F.
- Architecture governance iteration, dedicated to implementation and monitoring during phases G and H (Figure 2.5).

Typically, a cycle can run several development iterations (phases B, C, and D) in order to successively deal with business architecture, information system architecture, and technological architecture, before starting the transition and planning phases (E and F). This can result in the following phasing:

- Vision phase
- Iteration 1 (Business1, System1, Technology1)
- Iteration 2 (Business2, System2, Technology2)
- Iteration 3 (Business3, System3, Technology3)

2.3.2 Priority to target architecture or baseline architecture

These choices are partially guided by the perceived value or relevance of the existing architecture: priority can be given to the baseline architecture, or conversely to the target architecture.

For example, the first development iteration cycle (B1, C1, D1) will be dedicated to describing the existing architecture on all levels (business, information system, and technological), while the solution (the target) will only be outlined. The second iteration (B2, C2, D2) will focus particularly on the development of the target architecture on each of these three levels.

---

[7]TOGAF9, chapter 19.

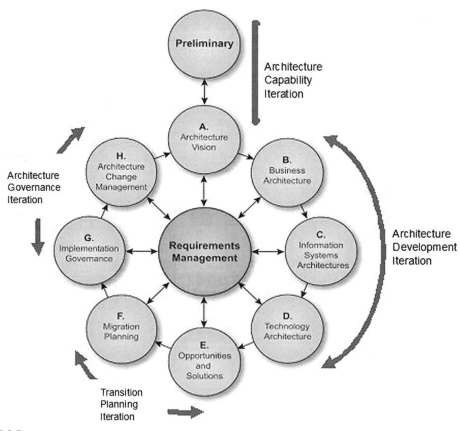

FIGURE 2.5

ADM and iterations—TOGAF9. (For color version of this figure, the reader is referred to the online version of this chapter.)

Source: © 2008 The Open Group.

The opposite choice is also possible, in other words, focusing first on the target architecture in a BCD cycle and then concentrating on the existing architecture during a later iteration. This technique can be useful when we want to work quickly on solutions, or if a large-scale revision of the existing architecture has been planned.

2.4 ADM TECHNIQUES AND GUIDELINES

Part III of TOGAF (*ADM Guidelines and Techniques*) is presented as a kind of "Swiss army knife," whose different parts are used according to our different needs. Most known themes related to enterprise architecture are found here, with recommended references on the subjects dealt with.

2.4.1 **The different techniques**

These different techniques (there are 14 of them) can be categorized as follows:

- Techniques linked to the organization and management of participants:
  - Stakeholder management
  - Business transformation readiness assessment
- Information system architecture techniques:
  - Architecture patterns
  - Architecture principles
  - Using TOGAF to define and govern SOAs
  - Interoperability requirements
  - Security architecture
- Techniques linked to architecture development:
  - Business scenarios
  - Gap analysis
- Techniques linked to the planning and deployment of the target architecture:
  - Migration planning techniques
  - Capability-based planning
- TOGAF adaptation techniques:
  - Applying iteration to the ADM
  - Applying the ADM at different enterprise levels
- Cross-organizational techniques:
  - Risk management

Given the density of certain themes would warrant a whole book in themselves, TOGAF provides a widely accepted summary of techniques, along with references and standards on the subject. This is notably the case with risk management and SOA. More generally, the aim is to provide a kind of "method of the method," enabling each theme to be appropriated in order that we can build our own guidelines from the examples provided.

2.4.2 **Techniques in ADM phases**

In the chapters dedicated to the different techniques, TOGAF links each technique to the ADM phases during which it is the most useful. Table 2.1 shows which techniques are used during which ADM phases. Techniques are also identified.

   We have chosen not to explain each technique in detail. For more information, readers can refer to the TOGAF document (part III). However, certain techniques are discussed in certain chapters of this book:

- Section 1.2.2: Gap analysis, capability-based planning
- Section 1.2.5: Stakeholder management, business transformation readiness assessment
- Section 12.1: Service-oriented architecture
- Section 2.3: Applying iterations to the ADM
- Section 2.2.6: The technique of business scenarios
- Section 12.3: Interoperability requirements

Table 2.1 Use of Techniques in ADM Phases

Techniques	Phases[a]	
Stakeholder management	Preliminary phase Phases A, E, and F	M
Business transformation readiness assessment	Preliminary phase Phases A, E, and F	R
Architecture patterns	Phases A, B, C, and D	S
Architecture principles	Preliminary phase Phase A	R
SOA	Phases B, C, and D	S
Interoperability requirements	Phases A, B, C, D, E, and F	R
Security architecture	All phases	R
Business scenarios	Phases A and B	R
Gap analysis	Phases B, C, and D	R
Migration planning techniques	Phases E and F	R
Capability-based planning	Phases E and F	R
Applying iteration to the ADM	Preliminary phase Phase A	M
Applying the ADM at different enterprise levels	Preliminary phase Phase A	R
Risk management	All phases	R

M, mandatory; R, recommended; S, supported.
[a]*We have indicated here the main phases during which each technique is used.*

2.5 FUNDAMENTAL CONCEPTS

The following fundamental concepts were introduced in this chapter:

- ADM cycle: Step-by-step approach and method to transform an enterprise architecture.
- ADM phase: Main stage of the ADM cycle, described by its goals, content, inputs, and outputs.
- ADM iterations: ADM cycle path with repetition of certain phases. TOGAF recommends the use of iterative paths in order to encourage the flexibility and adaptation of the ADM cycle.
- Business scenario: Prototype or model of a subset of the system, made up of a business process and a set of software components or applications, and of all the technical and organizational elements necessary to attain the desired result. Used to validate options and to verify the feasibility of a solution.

The Components of TOGAF Architecture

3

CHAPTER OUTLINE

This chapter is dedicated to part IV of TOGAF, which concentrates on the content framework, in other words, on the elements that will constitute the description of an architecture. This includes basic objects; deliverables; types of views such as catalogs, matrices, or diagrams; and the "building blocks" of the system.

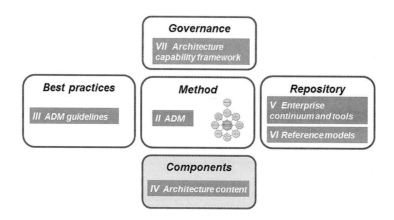

3.1 ARCHITECTURE COMPONENTS

3.1.1 Artifacts, deliverables, and building blocks

Part IV of the TOGAF document (Architecture Content Framework) focuses on architecture components and the media used to describe them. This is a fundamental point that will be widely discussed in Chapters 5 and 6. As we have already mentioned several times, architectural change projects are undertaken by a group of actors, who must understand one another and cooperate during each stage of the work, irrespective of their different concerns and specific viewpoints. A precise definition of the components, vocabulary, and representations used is therefore essential to efficient communication.

In this part of the document, TOGAF defines four types of architectural components:

- Basic architectural *elements* defined using a *metamodel*.
- *Artifacts*, which are a means of communication used to present a particular view of the architecture. Artifacts are organized into *catalogs*, *matrices*, and *diagrams*.
- *Building blocks*, which are the essential components of the architecture that constitute its skeleton.
- *Deliverables*, which are documents built based on earlier elements and formally validated as output of the different ADM phases.

Figure 3.1 presents the relationships that exist between these different components. The role of artifacts is particularly important, as architecture communication agents.

Here are some examples of these four types of components:

- Architectural elements: An actor, a requirement, an item of data
- Artifacts: The list of processes, the data/application matrix, a class diagram
- "Building blocks": An application, a business process
- Deliverables: The "architecture vision" document, in which we find the list of processes or class diagrams.

It should be pointed out here that some elements defined in the metamodel are potential "building blocks," inasmuch as they are identified as being reusable components of the system (see Section 3.4).

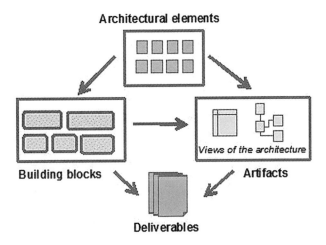

FIGURE 3.1

Architectural elements, building blocks, artifacts, and deliverables.

3.1.2 Using other content frameworks

An enterprise may prefer to use other content frameworks associated with the TOGAF ADM approach, such as Zachman or DODAF, or even a framework specific to the enterprise itself. This choice is justified when it turns out to be too costly to call the existing architecture into question or when business-specific standard frameworks must be used.

3.2 THE METAMODEL

The metamodel[1] describes the basic elements used to build an enterprise's architecture. The metamodel form enables all the elements and all their relationships to be represented through a simplified UML diagram (see Figure 3.3). The general structure of the metamodel is shown in Figure 3.2.

Here we find the four architecture domains (business, data, application, and technology), along with an additional domain (principles, vision, etc.). The business domain is broken down into three subdomains: motivation, organization, and function. Each architectural element belongs to one particular domain according to its nature, as we will see in the following pages.

The metamodel is also organized as follows: a "TOGAF core" part containing fundamental elements and an "extensions" part made up of elements that enrich the core" metamodel with regard to a particular aspect.

3.2.1 The "TOGAF core metamodel"

Figure 3.3 presents the "TOGAF core metamodel" in the form of a simplified UML diagram. The elements of the TOGAF core metamodel are organized using the structure presented earlier, in other words, the four architectural domains (business, data, application, and technology).

---

[1]TOGAF9, chapter 34.

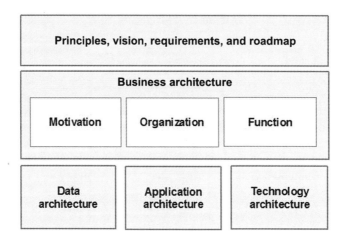

FIGURE 3.2

General structure of the metamodel.

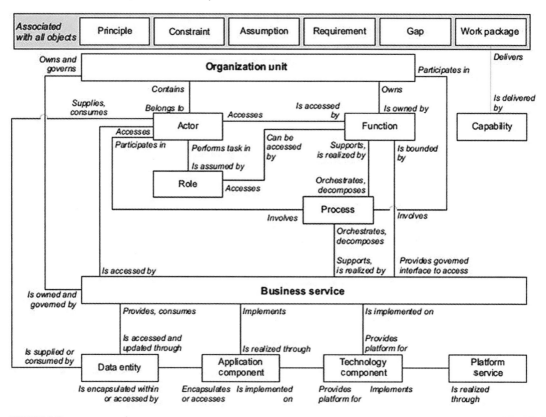

FIGURE 3.3

Architecture elements metamodel—TOGAF9.

- *Business architecture*
  - Organization unit
  - Actor
  - Role
  - Process
  - Function
  - Business service
- *Data architecture*
  - Data entity
- *Application architecture*
  - Application component
- *Technology architecture*
  - Service platform
  - Technology component

This breakdown is enriched by the elements used to describe requirements, principles, and the road-map: principle, constraint, assumption, requirement, gap, work package, and capability.

These elements play a slightly unusual role, inasmuch as they are potentially connected to all the other metamodel elements. These "omnipresent" links simply translate the fact that these elements constitute a set of justifications with regard to the architecture as a whole, and can be used as starting points for maintaining traceability links.

3.2.2 Metamodel extensions

The extensions used to enrich the "TOGAF core metamodel" are organized into several families, each of which adds additional elements to the "core" metamodel. The six extension families are as follows:

- *Motivation*
  - Goal or objective
  - Driver
- *Infrastructure consolidation*
  - Location
  - Physical application component
  - Logical technology component
- *Governance*
  - Measure
  - Contract
  - Service quality
- *Process modeling*
  - Event
  - Control
  - Product
- *Data modeling*
  - Logical data component
  - Physical data component
- *Services*
  - IS service

The goal of this organization into extension families is to make it easier to adapt the metamodel through the choice of such and such a family according to particular needs. Extensions are added to the "core" metamodel as particular modules, which will extend the vocabulary used.

As an example, Figure 3.4 shows the extensions dedicated to process modeling.

In this case, three elements have been added:

- The *event*: Enables events linked to processes to be represented, such as the event that triggers a process.
- The *control*: Typically acts on the execution of a process, by directing it to such and such a branch of the process.
- The *product*: Represents the input and output of the activities of a process.

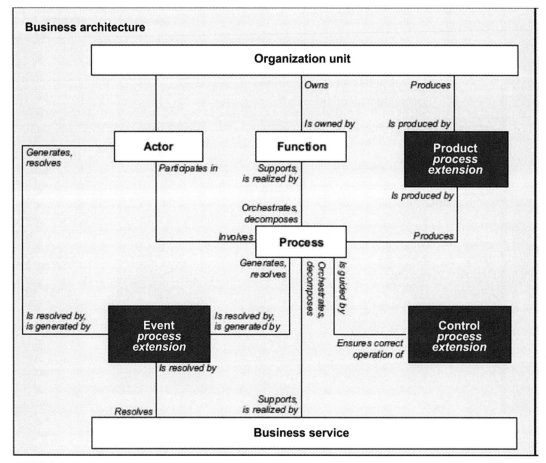

FIGURE 3.4

"Process modeling" extensions to the TOGAF9 metamodel. (For color version of this figure, the reader is referred to the online version of this chapter.)

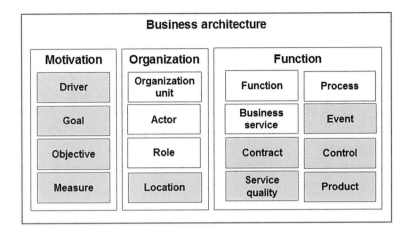

FIGURE 3.5

Complete set of elements (core + extensions) of the business domain.

This extension mechanism can be used as a means of specializing architecture descriptions within an enterprise. This manner of doing things is one element of the general approach to adapting the TOGAF framework.

Naturally, every element has its place in one of the parts of the general structure, whether it belongs to the TOGAF core metamodel or to one of its extensions. For example, Figure 3.5 shows the distribution of the different elements in the business part and its three subparts (motivation, organization, and function).

In this schema, gray elements are extension elements, while white elements are "core metamodel" elements.

3.2.3 Conceptual, logical, and physical

As in the previous figure, Figure 3.6 shows the contents of the data architecture, application architecture, and technology architecture domains.

The content of these three domains is relatively similar. Each domain is made up of a conceptual element, a logical element, and a physical element.

3.2.4 Relationship to ADM phases

What links exist between the phases of the ADM and the elements of the metamodel? A first approach, based on the structuring into domains, leads us to consider that there is a link between the breakdown of the metamodel and the three architecture development phases of the ADM (B, C, and D). When we consider that phase C is further broken down into two subphases, we find identical terms, with phases B (Business), C1 (Data), C2 (Application), and D (Technology). However, this equivalence turns out to be more subtle when we consider the elements contained in each domain.

For example, the "data entity" element is naturally positioned in the "data architecture" domain. However, the identification of data entities is a task that belongs to phase B of the ADM, "business

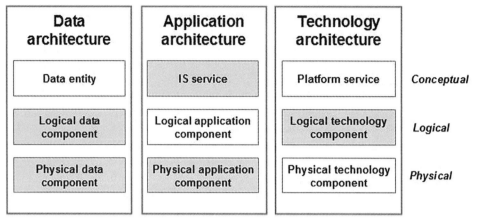

FIGURE 3.6

Complete set of elements (core + extensions) of the three domains.

architecture," which produces a model of these entities as output. Moreover, this approach is relevant, since business information (or business objects) is part of the business view of the system, and it would be a mistake to ignore it until phase C (in the "data architecture" subphase).

The "physical application component" element, located in the "application architecture" domain, is not really well located in phase C, which is dedicated to application architecture.[2] As a physical element, it is developed in phase D (technology architecture). Here too, the ADM cycle follows a traditional route, dealing first with a logical description, which is translated into technical components during the technology architecture phase (phase D).[3]

These two examples show that the structure of the two worlds (ADM phases and metamodel domains) does not always exactly match. This may seem surprising, especially as TOGAF tends to bring them together. However, this distinction between phases and architecture domains is realistic. On the one hand, the aim is strict classification; on the other hand, the objective is step-by-step development including all facets and constraints. In this regard, the ADM cycle is inevitably both more complex and more flexible than a formal classification grid, and this is what gives it its agility and efficiency.

3.3 ARTIFACTS

Artifacts designate the representation tools used as a means of communication. They show a part of the architecture in various forms and constitute a major part of the repository.

---

[2]TOGAF9, chapter 11.1: The goal of phase C states this clearly: "The applications are not described as computer systems, but as logical groups of capabilities" and further on: "The applications and their capabilities are defined without reference to particular technologies."

[3]In the organization of the metamodel, technology architecture designates the infrastructure, and application architecture is dedicated to business application components (logical or physical).

3.3.1 Viewpoints and views

The concepts of view and viewpoint play a key role in communication on architecture. A viewpoint designates a representational view of the architecture or addresses stakeholder concerns. The viewpoint of a business analyst and that of a project manager are different and require adapted representations. A viewpoint encompasses a collection of views, which define a particular form of representation.

The terms "artifact" and "view" in TOGAF are relatively close in meaning and correspond to a way or visualizing and communicating information captured in the metamodel for specific stakeholder needs. The term "artifact" is a generic concept designating all representations of the architecture, while "views" are organized methodically into "viewpoints."

3.3.2 Catalogs, matrices, and diagrams

There are three categories of architectural representation forms:

- *Catalogs*, which are organized lists of elements of the same nature. For example, the catalog of applications or the dictionary of business entities.
- *Matrices*, which show the relationships that exist between elements: the actors/processes matrix or the data/software components matrix.
- *Diagrams*, which show a subset of the architecture in the form of a graphical schema. UML diagrams are a good example.

Figure 3.7 shows an example of a diagram. This is a UML class diagram corresponding to a particular view, containing classes with their links but not showing their attributes. In general, other views will be used, for example, to describe all the properties of classes in detail, or conversely to provide a high-level outline of business entities.

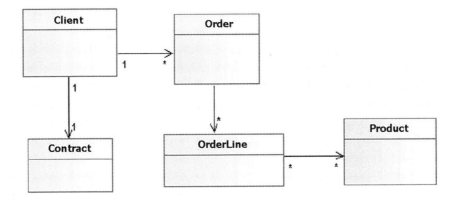

FIGURE 3.7

Example of a UML class diagram. (For color version of this figure, the reader is referred to the online version of this chapter.)

We will not go into further detail on these three types here; for more information, readers can refer to Chapters 5 and 6 in which we discuss this subject in detail, notably the major role of diagrams in the representation of enterprise architecture.

3.3.3 The catalog of TOGAF views

By default, TOGAF provides a list of views with a detailed description of their content. The viewpoints used to classify them are simply those of the ADM breakdown. Each phase of the ADM is considered a viewpoint that includes a set of catalog-, matrix-, or diagram-type views.[4] For example, the "business" viewpoint, which corresponds to phase B, defines the following views (extract):

- Organization/actor catalog
- Process flow catalog
- Actor/role matrix
- Functional decomposition diagram
- Process flow diagram

Each viewpoint (vision, business, data, application, etc.) defines the content of its views in the same way. Chapters 7–11 of this book present detailed examples of each of the TOGAF catalog's views.

This organization into viewpoints associated with ADM phases is highly pertinent, since each phase will consider the architecture from a particular perspective, depending on its objectives. However, in practice, this catalog has to be refined in order to better "suit" the actors (stakeholders) participating in the development of the architecture. This point was already raised during the description of the ADM phases (Section 2.2), which begins by identifying the viewpoints and defining the views that will be used. Naturally, the aim here is not to reinvent the wheel, and this stage will make widespread use of the TOGAF catalog, which, despite being open to criticism, does provide a significant starting point.

How can we build our own catalog of views? By being pragmatic. The main criterion here is efficiency of communication, which can only be developed by closely collaborating with participants, who are the most directly concerned. With this in mind, certain practices will contribute to the quality of the result:

- Start with what already exists, and link it to TOGAF catalog views. It is not unusual to find diagrams that are very similar to the diagrams defined by TOGAF; with just a few adjustments, we can avoid shaking up existing habits.
- Use concrete examples, wherever possible, rather than imposing abstract formulation.
- Communicate widely using different means, and pay close attention to feedback.

In most cases, this catalog can evolve, under the responsibility of the architecture board, which is in charge of validating modifications in order to safeguard its consistency.

3.3.4 Tools and languages

Without going so far as to define a fixed catalog of tools, TOGAF does recommend the use of standards wherever possible. This is notably the case for diagrams, with UML[5] and BPMN,[6] languages that are widely used in the modeling of information systems and business processes. In practice, enterprises

---

[4]TOGAF 9, chapter 35.6.
[5]www.uml.org.
[6]www.bpmn.org.

often use a set of various tools: office products, modeling tools, intranet, and so on. However, it is difficult to imagine not having structured tooling to ensure the consistency and management of all the different components of the architecture.

3.4 BUILDING BLOCKS

3.4.1 The game of building

"Building blocks" fundamentally represent the basic bricks that make up the system. More simply put, they satisfy the need to break down all representations of a complex system into subelements. For example, such and such an information system is broken down into domains, then into subsystems, which are themselves further broken down into applications. This example illustrates the composition relationship that exists between "building blocks," which, like matryoshka dolls, are built by aggregating lower-level "building blocks." However, this concept is more general, and the breakdown into "building blocks" applies whatever the type of architecture (business, system, or technology). Business processes, architecture foundations, or organizational units are good candidates to become architecture "building blocks."

TOGAF specifies the characteristics of "building blocks" as follows:

- Corresponds to a set of functions that meet business needs.
- Can be made up of other "building blocks."
- Interacts with other "building blocks."
- Can ideally be reused and replaced in the architecture.

The tasks of identifying and defining "building blocks" are central to architecture development, notably information systems. Fundamentally, a system is made up of a collection of interconnected "building blocks." Depending on the level of detail required, these building blocks "take on board" different types of element. In a large-scale organization, each subsystem can be made up of a set of actors, processes, applications, and technical platforms. If we consider the whole system without going into detail, these subsystems will be considered as "building blocks," each with a defined scope and defined exchanges between them. At this level, the description remains "black box." Naturally, other views will have the task of opening these boxes in order to describe the contents of such and such a subsystem in detail.

This way of looking at things is not revolutionary, and seems like simple common sense. The difficulty lies in choosing the best way of breaking down the system, in order to implement all business capabilities within a given timeframe and budget. Furthermore, this is the aim of the ADM method, which provides a structured approach and a set of practices to help the enterprise reach this objective.

"Building blocks" are elements that are conducive to capitalization and reuse. Consequently, they occupy a strategic position in the architecture repository (see Section 4.1).

3.4.2 Architecture building blocks and solution building blocks

We have already mentioned this terminology in Section 1.2.3. As a reminder, TOGAF makes a distinction between architecture building blocks (ABB) and solution building blocks (SBB) in order to separate purely documentary elements from physical components.

3.5 DELIVERABLES

3.5.1 Description and use

Deliverables play a special role in the progress of an ADM cycle. The approval of deliverables by stakeholders establishes formal consensus and defines a state of results from which future work can be carried out. This does not mean that each deliverable is provided and validated by one single phase. On the contrary, many deliverables are developed over the course of several phases, each progressively adding to and consolidating the deliverable in question. In this case, deliverables can be viewed as the gateways that involve the review and acceptance of outputs from one phase/activity as input into the next. This is the case for the "architecture definition document," whose different parts are developed during phases B, C, and D for the chapters dedicated to business architecture, system architecture, and technology architecture, respectively.

Deliverables are mostly documents, put together from architecture elements, "building blocks," and artifacts. However, certain deliverables are represented directly by models. This is the case for the "ABB" deliverable, whose aim is to formalize an architecture model.

TOGAF defines 22 deliverables and provides a description and a template for each. As an example, the template for the "architecture definition document" deliverable presents as follows:

- Scope
- Goals and constraints
- Architecture principles
- Baseline architecture
- Architecture models
  - Business architecture models
  - Data architecture models
  - Application architecture models
  - Technology architecture models
- Rationale and justification for architectural approach
- Mapping to the architecture repository
  - Mapping to the architecture landscape
  - Mapping to reference models
  - Mapping to standards
  - Reuse assessment
- Gap analysis
- Impact assessment

As we can see (and possibly regret), TOGAF provides a highly succinct description of the document template. It is described more as a typical table of contents, which must be further specified if it is to be effectively used within a particular organization.

Note that this deliverable includes several diagrams from business, application, and technological models.

3.5.2 Deliverables and ADM phases

Table 3.1 presents the main deliverables resulting from the different ADM phases.

Table 3.1 Deliverables and ADM Phases

No.	Deliverable	ADM Phases
L01	Request for Architecture Work	Pr
L02	Architecture Principles	Pr
L03	Tailored Architecture Framework	Pr
L04	Business Principles, Business Goals, and Business Drivers	Pr, A, B
L05	Architecture Vision	A
L06	Statement of Architecture Work	A
L07	Communication Plan	A
L08	Architecture Definition Document	B, C, D
L09	Architecture Requirements Specification	B, C, D, E, F
L10	Architecture Roadmap	B, C, D, E, F
L11	Transition Architecture	E, F
L12	Implementation and Migration Plan	E, F
L13	Architecture contract	F
L14	Capability Assessment	A, E
L15	Compliance Assessment	G
L16	Change Request	H

In this table, we have chosen to highlight the major deliverables corresponding to each ADM phase, without taking into account possible updates or adjustments that can always occur in other phases.

We have not included the architecture repository in our table. Although TOGAF classifies this as a deliverable, it is rather an information container, which is only validated through the documents that result from its contents (the same is true for ABB and SBB).

Deliverables linked to architecture work management

The *Tailored Architecture Framework* (L03), developed during the preliminary phase, plays a special role. Typically, it enables the TOGAF framework to be adapted to the enterprise's context. It is one of the results of the preliminary phase, which initiates the elements that are to be implemented by transformation projects on different levels: approach, contents, repository, and governance.

The *Request for Architecture Work* (L01), which results from the preliminary phase, triggers the start of a new ADM cycle. Note here that the response may be negative and the enterprise may decide not to start the architecture change ADM cycle (go-no go).

During phase A, the *Statement of Architecture Work* (L06) describes all the elements necessary to the organization of the ADM cycle, based on the request for architecture work: management, procedures, cycle planning, and scope.

The *Communication Plan* (L07), also produced in phase A, provides the internal communication framework: means, tools, and procedures.

Deliverables linked to principles, goals, and requirements

The *Architecture Principles* (L02), defined during the preliminary phase, establish the general architecture principles that apply to all ADM cycles.

The *Business Principles, Business Goals, and Business Drivers* (L04) specify the context and goals of an ADM cycle. Initialized during the preliminary phase, they are added to and consolidated during phases A and B (vision and business).

Requirements are recorded in the *Architecture Requirements Specification* document (L09).

Architecture description deliverables

During phase A, the *Architecture Vision* (L05) initiates future work by providing a macroscopic and cross-organizational view: goals, requirements, baseline, and target architectures.

The *Architecture Definition Document* (L08) is the main deliverable of the architecture development phases: B (Business), C (Information System), and D (Technology). In particular, it contains information on architecture (baseline and target), gap analysis, and impact analysis.

Deliverables dedicated to architecture transition

The *Architecture Roadmap* (L10) results from the development phases B, C, and D and establishes the progression of the transition, the definition of each stage, and macroscopic planning. These elements will be defined by the two following deliverables, during phases E and F.

The *Transition Architecture* (L11) describes the different stages of transition, and the breakdown of work into work packages, each with its content and dependencies. It also details the architecture expected at each stage.

The *Implementation and Migration Plan* (L12) provides the detailed schedule, implementation project, resources, and budget.

Deliverables linked to implementation

Architecture contracts (L13) formalize implementation project commitments with regard to the architecture board (phase F).

The results of compliance reviews are recorded in the *Compliance Assessment* document (L15). These reviews are conducted during phase G.

Once the new architecture has been deployed (phase H), *Change Requests* (L16) can be sent to and assessed by the architecture board.

3.6 FUNDAMENTAL CONCEPTS

The following fundamental concepts were introduced in this chapter:

- Artifact: Means of communication used to present a particular view of the architecture. Artifacts are organized into catalogs, matrices, and diagrams.
- Deliverable: Architectural work product that is contractually specified and formally validated as output of the different ADM phases.
- Metamodel: Describes the basic elements used to build an enterprise's architecture.
  The "metamodel" form enables all the elements and all their relationships to be represented through a simplified UML diagram.
- Building block: Essential components of the architecture that constitute its skeleton. Building blocks can be combined with other building blocks to deliver (target architecture).
- Catalog: Structured list made up of comparable objects, used as a reference.

- Matrix: Representation format that shows the relationship between two (or more) architecture elements in the form of a table.
- Diagram: Graphical view representing a part of a model.
- Viewpoint: Designates the most appropriate perspective for an actor or family of actors. A viewpoint is materialized through a certain number of views on the architecture, in the form of diagrams, documents, or other types of representation. A view is "what we see," whereas a viewpoint is "where we look from."

The Repository and Governance

This chapter deals with both the architecture repository and with governance (parts V and VI and part VII of TOGAF, respectively). First, we specify the relationships between the architecture repository and the ADM cycle and the dynamic structure of its content. Second, we then deal with the governance of the architecture, which includes repository management and the organization of the monitoring and checking of architecture work.

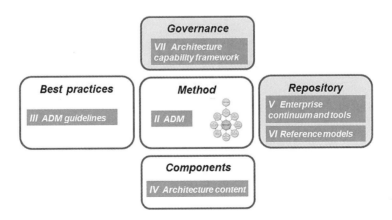

4.1 THE ARCHITECTURE REPOSITORY

4.1.1 The repository and the ADM

The architecture repository occupies a central position in TOGAF as a tool for capitalizing, reusing, and structuring information. The goal consists of finding practices accumulated during previous ADM cycles to progressively constitute an asset available to the entire enterprise. From this point of view, the TOGAF ADM cycle can be considered in two ways: as a provider of information that feeds the repository during its construction or as a consumer that draws elements from the repository according to its needs (Figure 4.1).

In practical terms, certain elements are selected to feed the repository at the end of each phase. This virtuous cycle enriches the enterprise's know-how and contributes to the minimization of risks and costs through the reuse of architectural practices and structures.

4.1.2 The structure of the repository

The repository contains various elements such as models, patterns, architecture descriptions, or deliverables resulting from earlier work and also external elements from standards or other organizations. TOGAF proposes that the repository be partitioned in the following way:

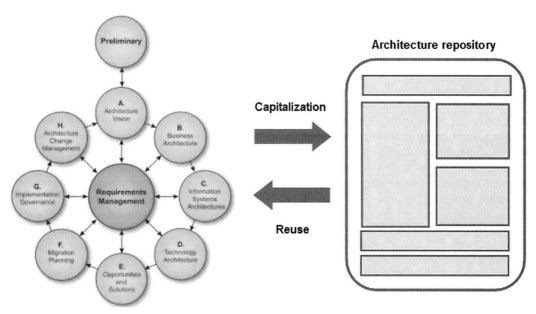

FIGURE 4.1

ADM and architecture repository. (For color version of this figure, the reader is referred to the online version of this chapter.)

Source: © 2008, The Open Group.

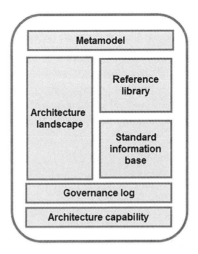

FIGURE 4.2

Structure of the architecture repository.

- The *metamodel*, which establishes architecture elements and the relationships[1] between them.
- The "*architecture landscape*," which describes the existing architecture.
- The *reference library*, in which templates, patterns, guides, and all elements already implemented and available for reuse are located.
- The *standard information base*, containing international norms, tools, and services that must be conformed to.
- Two parts related to the *governance* of the repository itself: the governance log and the architecture capability (Figure 4.2).

4.1.3 The landscape

The landscape contains models of the existing architecture across the entire enterprise. Its content varies from one enterprise to the next. The models found here most frequently deal with business processes, applications, and data.

    This view of the architectural landscape is found in some enterprise architecture approaches that have developed over the past few years.[2] For example, the application mapping includes all applications and their links (interapplication flows). This model is essential to the overall understanding of the system and constitutes a major tool for driving its evolution. Naturally, its content is constantly evolving as architectural transformations take place.

---

[1]For example, this is the metamodel described in Section 2 in Chapter 3.
[2]L'Architecture d'Entreprise, CIGREF, 2008.

4.1.4 Classification plan: Architecture continuum

The role of the architecture continuum (part V of the TOGAF document) is to provide a classification plan of the enterprise repository, focusing more particularly on the "reference library" part. This part plays a major role as both a storage area and a basis for reuse in the context of the execution of an ADM cycle.

This classification plan includes four types of elements in order of decreasing abstraction: foundation architecture, common system architectures, industry architectures, and organization-specific architectures.

- *Foundation architecture*: Deals with the foundations of generic architectures, in which we find high-level specifications and architecture patterns that can be applied to all types of enterprises. TOGAF provides an example of foundation architecture, the TRM (*technical reference model*).
- *Common systems architectures*: Represent high reusable systems dedicated to very cross-organizational services, such as security, network, and communication. The III-RM (Section 4.1.5) included in TOGAF is an example of a common system.
- *Industry architectures*: Here we find structures destined for a particular industry, such as telecommunications, banking, or insurance.[3] These structures range from data models to information system frameworks, or any other structure dedicated to a given domain.
- *Organization-specific architectures*: Dedicated to content that is specific to the enterprise or a part of the enterprise. It is typically here that we will find different elements of all different types resulting from the execution of ADM phases, elements that we want to capitalize on and potentially reuse.

The term architecture "continuum" characterizes the type of breakdown used, which partitions elements from the most general to the most specific (from foundation architecture to organization-specific architecture, respectively).

As with building blocks, two types of elements coexist within this classification: the "architecture" part and the "solution" part, with the latter being the physical translation of the former. For example, the specification of a workflow tool will be positioned in the "architecture" part, which describes the functions, use modes, and components that a tool of this category must provide. Conversely, a marketplace tool recommended by the enterprise will be found in the "solution" part. In this way, we end up with a double classification plan, illustrated in Figure 4.3.

4.1.5 TOGAF reference models

In part VI of the TOGAF document (TOGAF reference models), TOGAF presents two detailed examples of architecture continuum elements: the *technical reference model* and the III-RM (*integrated information infrastructure reference model*).

The technical reference model

The TRM is positioned as a foundation architecture within the architecture continuum. It defines the components of an information system infrastructure by providing terminology, structure, and rules for interconnection between different components. Figure 4.4 presents this structure.

---

[3]For example, Etom for telecommunications (www.energistics.org), ACORD for insurance (www.acord.org).

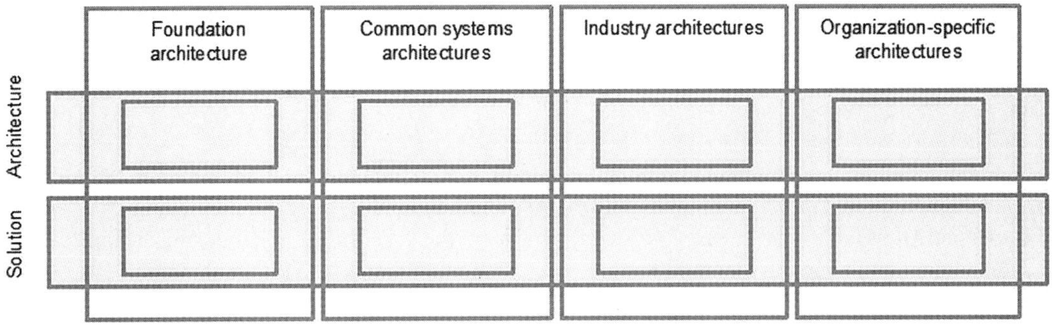

	Foundation architecture	Common systems architectures	Industry architectures	Organization-specific architectures
Architecture				
Solution				

FIGURE 4.3

Architecture continuum.

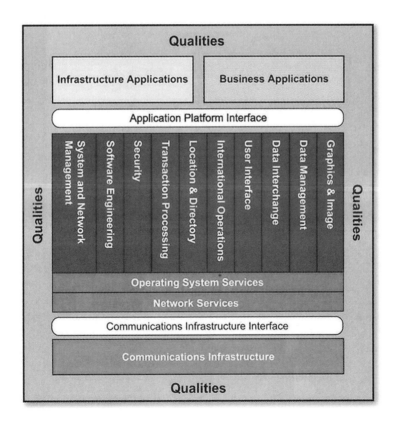

FIGURE 4.4

Structure of the TRM (technical reference model)—TOGAF9. (For color version of this figure, the reader is referred to the online version of this chapter.)

The TRM breaks down into several levels, from the communications infrastructure to applications. Applications use a dedicated interface, the Application Platform Interface, which provides a collection of common services used by all the system's applications (graphical user interface, security, transaction, etc.). These common services are built on two lower-level layers: network services and operating system services.

The integrated information infrastructure reference model

This second reference model can be considered a subset of the first (the TRM), focusing on applications by describing the following elements:

- Business applications
- Infrastructure applications, such as utilities or development tools
- The application platform, which handles application management services, including access, deployment, or location
- Interfaces between components, with details on protocols, exchanges, and programming interfaces
- Service quality

The emphasis here is on pooling and information sharing through the implementation of interfaces between service providers and service consumers, which is similar to the SOA (service-oriented architecture) view.

These two reference models are above all examples of what can be found in the "reference library" part of the architecture repository.

When first looking at TOGAF, they can simply be looked over, before being used later when real architecture work begins, or when an architecture repository is constituted.

4.1.6 **Repository tooling**

It is difficult to imagine an architecture repository without thinking about its tooling. The choice of this tooling is one of the actions planned during the preliminary phase of the ADM (if it is not already in place), and a chapter of the TOGAF document is dedicated to this subject.[4]

In this type of context, the choice between an "all in one" solution or a suite of tools remains a common question.

If the repository is to take into account all the expected functions, it will be difficult to find a single tool that will efficiently meet all needs, since the repository must include everything from structured models to documents, from software components to follow-up or communication elements.

Moreover, we must distinguish between the two facets of the repository: the "construction" facet and the "communication" facet. There is no guarantee that the tool used to build the repository will be perfectly adapted to the distribution of information. As far as models are concerned, we often see different tools being chosen for development and for communication. Models are built using modeling tools, which are able to provide designers and architects with an adapted interface; however, models are consulted via intranets, which provide a homogeneous framework for browsing, one that is simpler to use and that is workstation-independent. In this scenario, we must make sure that the modeling tool allows models to be available from a web[5]-type environment.

---

[4]TOGAF 9, chapter 42.

[5]This type of export is now available in most modeling tools, even if they have to be adapted using scripts or a programming language.

4.2 ARCHITECTURE GOVERNANCE

4.2.1 Architecture management

Like any enterprise activity, enterprise architecture management requires the setup of a particular organization: governance rules, processes, roles and responsibilities, and tools. This subject is dealt with in part VII of the TOGAF document, "Architecture Capability Framework," which describes the capabilities necessary to enterprise architecture management. The main points discussed are as follows:

- Architecture board
- Architecture contracts
- Compliance management
- Architecture governance
- Maturity models

On a fundamental level, architecture governance has two facets:

- The strategic facet, which handles repository management and the overall view of the enterprise architecture in the long term.
- The operational facet, which manages particular transformations, provides assistance to entities, and ensures the compliance and consistency of the solutions implemented.

This double facet is a well-known difficulty: How can general goals be translated to different transformation stakeholder entities? Complex organizations naturally establish entities that must attain specific objectives, objectives that are sometimes perceived as being paradoxical with regard to strategic goals.

In view of this fact, several types of responses are necessary: the establishment of a dedicated, centralized organization (the architecture board); a contractualized mode of governance; and an awareness of what is happening on the ground. In any case, the use of a collaborative mode (through web tools) will involve more stakeholders and can facilitate the management of architecture.

4.2.2 The architecture board

By its very nature, enterprise architecture requires centralized organization. This does not rule out operational delegations or a certain degree of federalism, but it does mean that a decision center is essential. This is the role of the architecture board, who reports back to the executive management on the compliance of implemented solutions with regard to enterprise architecture principles and decisions. The architecture board also manages the architecture repository, guaranteeing its consistency and the quality of its content.

> How many people should be on the architecture board? It is recommended that this number should be limited (fewer than 10 people) in order to safeguard the efficiency and reactivity of the architecture board. A certain level of rotation will encourage the board to be dynamic, but a stable core is important for the durability of long-term actions.

As a cross-organizational organism reporting to the executive management, the main functions of the architecture board are as follows:

- Creating and managing architecture projects, responsible for driving ADM cycles
- Controlling and validating implemented solutions
- Guaranteeing the consistency and convergence of the architecture
- Managing conflicts
- Developing and communicating norms, references, and guidelines
- Managing the architecture repository
- Organizing work to reduce divergence with regard to principles and goals
- Ensuring regular follow-up of activities and reporting to the executive management

Who participates in the architecture board? Experienced architects, of course. Also, the inclusion of high-level managers can make it easier to obtain consensus, which remains a major goal. Moreover, depending on the nature of the work, the architecture board can request assistance on particular subjects.

4.2.3 The architecture contract

Architecture contracts establish the relationships between the architecture board and all the stakeholders involved in an architecture project. They formalize expectations, constraints, goals, and appropriate means of measurement.

Architecture contracts are used at several points in the ADM cycle:

- During phase A, between the sponsor and the architecture board, who define the schedule and the goals of the ADM cycle: deliverables, organization, milestones, and key indicators. The content of the "Statement of Architecture Work" deliverable is found here.
- During phase F, with the elaboration of architecture contracts concluded with implementation projects.
- During phase G, with the validation and signature of these contracts.

4.2.4 Compliance reviews

As one of the main activities of the architecture board, compliance reviews evaluate whether or not solutions are appropriate, with regard to general rules and contracts included with implementation projects. Reviews are carried out using precise checklists in order to objectify results.

TOGAF provides an example of a detailed checklist with nearly 200 typical questions organized into eight major themes[6]:

- Hardware and operating system checklist
- Software services and middleware checklist
- Applications checklists
- Information management checklists

---

[6]TOGAF9, chapter 48.5.

- Security checklist
- Information system management checklist
- System engineering/overall architecture checklists
- System engineering/methods and tools checklist

The organization of these reviews is also described in the form of a dedicated process, which explains the approach and the role of each participant.

4.2.5 "Good" governance

All the points that we have just discussed constitute a working base for the implementation of enterprise architecture governance. However, when put into practice, this governance comes up against certain difficulties. Earlier we discussed the main difficulty, namely the dichotomy between the strategic view and the reality of teams on the ground. An inaccessible and "disembodied" organization cut off from organizational units will only encourage this tendency.

A more pragmatic approach will encourage closer collaboration between the architecture board and teams. For example, the active participation of enterprise architects in the elaboration of choices, without limiting themselves to a validation role after the event. This participation can go as far as the temporary integration of enterprise architects within teams. This organization has two advantages: first, for the project manager, whose team is strengthened at no extra cost, and, second, feedback to the architecture board, which can adapt and react to what is happening on the ground in real time.

Efficient communication is the other area of work on which to concentrate. Particular attention must be paid when distributing strategic elements in the architecture repository. The quality of the information (legibility, availability, pertinence, etc.) will condition the efficiency of its use. Patterns, guides, methods, and examples will be that much more easily accepted if they provide real added value and concrete help to operational teams.

More generally, finding practical means of bringing viewpoints closer together is essential, if convincing results are to be attained. Real commitment to operational projects on the part of enterprise architects contributes significantly to this: it is a question of switching from a purely contractual mode to a more dynamic collaboration.[7]

4.3 FUNDAMENTAL CONCEPTS

The following fundamental concepts were introduced in this chapter:

- Architecture repository: System that contains and manages all the enterprise information that is useful to enterprise architecture (processes, data, components, deliverables, artifacts, patterns, norms, etc.). The repository saves and manages all model elements and their links, in particular traceability links between model elements. It also saves diagrams and manages the connection between diagrams and the model elements represented.

---

[7]Governance of Enterprise Transformation and Different Faces of Enterprise Architecture Management, Daniel Simon, Journal of Enterprise Architecture, May 2011.

- Architecture board: Cross-organizational instance of the enterprise responsible for its entire architecture. Responsible for controlling architecture, managing the architecture repository, and launching new architecture transformation cycles.
- Architecture contract: Establishes the relationships between the architecture board and all the stakeholders involved in an architecture project. They formalize expectations, constraints, goals, and appropriate means of measurement.

Key Modeling Techniques

5

CHAPTER OUTLINE

TOGAF places particular emphasis on models and on the construction of a repository. Modeling languages help to better formalize knowledge, analyze problems, and design solutions. However, they constitute a toolbox whose uses, potential benefits, and limitations must be clearly understood. Architects need to understand how to use and benefit from models.

5.1 MODELS: BENEFITS, USES, AND CHARACTERISTICS

5.1.1 Definition

What is a model?

According to TOGAF, a *model* is a representation of a particular subject. The model provides this representation on a reduced scale, in a simplified or more abstract manner depending on the subject in question. In the context of enterprise architecture, the subject is the enterprise or some of its parts. The finality of the model is the elaboration of views that address stakeholders' concerns; in other words, their viewpoints on the enterprise.

The model concept can be considered in a restrictive way, where the model is made up of and limited to what has been formalized in the modeling tool repository. Alternatively, it can also be looked at in a more extensive manner, where the model includes all the informal elements gathered during enterprise architecture work (texts, images, etc.).

A universal need

The need to build models is universal, reaching far beyond enterprise organizations and information systems. It would be impossible to imagine the absence of models in the construction business, where plans are needed to define what needs to be built, to coordinate the problems of different building trades, and to define who needs to do what. In this domain, models have a legal dimension, for the authorization of building permits, declarations of taxable surface areas, or contractual aspects between the client, the business owner, and the project manager. Plans and maps constitute another example of essential models, ones we could not imagine living without. In most domains, dedicated models have thus been defined and become widely used (mechanics, building architecture, CAD, avionics, and electronics are just a few examples).

Although the need for models is universal, enterprise architecture and information technology present particular difficulties that have delayed and reduced their implementation. Both fields are immaterial and theoretical, making them more difficult to represent than more concrete domains. Thus, while blueprints for a building pose no interpretation problems (everyone understands what a wall is, and that a wall is represented by a solid line), the same is not true in our field: How do you represent a concept, a state, an event, an application, a function, and so on? Conventions have to be fixed in the field, conventions whose technicity will prevent them from being as universally accepted as those of building plans. It is only during the last decade[a] that modeling standards have stabilized, finally paving the way to standardized support for the construction of enterprise architecture models.

History

In the field of information technology, models have been around since the very beginning, with significant growth during the 1980s. Essential modeling techniques have been known since the start of the 1990s. However, there was great heterogeneity among models, with significant differences between countries and IT fields, as well as unsuccessful cooperation between these models (Merise was a method and model specific to the IT management field in France, the Yourdon method was popular in the Anglo-Saxon world, use of the IDEF0 model was widespread in technical systems, the first

---

[a]Notably BPMN and UML, mentioned in this book.

object-oriented models were highly specialized and few and far between, and so on). Modeling standards were born in the 1990s/2000s UML and then BPMN), enabling modeling techniques to be harmonized.

Standard architectures have also evolved, resulting in the emergence of SOA architectures in the field of information systems. Since 2000, the UML and BPMN standards have matured and stabilized, together with their adaptations to specific applications (such as SysML for large-scale systems). The field of enterprise architecture, which has gradually emerged since the 1990s, can use these standards to model the entire enterprise. TOGAF thus recommends the use of UML and BPMN. However, TOGAF has its own metamodel. An architect who has to use models must first decide how to use UML for TOGAF and how to map UML concepts to TOGAF concepts. The goal of Chapter 6 is to provide an answer to this question.

5.1.2 Usefulness of a model
Understanding and thinking about a problem
Models are used to meet several types of needs. By formalizing knowledge, they enable a problem to be understood and clarified. Using models, the different components of a field of study are represented, with different types of links used to position them. These components are further developed by allocating properties to them. Thus, models help participants think, and are then enriched by the results of this thought process. By materializing the understanding of a problem, models describe both the context and the target domain and reflect the intention, in other words, the construction project envisaged.

Models thus support two essential activities, namely, analysis and design. Analysis defines the description of the problem, and details the areas where intervention is needed. Design focuses on the solution, describing how the problem will be solved and detailing which techniques and activities will be used.

Communicating, sharing, and collaborating
Communication is essential within enterprises, and models provide important support in this area. Enterprises use models to represent their organization, and these models are used both to map the elements of the enterprise (such as roles within the enterprise, sites, business processes, material resources, applications, etc.) and to provide details on its components and its functioning (such as the progress of a business process). Mapping consists of listing, classifying, and positioning what already exists in order to share knowledge and enable everyone to situate the different components of the map.

In the same way as a map of the London tube helps passengers get around and supports designers in their study of its future development, recipients of data schemas know, for example, how to use or add to the data.[b]

Models also help establish dialog between the different experts in an enterprise, typically between business owners and project managers, or between users and business analysts. Thus, models can be used to represent the business needs of users, which are then precisely codified in order to prepare the work of architects and designers.

---

[b]However, these models are too often oriented toward the description of the structure of data, and not its meaning. Conceptual models, oriented to defining the semantics of a domain, are of high value for enterprise architecture.

Models help share knowledge and contribute to its construction. Collaborative work can be carried out on models, which are enriched by each person's contributions and shared by all team members. This is typically the case for engineering work, which consists in building and consolidating models.

Modeling knowledge of the business, organization, processes, and IS enables the enterprise to constitute a legacy that can be used and reused in many different ways. The usefulness of this knowledge sharing goes beyond the walls of the enterprise, since it allows improved formalization of cooperation and exchanges between enterprises, partners, and clients. Last but not least, models allow preexisting business solutions to be reused by aligning the enterprise architecture model with shared business models, such as those that exist in the domain of insurance or certain banking fields. This alignment also makes it easier to guarantee that imposed business norms and standards are respected. For example, this can concern information that has to be kept or procedures that must be respected.

Planning and simulating

Frequently used in all sorts of engineering projects, models are also used to *plan and simulate* the behavior of the system to develop, as well as the work involved in the actual construction of the system. By providing a view of the whole, the model enables changes to be applied more easily, in accordance with a particular strategy. Hypotheses can also be tested and variations thought up. These activities are not possible when the project is actually being carried out, as they are too costly in terms of both time and money. Moreover, models are often used to identify work packages within a project in order to delegate and monitor work.

Producing

In some domains, such as CAD or IT, models are used to guide, check, and automate production. Thus in mechanical CAD, the modeling of parts enables complex systems to be defined, precise specifications to be provided to subcontractors, and workshop construction of parts to be automated. IT also uses models to automatically generate more detailed IT productions (for example, code, database schemas, or documents).

As they evolve over time from vision to realization, models become more and more precise and formal, guiding or even automating the work of architects, designers, and then developers.

The drawback to this approach is that once models become precise enough to be executable or compiled into code, they become much less useful for understanding and reasoning on complex systems. Enterprise architecture is more about planning and less about building, and therefore requires less precise, less formal models.

5.1.3 Characteristics of models
Abstraction

Models provide *abstraction* mechanisms, which enable users to consider the system at more macroscopic levels, by aggregating detailed elements, only showing significant parts or generalizing notions and mechanisms. Abstraction helps manage complexity, which is one of the main brakes within an enterprise, causing the lethargy and inertia that prevent many enterprises from being reactive. When there are thousands of applications in an enterprise, dozens of repositories, hundreds of processes, and consequently thousands of tasks, and when the volume of application code is counted in millions of lines of code, the problem of complexity linked to volume and diversity cannot be ignored. Abstraction is necessary for primary management and classification needs, as well as for more sophisticated needs, such as pooling, reconciliation, and rationalization. For pedagogical reasons, abstraction is also used to adapt the level of detail presented to the participants in question.

We will see that models for TOGAF will be separated into different viewpoints dedicated to specific stakeholders. The level of abstraction therefore needs to be carefully defined for a model's targeted purpose and stakeholders.

Standardization

Model *standardization* greatly increases the benefits they bring. Standardization ensures notation that is unique, used by everyone, and shared between all countries and all fields related to enterprise architecture (organization, business processes, data, applications, and IT). Standardization provides formally developed semantics; in other words, a formal definition of all its terms, mechanisms, and constructions, thereby limiting the number of possible interpretations of a model. Standardization also guarantees a market for a large number of associated tools (modeling tools, generation tools, etc.) and enables interoperability between modeling tools, allowing users to avoid being locked into one particular tool. Models developed for the enterprise have greater value because they can be used by a large number of people and tools.

However, models such as UML and BPMN constitute a vast toolbox, and it is up to each organization to define its conventions, which parts of these models will be used and to what ends, and which extensions are provided. This book provides an example of conventions and extensions for TOGAF, whose implementation facilitates the work of participants, the sharing of information, and the building of a common repository. By defining these conventions and extensions of UML and BPMN, we naturally also introduce extensions and adaptations to TOGAF as described in Chapter 6.

Formal or informal models

Informal models do not respect rigorous formalism. They are often free images, media for ideas, or spontaneous means of communication. They are naturally used during meetings and facilitate spontaneous communication. During early analysis phases, where the problem has not yet been clearly established and consensus is needed to scope the area of intervention and the work to be carried out, or where there is a need to communicate with participants who have no experience of the models used, informal models can be used.

During phase A (Vision), these informal models can, for example, be used to produce solution concept diagrams or value chain diagrams. They will then be used as a basis for building more precise "formal" models, which will be managed by modeling tools.

However, as we progress toward the technical solution, models must be more precise and must provide a high level of detail regarding the functioning of the solution. In this way, we end up with more formal models, which describe in detail the structure of data or the logic behind activity sequencing in a process. Here, we are addressing more experienced participants, which means that more technical models can be used. As a result, the development phases of the ADM will make greater use of formal models. The viewpoint related to a model drives the domain, scope, time horizon, and level of detail of a model.

5.1.4 **Limitations of models**

The model is only a component within TOGAF, the main point being the ADM cycle. The ADM provides the processes and activities that produce and consume the models, and motivate their change over time for some purpose.

Models are tools that must be pertinently used in the context of the enterprise. In Section 5.6 we look at the limitations of models (incompleteness, difficult to update, etc.), which necessitate adapted calibration and governance.

Moreover, models do not provide the contextual information that is necessary to their being understood correctly. Why was this model developed? Which problem is it to deal with? How will it be used? This last point will be addressed by specializing models using the different "diagram" type TOGAF artifacts, and by structuring them into viewpoints: every time a model is used in a TOGAF artifact (see Chapters 6–11), TOGAF and the *viewpoint* affected will indicate the main issues that are being targeted and the participants at which the models are aimed.

5.2 THE CONCEPT OF VIEWPOINTS

5.2.1 **The angle from which a problem is looked at**

Complex systems imply the involvement of a wide variety of expertise and stakeholders. Each type of expertise requires a specific view of the system, and will only be interested in a part of the model of the system, according to a particular representation. This angle of vision or these concerns being addressed, which target(s) certain categories of stakeholders, constitute(s) a *viewpoint* on the model.

Figure 5.1 successfully illustrates the need for different views, according to who the participants are and what problems are to be managed. When dealing with a client and future user, attractive and/or functional views will be chosen. However, when working with different building trades, views dealing with trade-specific problems will be developed (structural plans, electric networks, plumbing, etc.).

A similar problem exists for information systems. For example, users can attach importance to *ergonomics*, security managers to the *security* of the system, system administrators to *technical deployment*, data administrators and database designers to *data schemas*, business analysts to *business processes*, or service architects to *technology architecture*, and so on. Figure 5.2 shows an example of a business analyst contemplating a process model, and an application architect faced with an application architecture.

This leads to the identification of a number of viewpoints in the enterprise, which materialize both the principal groups of issues that will have to be managed and also the participants concerned. Determining viewpoints provides real structure to the organization and the work to be carried out, by configuring the types of problems to be dealt with and the nature of the people who will be involved. This is why this concept has become increasingly important since the 1990s in modern methodologies, such as RM-ODP (for network architectures), RUP, Zachman (the reference in terms of enterprise architecture), Praxeme[c] (enterprise method), MODAF,[d] DODAF,[e] and of course TOGAF. The concepts of viewpoint and view are standardized in the IEEE 1471-2000 norm.

---

[c]www.praxeme.org, http://en.wikipedia.org/wiki/Praxeme.

[d]UK Army Enterprise Architecture Framework, http://www.modaf.org.uk.

[e]DOD Enterprise Architecture Framework, http://dodcio.defense.gov/dodaf20.aspx.

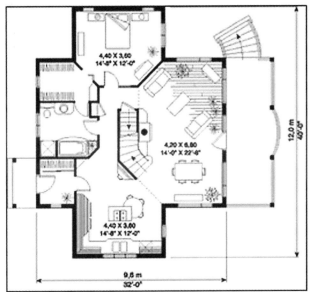

FIGURE 5.1

"Technical" and "marketing" viewpoints of a building. (For color version of this figure, the reader is referred to the online version of this chapter.)

5.2.2 View and viewpoint: Definition

One of the objectives of enterprise architecture is to produce representations that cover all stakeholders' concerns. These specific representations must be linked, and must reflect all the compromises and adjustments that manage potential conflicts between concerns (for example, performance and security).

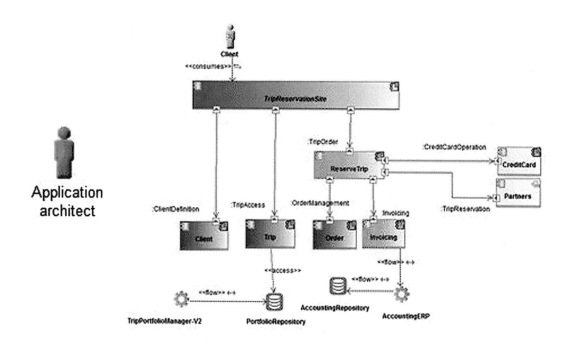

**Application
architect**

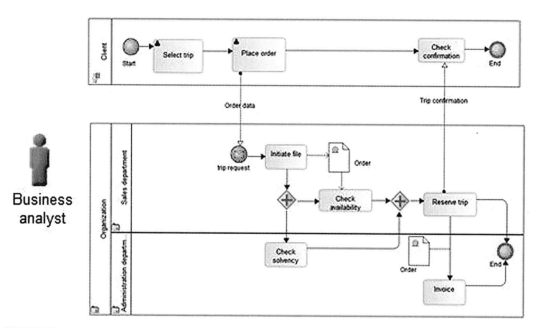

**Business
analyst**

FIGURE 5.2

Different TOGAF models according to different viewpoints. (For color version of this figure, the reader is referred to the online version of this chapter.)

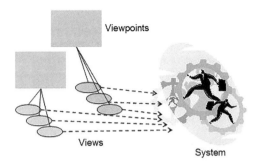

FIGURE 5.3

Viewpoints, views, and the system. (For color version of this figure, the reader is referred to the online version of this chapter.)

Viewpoints constitute different perspectives of a system, developed according to the main concerns of stakeholders. A viewpoint focuses on one or several issues, and therefore on the stakeholders concerned by these issues, and defines a set of conventions to develop adapted views.

A *view* is a representation of the system from the perspective of a set of issues (the viewpoint). A view is what we see of a particular system, while the viewpoint is the angle from which the system is looked at. Viewpoints are defined generically (independently of any particular system). Figure 5.3 shows two viewpoints and six views, each related to one of the viewpoints and each providing a particular representation of the same system.

The viewpoints (or concerns) we can have for an enterprise and its IS can be related to:

- Security (access rights, intrusions, etc.)
- Persistent data (data models, databases, etc.)
- The organization of the enterprise (actors, organizational units, etc.)
- Application architecture (applications, messages, etc.)

Generally speaking, several views exist for each viewpoint, and for this reason, Chapter 9 presents several views related to application architecture.

5.2.3 Usefulness of views

Views help manage complexity by separating problems into different skill domains related to business, technology, or organization.

In contrast, when considering a given model, it is difficult to interpret it if we do not know the *viewpoint* to which it is related. Is it a business model? A technical solution? A design model? A technology architecture model? With regard to the concerns being addressed, does this address the structuring of the application, the combination of legacy applications and new evolutions? Does it describe the conceptual business domain, or does it specify how a business process should be optimized? Is it an example or an illustration? Does it reflect what exists or what is intended; in other words, the project that is going to be developed? In itself, the model determines neither the context in which it is defined nor the intentions that led to its development. Knowing the viewpoint from which a model should be looked at allows the spectator to interpret it and find out how to use it. This is not only true for spectators but also for tools, which can apply different checks and usage services according to the viewpoint in question. For example, code generation, matrix or report generation, and consistency checks are features that are closely linked to the viewpoint.

Viewpoints are used to break complex models down into different aspects, and to present these aspects to the different participants according to their field of interest. In this way, they help provide different formalisms, which are adapted to different participants. They provide assistance in organizing teamwork within large-scale teams and in structuring models and deliverables, by allowing each contributor to participate according to his or her level of expertise.

Recent methods use viewpoints to organize work and skills, such as in the Zachman framework, the DODAF and MODAF architecture frameworks, or the Praxeme enterprise method.

5.2.4 **TOGAF viewpoints**

The implementation of TOGAF implies the definition of several viewpoints. By default, we can consider TOGAF's four architectural domains as being predefined viewpoints. The examples of views provided in Chapters 10–15 are based on this structure.

However, TOGAF recommends that viewpoints relevant to the ADM cycle be identified during the preliminary phase (see Section 2.2.1). For this, we have to think about which architectural views and viewpoints have to be established if we are to satisfy the requirements of the different stakeholders. One of the essential uses of viewpoints is to allow architects to show how stakeholder concerns have been dealt with in the different TOGAF architectures (business, data, etc.). Table 7.2 (Section 7.2) shows an example of a stakeholder matrix consolidated in phase A, which helps determine which viewpoints to develop. For any given viewpoint, appropriate types of diagrams must then be defined, as well as adapted tools and methods (for example, by selecting diagrams from those presented in Chapters 6–11).

The TOGAF architectural domains are already viewpoints that deal with the typical concerns of stakeholders. For example, if we use some of the capabilities that appear in Table 7.2:

- Business architecture deals with the needs of users, organizational unit directors, business analysts, and business managers.
- Data architecture deals with the needs of data architects and software designers.
- Application architecture addresses the needs of application architects, technology architects, and CIOs.

Table 7.2 Stakeholder Matrix (Extract)

Participant	Concern	Decision-Making Power	Level of Interest
CEO	Goal orientation, decisions	High	High
Organization unit director	Requirements orientation, decisions	Quite high	Medium
Business architect	Business, architecture	Medium	High
CIO	Project management, IS	Quite high	High
Data architect	Data architecture	Low	Quite high
System and network engineer	Hardware, systems, network	Low	Medium

Table 5.1 Development of Viewpoints According to the Issues to Deal with Extract from the TOGAF Guide

Need	Stakeholder	Goal	Example
Design	Architects, software designers, BPM analysts	Design, explore, establish a basis for decisions, compare the alternatives	UML or BPMN diagrams
Decide	Managers, CIOs	Make decisions	Cross-referenced tables, mappings, lists, and reports
Inform	Users, clients	Explain, convince, obtain support	Animations, images, prototypes, model illustration

- Technology architecture targets the needs of operations managers, system and network engineers, and technical architects.

Table 5.1 gives a general overview of the expectations of each different category of stakeholder.

5.3 SPECIAL ROLE PLAYED BY DIAGRAMS
5.3.1 Models and diagrams

Enterprise architecture develops a model through different views, each related to one or more viewpoints. Some of these views are diagrams.

A *diagram* is thus a graphical view that represents a part of a model. The model of an enterprise can be considered to be a repository that includes all concepts, properties, processes, tasks, actors, and so on, and all the different types of links that associate them. Diagrams are only one of a number of representation forms that exist for a model, some of which take graphical form (for example, class diagrams or process diagrams), others textual or syntactic form (for example, business rules), and still others table form (for example, TOGAF matrices), as well as other forms, such as model element hierarchies. For this reason, Figure 5.4 shows the classic layout of a modeling tool. The explorer on the left is used to browse the entire model, while the diagram on the right-hand side graphically represents a small subset of the model.

5.3.2 Diagrams for communicating

The main function of diagrams is communication between participants. Diagrams help position elements based on specific visuals (schemas or images) that would be hard to do without. Their aim is therefore not to present the entire model, but rather to illustrate it and to explain it. To this end, diagrams filter the elements to present, starting from models that are sometimes very large. Diagrams are dedicated to particular participants, and focus on a part of the model. UML and BPMN provide several types of diagrams, each of which represents a specific facet of a problem, with a different representation mode. For a given model, there exist several diagrams of the same type, each dealing with a different part of the model (for example, several process diagrams for several processes, several class

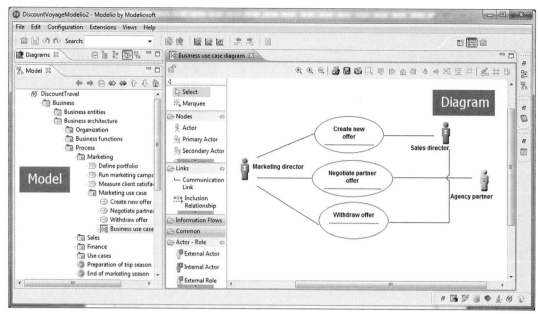

FIGURE 5.4

A model and a diagram in a modeling tool. (For color version of this figure, the reader is referred to the online version of this chapter.)

Table 5.2 Questions Dealt with by Different Types of UML and BPMN Diagrams

The Question ...	Is Handled by ...
What?	Class diagrams, package diagrams, object diagrams, component diagrams, state diagrams
Who?	Use case diagrams, process diagrams
How?	Process diagrams, use case diagrams, sequence diagrams, collaboration diagrams
Where?	Deployment diagrams
Why?	
When?	Process diagrams, state diagrams

diagrams for different parts of the model, different representation levels, etc.). One model element (for example, the "Order" class) can be represented in several different diagrams.

Table 5.2 shows which types of UML and BPMN diagrams can be used to answer essential questions (defined in the "Zachman framework"). As we can see, these standards do not answer the question "why," despite its fundamental importance. This question is handled notably using goal diagrams and requirement diagrams (see Sections 7.3 and 7.4), which are neither UML nor

Table 5.3 Use of Different Types of UML and BPMN Diagrams (Example)	
Diagram	**Example of Use**
Use case diagram	Expression of requirements; functional requirements
Class diagram and package diagram	Conceptual model, data model, software models
Sequence diagram	Example of functioning
State diagram	Entity lifecycle; functioning dynamic
Collaboration/Object diagram	Cooperation between objects; architecture illustration
Process diagram	Business process and workflow modeling
Component diagram	Logical and physical architecture models
Deployment diagram	Hardware architecture; geographical distribution

BPMN. The extensions to UML and BPMN presented in this book are used to better answer these questions in order to cover the entire scope of TOGAF by completing all the boxes of this table (Table 5.2).

Table 5.3 Diagrams play an essential role in communication between the participants involved in handling a problem, as the table 5.3 shows for UML and BPMN. Their aim is therefore not to present all the information modeled. Due to their role of exchange and communication, they must be understandable by all stakeholders. Diagrams which are too "technical" will not be understood by management personnel, users or certain "business" participants. Organization diagrams, process diagrams or use case diagrams can, for example, be presented to users or directors, while class diagrams or state diagrams will be reserved for more "expert" participants (analysts, architects, and designers). These considerations help determine which types of diagram should be used with regard to the different viewpoints identified. We will see that the adaptations that we propose to cover TOGAF will address these issues, and that the technical parts of UML, in particular, will be filtered out.

5.4 CONSISTENCY AND TRACEABILITY

5.4.1 What is a "good" model?

There is no one right answer to this question, which is subject to lengthy discussion. However, there exist three important criteria that help qualify a model:

- Its consistency: A model is consistent when it satisfies the consistency rules imposed by the modeling language used. The model must be consistent, in other words structurally sound, although this does not in itself guarantee that the model is good. For example, the blueprints of a building may respect construction rules (roofs are supported by walls, there must be an entrance and an emergency exit, etc.), but this in no way determines whether or not the building is appropriate.
- Its relevance: A model is relevant when it successfully represents the problem that is to be dealt with. The model must describe the problem using the correct concepts, with an appropriate level of detail. All necessary elements must be present, and all the elements present must be necessary. This criterion is both the most important and the most difficult to judge.
- Its justification: Justifying the existence of a model's elements helps ensure its relevance. A model element is justified by the fact that it meets a defined need, or a goal, or that it represents one of the

aspects of the domain to be dealt with. Model elements are essentially justified through traceability. In this way, the elements necessary to the completion of the model are built based on known and desired elements.

When modeling languages are used, their consistency rules must be respected. This consistency can be naturally imposed by modeling tools, or else checked later by model checks. Furthermore, each "viewpoint" predefined for enterprise architecture will add specific consistency rules. These rules act as a guide for the model designer and as a guarantee for readers.

Model consistency rules on models essentially concern models located at the same level of representation, or the same level of TOGAF architecture (or inside the same viewpoint). If several levels coexist, for example, when building a model based on higher level models, such as an application architecture model based on a business model, then intermodel links will essentially be "traceability" links.

5.4.2 Traceability links

The term "*traceability*" designates the ability to link artifacts (see Section 4.1) produced by enterprise architecture and subsequent technical realization activities to other artifacts from which they originate or to which they refer. This practice is widely used, notably in requirements management, either to check that all requirements are traced to at least one artifact describing their satisfaction (completion of the artifacts realized), or conversely to find out which requirement is linked to an artifact. Traceability links are also used to carry out impact analyses, which indicate what will be affected if a requirement is modified and calculate the consequences. Traceability links form a network between artifacts and/or model elements, which constitutes a graph. More precise types of traceability links can be defined, for example, to express that a model element "refines," "satisfies," or "verifies" a requirement (see Chapter 11 and the "Requirement analysis diagram" artifact for the definition of these different types of links). By extension, we use the term "traceability" link to designate any dependency that is not predefined by modeling languages and that a designer creates between two different levels of representation or architecture. Thus, an "assign" link from a goal to a process or an actor, or an "implements" link between an application component and a process, will be classified in the very generic category of traceability links. Figure 5.5 uses the "trace" link, which is very vague about the meaning of the dependency in question. We recommend the use of more precise links ("refine," "implements," "satisfy," etc.) to express the nature of the dependency or relationship between a model element and its reference.

A traceability link is always oriented toward the reference element. So in Figure 5.5, the "model" element refers to the definition of the "reference" element. For example, a business process may have been built based on one of the enterprise's goals, or an application component may have been defined based on a business process. Note that this does not mean that the reference element has to be defined *before* the model element. The identification of a model element often leads to the subsequent identification of a reference element.

FIGURE 5.5

Traceability between several model elements. (For color version of this figure, the reader is referred to the online version of this chapter.)

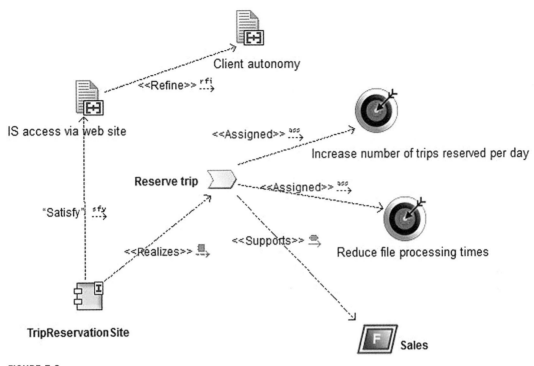

FIGURE 5.6

Example of traceability. (For color version of this figure, the reader is referred to the online version of this chapter.)

In the example shown in Figure 5.6, the "TripReservationSite" application component has been defined to partially realize the "reserve trip" process, and to satisfy the "IS access via web site" requirement. The "reserve trip" process has been realized to meet the "Increase number of trips reserved per day" and "Reduce file processing times" goals. This process supports one of the enterprise's functions, namely, the "Sales" function.

5.4.3 Using traceability in enterprise architecture

The origin of traceability links is generally established on the basis of knowledge obtained prior to the development of the model, and by elements that have justified the launch of an ADM cycle. Thus, the fundamental elements of the business (business terms, business entities) can constitute preliminary knowledge that initiates traceability links. The enterprise's goals (see Section 11.3) and drivers are elements that are essential to the motivation of the ADM cycle. Enterprise organization and business processes are therefore traced to these initial elements, and then the application model traced to business architecture elements. We obtain a sort of traceability graph, which clearly shows where all intermediate model elements come from, right up to the solution. The description of what already exists is also an essential origin of traceability; here the model is simply justified by the retranscription of elements resulting from the description of what already exists.

Table 5.4 Retranscription of Figure 5.6 in the Form of a Matrix

	IS Access via Web site	Reserve Trip	Client Autonomy	Reduce File Processing Times	Increase Number of Trips Reserved Per Day	Sales
TripReservationSite	Satisfy	Realize				
IS access via web site			Refine			
Reserve trip				Assigned	Assigned	Supports

Traceability enables us to see what justified the construction of a model element (justification), and conversely to find out which model elements are based on a given element. In the latter case, starting with a model at a certain level, we can determine its coverage by lower-level models, and thus get an idea of how exhaustive a model is with regard to a reference. Another use of traceability is impact analysis, for example, to find out the cost of changing a requirement or altering a technical component.

We have already seen that a model constitutes a database of model elements and links. Traceability links are part of the model, and can therefore be systematically used from this database. Generally speaking, the term "traceability" designates the use of any links in this model database, to clarify if and how several elements are connected.

In practice, traceability links can appear in diagrams, but their systematic use is more often presented in the form of matrices. Most of the matrices defined by TOGAF result from the use of these links (Table 5.4).

5.5 ARCHITECTURE REPOSITORY

During the activities defined by the TOGAF ADM, a large number of elements will be produced as a result of the work carried out. For this reason, TOGAF defines *deliverables*, *artifacts*, and *architecture building blocks*. The definition of these elements is provided in Section 3.1.1.

These elements are part of the assets of the enterprise, which will be able to reuse them during future evolutions, as well as in the current project. It is, therefore, essential to set up an enterprise repository for all these elements. The model is a fundamental part that must be taken into account by the repository, since a very large proportion of the types of elements that must be stored in the repository are model elements.

The *repository* saves and manages all model elements and their links, in particular, traceability links between model elements. It also saves diagrams and manages the connection between diagrams and the model elements represented. The "content *metamodel*" recommended by TOGAF defines which types of elements are stored in the repository. For example, all the model element types used in this book (Actor, Business Service, Business Entity, etc.) must be defined by the metamodel. The repository (content framework) is the medium for the activities of the TOGAF ADM, with each phase using repository elements as input, and producing other elements as output.

As an architectural framework, TOGAF can be extended. It must be adapted to each enterprise, which means that the metamodel must be able to adapt to each context.

In TOGAF the concept of the repository includes all elements created or modified during the ADM, which means that the scope of the repository covers a set of elements far beyond models. TOGAF indicates some of its components: elements linked to governance, the definition of business and application services, the modeling of business processes, the modeling of data, elements linked to application or technology architecture, and elements linked to vision, for example, goals. These examples should all be part of the model.

The repository allows viewpoints to be developed on the enterprise. Viewpoints do not organize models into separate, disjointed parts, but rather act as filter for models which are too large and too complex to be handled in their entirety. If we use the example of a building again, general plans interact with specialized plans concerning structure, plumbing, electricity, and so on. Overall consistency is essential. The repository and modeling tools guarantee this overall consistency, notably consistency between viewpoints, so as to ensure that the interactions between model elements handled by the different participants complement one another harmoniously. In Section 6.1 we provide an example of how to structure the model repository.

Typical uses of a repository include recording the results of enterprise architecture work, providing access to these results to each participant according to his rights, ensuring overall consistency, and enabling requests and extractions (matrices, reports) to be carried out.

5.6 RISKS AND MAIN DIFFICULTIES

5.6.1 Limitations inherent to any model

Intrinsic limitations of models

Modeling is all about choices, and is largely down to analysts and architects. The famous painting "The Treachery of Images" by Magritte (1929) representing a pipe reminds us that all models are false and can never get very close to reality. For example, geographical maps are marred by approximations, despite being meticulously realized.

Modeling therefore consists in building a theory that we want to conform to reality. This task is easier in domains that are themselves man-made, such as insurance contracts or bank accounts, rather than in real-world phenomena. For example, it is extremely tricky to model human cooperation processes, since it is so difficult to take into account all possible interaction modes between people and to define a generalization that everyone in the enterprise must apply.

A partial description of the problem

Models do not enable all the problems and all the knowledge of an enterprise to be represented. In general, they cannot do without related explanations and precisions, which can only be provided through associated documents, but also through direct communication between participants, in order to guarantee a good level of mutual understanding. Models are only a medium.

Figure 5.7 illustrates this point. The model shown highlights the concepts of "Holiday" and "Trip" in the field of a travel agency. Associations determine the possible links between the concepts of this domain (participants, range, and order for a holiday, for example). Without textual additions, this

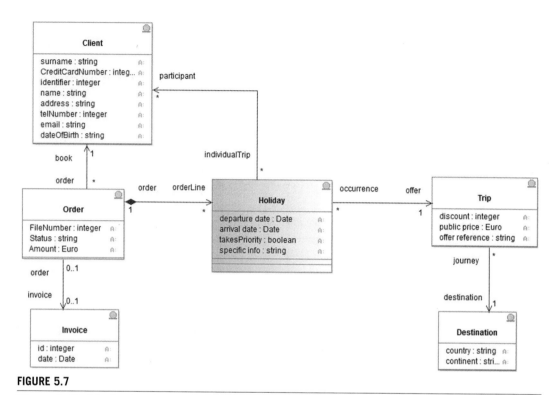

FIGURE 5.7

"Concept of holiday in a travel agency" class model. (For color version of this figure, the reader is referred to the online version of this chapter.)

model lacks detail. For example, the following information, which is important to the business, is absent from the model:

- There is client uniqueness.
- A single client cannot take the same holiday several times.
- If a client participates in several holidays, there can be no conflict of dates.
- A holiday is only confirmed if an order is placed.
- A holiday only exists if the trip is still available.
- The departure and arrival dates of a holiday must correspond to the duration of its offer (trip).

In this example, this information can be expressed in the form of business rules, and defined using adapted rule languages, but it is never possible to provide all the information. A model, like a document, cannot describe everything.

Confining modeling work

The benefits of high levels of detail must be evaluated. A detailed model supposes a larger volume of information, which has required a greater amount of work in its development. The effort involved in reviewing, understanding, and updating evolutions increases, thereby limiting the number of possible participants. Thus, investment in modeling increases significantly, compared with the benefits obtained. This forces us to define a practical limit regarding the degree of detail that should be provided by models. This limit is guided by considering the return on investment (ROI). For example, for parts of systems where security issues exist (nuclear power plants, transport systems, etc.), a higher level of detail is required. When generation services are applied to models (documentation, code, DBMS schemas, etc.), model designers will tend naturally to provide the level of detail necessary for the generation in question, and the model is then productive. However, where the goals are a general understanding of and a consensus on architecture, the level of detail will be reduced to what is strictly necessary pedagogically speaking.

Making a model a reference

The main difficulty of an enterprise architecture model is its constant evolution, and consequently its permanent update. Unlike building plans, which we can assume will remain stable over a very long period of time, enterprise architecture models quickly become obsolete if they are not updated. The organization, IS, procedures, business, and goals are constantly evolving, making it essential to rework models in order to reflect changes.

The situation can deteriorate very quickly. If analysts or architects do not trust in the relevance of existing models, the pressure of deadlines may force them into rebuilding models ad hoc, focusing on the requirements of the moment, which are even more short-lived. Worse still, they may decide to do without models altogether, in order to continue on to the actual realization of projects. If this happens, the enterprise is back at square one, where knowledge is neither controlled nor recorded, but rather scattered across detailed realizations.

This difficulty requires vigilant governance (see Section 4.2) and significant involvement of the architecture board.

5.6.2 Usefulness and support: Major criteria

Modeling therefore demands great modesty on the part of designers, who must realize that their models will never be perfect. They will simply aim to build models that are useful with regard to identified needs. Thus, the London tube map is a model that is geographically false, but that is very useful in practical terms. It is recognized by everyone (designers and users) as being a reference, which makes it extremely valuable.

Besides the criteria identified in Section 5.4, the value of a model essentially resides in how well it is accepted by all the stakeholders. A business process model, which is understood and accepted by users, business analysts, and, where necessary, IT engineers, is of tremendous value. The same is true of an organization model shared by decision-makers and business analysts. A model designer must therefore avoid working alone on an individual task, and must use all possible means to obtain the support of stakeholders, using a pedagogical approach when presenting a model. The organization of reviews also contributes to the quality of models. The earlier the model is produced, the more these exercises are necessary. This means that the models produced must be understood by everyone. Later on, models become more technical and more detailed, meaning they cannot easily be presented to users, for example. These models will have to be based on earlier models, notably using traceability links, in order to justify choices and the reasoning behind them.

As we have already mentioned, models cannot do everything. They cannot replace the willingness, discipline, organization, and skill of human beings. However, they are a powerful tool that facilitates the analysis, design, and communication of solutions.

Designing a model requires significant pragmatism. Model design is not concerned with covering a whole array of model types, nor with aiming for maximum detail, which will prove to be useless. For every problem to be dealt with, the models built must bring added value, and we must only model what is absolutely necessary. Models must clarify the problem. For example, modeling a business process clarifies its functioning and procedures. If the process is realized differently depending on the participant, then producing a generalization that satisfies all participants becomes a complex activity. Similarly, realizing a conceptual class diagram clarifies a business domain. Models must make sure that construction of the solution is secure. For example, a conceptual class diagram brings significant added value to the definition of a repository or software application. Models must clarify intention, share knowledge, and encourage consensus. For example, application and technology architectures constitute an area of negotiation and sharing between business owners and project managers, enabling them to contractualize what has to be done and apply decisions to what already exists.

5.6.3 *"Bottom-up"* or *"top-down"*: Two limited techniques

Two major approaches to modeling exist. The *"top-down"* approach starts with general models, and progressively builds models that are more and more detailed, right up to the complete definition of the solution. This is a highly analytical approach, which has the advantage of covering the entire scope of the problem and of positioning all components. The risk of this approach is that it can be too general, too theoretical, and too disconnected from reality. By arriving at the solution relatively late, we then realize that overall solutions cannot be applied to real situations, which sometimes calls the entire theoretical construction into question. Conversely, a *"bottom-up"* approach has the advantage of focusing on a specific part of the problem by providing a solution that will be a tried and tested brick in the construction of the entire edifice. This approach can start with a prototype of the solution, which will be used to validate its viability. The disadvantage is that this approach provides no overview, and does not guarantee the consistent integration of bricks that is necessary to a pertinent view.

A combination of the *bottom-up/top-down* approaches should be used. For any given problem, we have to define what should be carried out in *top-down* mode and what should be realized in *bottom-up* mode. A specific strategy must be established each time. Risk analysis is a guide when defining this strategy: insufficiently known parts, subject to functional or technical risks, are good candidates for a *bottom-up* approach.

5.7 REPOSITORY GOVERNANCE

The goal of the *repository* is to constitute an asset of knowledge for the enterprise, which can be used as a basis for reusing information about the business, process, organization, application architecture, database schemas, and so on. A properly managed repository is of tremendous value, as it provides an immediate framework for defining evolutions, building specifications, and evaluating the feasibility and consistency of new projects, among other things.

However, the correct use and durability of the repository depend greatly on its quality. If close attention is not paid to what is going into the repository, an abundance of produced models will find their way in, without their relevance, completeness, and overall consistency having been established. In other words, the value of the model is thus reduced, and participants cannot use existing models as a basis for their development. Any reasoning on existing models is marred by the errors and imprecisions they include. Enterprises frequently have a large number of nonmanaged models, obsolete process models, and application mappings that do not correspond to reality and do not meet the expectations of a repository. The absence of investment in governance leads to the depressing impression of a heap of models that must constantly be reworked depending on current needs and emergencies.

Thus, construction of a repository must be organized and its *governance* ensured, if its quality is to be guaranteed. Repository evolutions must be managed, as well as evolutions of the enterprise and its IS over time, which must be properly reflected in the repository. Participant rights on identified parts must be identified. The quality of elements must be checked before they are added to the repository. The data located in the repository must also be audited, and corrected or updated where necessary, in order to align the repository with enterprise evolutions. Everything that is in the repository must be managed in the long term, which means significant management costs.

This update presents the challenge of having a large amount of information updated by a dedicated team that does not always have all the business knowledge. When architects are in pure production mode, similar to project mode, they systematically give priority to their own emergencies, thereby neglecting update operations. This is the core difficulty of governance: managing the conflict between the needs of individual projects, delivering work products that meet specific project requirements within a specific timeframe, and the needs of longer-term enterprise asset management. This is generally handled by having different streams represent changes to model elements over time for a given purpose. Governance then controls the flow of changes between these streams.

As such, a pragmatic approach must be taken. Only essential information should be put in the repository, information in which we are willing to invest (checking, monitoring, and updating). This confirms the fact that the level of detail required in a model must be adjusted to include only what is absolutely necessary. Having the necessary and sufficient level of information in the repository is one of the key points in repository governance.

The repository enables enterprise knowledge to be managed. In order for this knowledge to be procured, all stakeholders must contribute; knowledge must be extracted, collected, and federated from all participants. Participants must be encouraged to open up and fight their natural tendency to keep their individual knowledge to themselves and to appropriate skills for themselves alone. This is a knowledge management and collective intelligence project in itself, whose accomplishment is at the heart of the success of any enterprise architecture project.

We have seen that the ADM is correlated to the repository, as its activities withdraw and deposit information. The constitution of the repository and the nature of the stored elements have an influence on the definition of the ADM.

The TOGAF architectural capability framework handles these organizational aspects, notably the need to define an organization, roles, responsibilities, and skills when setting up enterprise architecture. Managing the repository is not a project but rather a continual, long-term operation. The governance of the repository is a cross-organizational function in the enterprise under the responsibility of the architecture board, which brings together a limited number of representatives of the stakeholders.

As shown in Figure 5.8, governance has a much wider spectrum than the constitution of the repository, the chosen field of architects. It must also check that projects respect enterprise architecture, as well as deployment and operational system management operations.

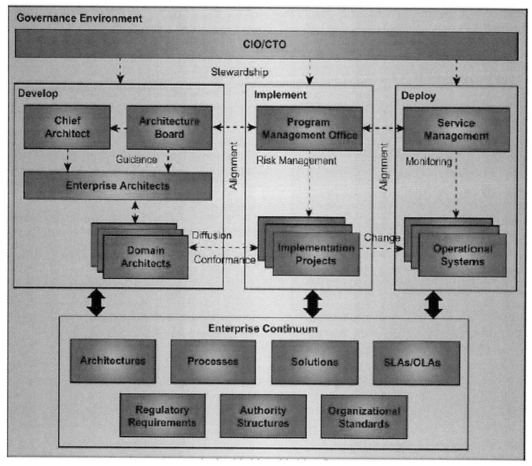

FIGURE 5.8

TOGAF architectural governance framework. (For color version of this figure, the reader is referred to the online version of this chapter.)

5.8 TOOLS AND LANGUAGES

5.8.1 Modeling tools: A necessary medium

Modeling, tooling, and the repository cannot be dissociated. The main function of enterprise architecture modeling tools is to:

- Provide graphical editors that support TOGAF models
- Guarantee the correct use of TOGAF concepts
- Manage the part of the model repository
- Support and coordinate teamwork between participants
- Generate useful products for artifacts or deliverables (for example, matrices or documents)
- Provide a set of services associated with models (such as model requests, impact analysis, redundancy searches, searches for unused elements, statistical reports, service and application component reuse rate analysis, and consistency and quality analysis).

In short, the purpose of the model is to capture, communicate, validate, reason, and act upon shared information, and tools make this possible.

Tools thus provide a "content *metamodel*," which includes TOGAF elements. All these tools must be adaptable, so as to take into account adaptations of the generic TOGAF framework. It must also be possible to customize the assistance they provide in the production of other TOGAF artifacts and deliverables, typically catalogs and matrices.

These tools generally structure models according to TOGAF viewpoints, thereby presenting diagrams adapted to the people concerned. They guarantee the overall consistency of models by managing element uniqueness, the update of elements in all the diagrams in which they appear, and the overall consistency of the model. By managing cooperation between the participants involved in building models, they help organize teams, coordinate work on the model by avoiding access conflicts, and manage model versions and configurations.

When an enterprise architecture approach is set up within an enterprise, everything must be taken into account: the architectural framework, the tooling, the adaptation to the enterprise's approach, and the adaptation to the participants' work mode.

Successful implementation of tooling will help improve communication between participants and record the work carried out. It will also help manage the enterprise continuum on a carefully controlled enterprise architecture repository, as well as facilitating overall governance.

Modeling tools do not do everything. They should be included as part of a wider toolset, in order to cover all services linked to a complete repository in the TOGAF sense of the term. For example, listings, deployment configurations, library versions, and production or tooling statistics producing matrices or architectural structures are frequently managed by integrated, third-party tools. The definition of tools is carried out during the TOGAF preliminary phase (see Section 2.2).

5.8.2 Tools available in the marketplace

There exist several tools capable of modeling enterprise architecture, all of which manage the model in a database and provide graphical editors.

Purely graphical tools such as PowerPoint or Visio should be ruled out. These tools can be used to build isolated diagrams, but provide no assistance when constituting a model repository. Simply using two or three diagrams that reference the same model elements is enough to be sure of ending up with a set of inconsistencies between these diagrams.

Two families of tools can be distinguished in the marketplace: tools dedicated to enterprise architecture, and UML and BPMN modeling tools providing extensions for enterprise architecture.

Tools dedicated to enterprise architecture, such as IBM's Rational System Architect, Mega, ARIS, or Case Wise, provide a general solution to enterprise architecture, and are customized for each enterprise context. They provide BPM (business process modeling) solutions and enterprise architecture solutions. The modeling language supported is often proprietary, but frequently includes BPMN. All propose predefined TOGAF customization, which means each provides a specific solution for TOGAF. However, it is possible to customize these tools to support the approach presented in this book.

This book presents an enterprise architecture modeling approach that uses TOGAF, UML, and BPMN modeling standards, and UML extensions dedicated to TOGAF in the form of "UML *profiles*" (see Chapter 10). The advantage of this extension technique is that it can be applied to all UML and BPMN tools.

Tools dedicated to enterprise architecture successfully cover functional needs through their focus, while UML and BPMN tools bring the benefit of their support of very widely used standards. TOGAF 9.1 recommends:

> *"It is highly desirable that the description of the architecture be encoded in a standard language in order to enable a standard approach for the description of architecture semantics and to facilitate its reuse by different tools."*

This addresses the use of TOGAF as a standard approach, but can also be extended to the modeling techniques used for TOGAF.

Additional elements online

The examples in this book were developed using the Modelio modeling tool, which provides the following useful features to support TOGAF modeling:

- UML and BPMN support
- Support of the "UML profile" extension mechanism
- Catalog and matrix generation
- Support of goal analysis and requirement analysis
- Traceability management

An open source version of the Modelio tool can be downloaded from the www.modelio.org web site. This version enables users to access the model database containing the examples presented in this book.[f]

---

[f]The model database can be downloaded from www.togaf-modeling.org/togaf-en-pratique/.

5.8.3 **Summary of the appropriate use of modeling techniques**

Modeling is an investment, but to what end? Keep in mind the reasons for which you are investing in change.

- Goals, requirements, and domain

A model must have the agreement and consent of all those working on it.

- However, formalism can be an obstacle.

Modeling work includes establishing a consensus.

- Agreeing on goals and terminology sets the foundations for consensus on models.

Relevance is a model's most important quality.

- A model must correspond to the reality of the business and the company.
- Does a given model serve its purpose?
- What is the purpose of the model?

5.9 FUNDAMENTAL CONCEPTS

The following fundamental concepts were introduced in this chapter:

- Model: Representation of a particular subject.
- Abstraction: Mechanisms that enable users to consider the system at more macroscopic levels.
- View: Representation of the system from the perspective of a set of issues (the viewpoint).
- Traceability: Ability to link artifacts produced by enterprise architecture and subsequent technical realization activities to other artifacts from which they originate or to which they refer.
- Modeling tool: Enables the realization of the goal of the model—to capture, communicate, validate, reason, and act upon shared information.

Introduction to TOGAF Models

CHAPTER OUTLINE

TOGAF defines a large number of different kinds of artifacts. This chapter provides examples of artifacts and interpretations of how they can be realized and modeled. This will help you to get to know TOGAF artifacts and how to use them and will provide useful modeling techniques to realize them. The progress of artifact construction is illustrated through an example of an enterprise.

6.1 TOGAF ARTIFACTS

6.1.1 Using models to realize artifacts

The notion of the TOGAF *artifact* was described in Section 3.3. Artifacts are a means of communication that present a particular view of the architecture. Catalogs, matrices, and diagrams are three types of artifacts. Architecture objects (for example, actor, business entity, business process) will be represented in these artifacts, along with their properties and links. TOGAF provides a list of recommended artifacts by architecture domain and also indicates which ADM phase uses or produces which artifacts.

    Based on the list of artifacts recommended by TOGAF, this book describes how these can be represented using the Unified Modeling Language (UML) and Business Process Modeling Notation (BPMN) modeling standards or specific extensions.

> The model examples provided in this chapter and in Chapters 7–11 can be downloaded from www.togaf-modeling. org/downloads-menu.html and used with the open source Modelio tool.[1]

---

[1] www.modelio.org.

Of course, in the first instance, models support "diagram"-type artifacts. However, matrices and catalogs can also be produced (generated) from models too. Consequently, we sometimes propose diagram-type artifacts to support certain TOGAF catalogs.

It should be noted that TOGAF does not describe how to model artifacts in detail. The implementation of the models in this book is therefore a specific creation on the part of the authors and is the result of their choices.

6.1.2 Preliminary phase: Determining useful artifacts in the context of the enterprise

Let's remember that TOGAF is a generic methodological framework. Every enterprise and every context will require that TOGAF be adapted. This adaptation takes place during the *preliminary phase*, in the context of the "Tailored Architecture Framework" deliverable and, more particularly for artifacts, the "Tailored Architecture Content" section. For this reason, TOGAF proposes a list of artifacts but does not impose that they all be realized, and does not claim that the list is exhaustive. This book has, therefore, partially carried out this adaptation work in order to facilitate the support of TOGAF by modeling standards. It has made a selection, which includes a large majority of TOGAF artifacts, as well as other artifacts that are considered useful for enterprise architecture. Readers can use this work as a basis for the completion of this adaptation to their own context.

The aim of the preliminary phase (see Section 2.2.1) initiating the TOGAF ADM is precisely to determine the viewpoints and artifacts that are considered to be important in the context of an enterprise. Stakeholders participating in enterprise architecture work must therefore be identified. Once we have identified these actors' specific issues, we can then determine the necessary representation viewpoints. By default, TOGAF architecture domains can be used (this is the choice made in this book) or specific viewpoints can be defined.

From a pragmatic standpoint, we recommend that participants in enterprise architecture work be identified (as TOGAF actors), that artifacts be reviewed and only those relevant to the enterprise be retained, and that their characteristics be redefined, notably by specifying the nature of the participants involved in each artifact for the enterprise.

To facilitate this selection, we have characterized each artifact using the following properties:

- Name
- Participants: The aim of the preliminary phase is to identify the enterprise stakeholders who are involved in enterprise architecture activities. For each artifact, we must indicate which of these participants contributes to its elaboration. Among participants, the following categories[2] can be distinguished:
  - Experts: Those who bring knowledge. For example, the executive management of the company is responsible for determining goals.
  - Designers: Those who realize the artifact. For example, business analysts can elaborate the goal model.
  - Recipients: Those for whom the artifact is destined. For example, the definition of goals is essentially destined for business analysts and architects, who must refer to them. These participants are generally involved in the review of the current artifact.

---

[2]These categories are usually formalized through a RACI (responsibility assignment matrix showing the "responsible, accountable, consulted, informed" roles per deliverable).

- Aim: What is the benefit and usefulness of the artifact? To do what? How is it used? This information is decisive when deciding whether or not the artifact should be included in the enterprise architecture work of a given enterprise (benefits versus cost of construction).
- Incoming elements: List of information extracted from other artifacts and useful in the development of the current artifact.

6.1.3 Structuring artifacts

The models presented in this book are based on the artifacts provided by TOGAF, as shown in Figure 6.1. In this figure, artifacts are organized either by type of architecture (for example, data architecture) or by phase (for example, Phase E—opportunities and solutions).

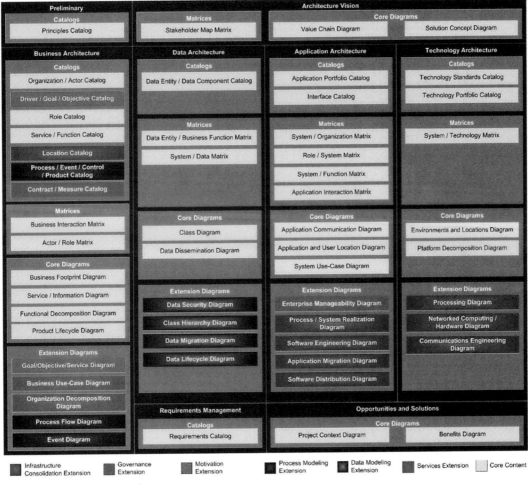

FIGURE 6.1

Different artifacts defined by TOGAF (extract from the reference document). (For color version of this figure, the reader is referred to the online version of this chapter.)

Generally speaking, several phases contribute to the development and consolidation of an artifact. Thus, certain artifacts may be initiated during the vision phase, which presents the initial architectural intentions in a very general manner, before being consolidated, notably during phases B and C. This book structures these artifacts according to the phase they are most involved in.

The chapters dealing with artifacts are organized as follows:

- Chapter 7—Vision (essential artifacts of phase A)
- Chapter 8—Phase B (business architecture)
- Chapter 9—Phase C (application architecture)
- Chapter 10—Phase D (technology architecture)
- Chapter 11—Phase E (opportunities and solutions)

In Section Organization of the model, we see that data architecture will be split into two parts, one related to business architecture and the other to data architecture.

Quite logically, these chapters focus more on the development phases (notably A, B, C, and D), which are more concerned with the development of artifacts linked to models (Table 6.1).

6.1.4 Organization of the model

It is a common practice to organize TOGAF enterprise architecture model using a structure that resembles the viewpoints retained for the approach (see Section 5.2.4) as closely as possible. Since UML and BMPN modeling tools do not use the concept of viewpoints, the model must be organized using *packages*,[3] which represent these viewpoints. By default, viewpoints span at least the four TOGAF architecture domains: Business, Application, Data, and Technology. The separation of concepts and models is easy with regard to business, application, and technology architectures and is naturally supported by UML packages that are specialized for TOGAF.

Data architecture partially spans business architecture and application architecture, depending on the level of representation used. We will see examples of these two data architectures at the business level in Chapter 8 and at the application architecture level in Chapter 9.

Two subpackages are therefore created inside the business architecture and application architecture packages to support data architecture.

This structuring is by no means mandatory (Figure 6.2). In particular, the definition of viewpoints specific to an enterprise can lead to different structuring. For example, an additional viewpoint dedicated to system security could be envisaged.

The structure is then further broken down in a functional way, relevant to the enterprise's business.

---

[3]UML concept enabling model elements to be structured.

Table 6.1 Examples of "Diagram" Artifacts Organized by Phase

Artifact	Main Phase	Description
Solution concept diagram	A: Architecture vision	High-level orientation of the envisaged solution (its main components) to reach the goals of the enterprise architecture
Organization/actor catalog	B: Business architecture	Definition of the actors, their duties, hierarchical links, and responsibilities
Functional decomposition diagram	B: Business architecture	Graphical representation of the functions of the enterprise, structured hierarchically
Process flow diagram	B: Business architecture	Detailed view of the functioning of a process, broken down into tasks
Class diagram (business level)	B: Business architecture	Modeling of business entities and their properties and associations
Application communication diagram	C: Application architecture	Representation of interconnections and communication between the system's applications and application components
Application migration diagram	C: Application architecture	Representation of the IS's evolution path, with its different stages
Networked computing diagram	D: Technology architecture	Representation of the hardware and network architecture (servers, networks, etc.)
Requirements analysis diagram; requirements catalog	Requirements management	Definition of requirements and their properties and links
Benefits diagram	E: Opportunities and solutions	Representation of opportunities and solutions at application architecture level

FIGURE 6.2

Structuring of different TOGAF architecture into packages. (For color version of this figure, the reader is referred to the online version of this chapter.)

6.2 UML AND BPMN FOR TOGAF MODELING

6.2.1 Choosing a representation mode for TOGAF models

TOGAF refers several times to the UML and BPMN modeling languages to support enterprise architecture modeling. However, some explanations are still required on how these standards should be used to apply TOGAF, and on which model parts to show for each viewpoint.

UML and BPMN will be used to represent basic architectural objects, defined in the TOGAF metamodel (see Section 3.2.1). This means that we must therefore decide which UML or BPMN element will be used to represent each TOGAF object. In this way, a BPMN process will naturally represent a TOGAF process, a UML actor will represent a TOGAF actor but also a TOGAF role, and a UML class will represent a TOGAF business entity but also a TOGAF product.

As we saw in Chapter 5, models must be adapted to facilitate communication between participants. UML and BPMN, both extremely rich standards, must be filtered according to viewpoints so as only to present useful concepts and must also be adapted to correspond to TOGAF terminology (such as a role, a business entity, etc.). They sometimes have to be extended to support concepts that are absent from these languages (for example, a function, an organization unit, a goal).

6.2.2 Modeling standards for TOGAF

Panorama of standards that are useful for TOGAF

Most modeling standards used in this book stem from the OMG organization. The OMG has standardized very well-known standards such as UML and BPMN and has workgroups that provide standards for modeling domains linked to enterprise architecture (vision, enterprise organization, process modeling, requirements modeling, SOA architecture modeling). It is therefore a very rich and useful source for selecting modeling techniques adapted to TOGAF.

- UML and BPMN are essential standards defined by the OMG and used in enterprise architecture modeling.
- Service component architecture is a reference in the field of SOA architecture definition. SoaML is an OMG standard based on UML and used in SOA architecture modeling.
- SysML is an OMG standard dedicated to modeling technical systems. It models systems by breaking them down into components, fitting together systems, subsystems, and components (the concept of "blocks"). It provides a requirements modeling standard reused in this book.
- Business motivation metamodel is an OMG standard providing a detailed metamodel for the "who, what, why, and how" of business motivation (vision phase, goal definition).
- Organizational structure metamodel is an OMG specification (not an adopted standard) defining useful concepts for organization modeling. Here, we find concepts similar to those of TOGAF, such as the concept of the organization unit.
- Ontology definition metamodel is an OMG standard, providing a metamodel for the definition of ontologies. Part of this metamodel is used to support the concept of the dictionary.

The UML standard

UML was standardized in 1997, and a major new version was published in 2005. UML groups together a large number of modeling techniques that were previously scattered among different domains (entity relationship, object model, state diagram, sequence diagram, process modeling, etc.). It is widely accepted and used in the modeling of software systems.

UML enables data to be modeled through class diagrams. Behavior is modeled through object modeling (object behaviors, operations, etc.) and the support of sequence diagrams, state diagrams, and activity diagrams. Systems and architectures are also modeled using the concept of components and component assembly techniques.

Extending and adapting UML: The profile mechanism

UML is used for a wide variety of domains and targets and must therefore be adapted to correspond to the concerns and concepts specific to each target. For example, the concept of persistence must be introduced when modeling database schemas, while concepts specific to programming languages must be added for targets. Similarly, the concept of service is required when modeling SOA architectures, while the concept of the system is central to large system modeling.

A UML *profile* is a set of extensions brought to UML to adapt it to a particular target. For example, SoaML or SysML (Figure 6.3) are UML profiles standardized by the OMG.

We will see that in order to better target TOGAF, a UML profile has also been defined in this book.

The BPMN standard

BPMN is a standardized, graphical notation used to model business processes and workflows.

The main goal of BPMN is to provide notation that is truly understandable by all enterprise users, from business analysts who create initial sketches of processes, through developers in charge of setting up the technology that will run these processes, right up to enterprise users who will manage and supervise these processes.

BPMN was standardized by the OMG in 2006, and a major new version (BPMN2) published in 2010.

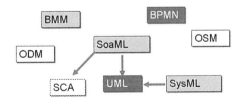

FIGURE 6.3

Reference standards for supporting enterprise architecture modeling. (For color version of this figure, the reader is referred to the online version of this chapter.)

Although the UML standard also has notation for modeling processes (activity diagrams), BPMN is an OMG standard that is independent of UML. In practice, several modeling tools support both modeling languages.

Adapting standards to TOGAF: The Enterprise Architecture Profile

TOGAF provides a metamodel that describes the key concepts (TOGAF objects) that have to be linked to the concepts provided by UML and BPMN. This is why this book provides a UML profile dedicated to TOGAF.[4] This "UML *profile*," named EAP (*Enterprise Architecture Profile*) extends the relevant UML concepts in order to represent all TOGAF objects. For example, a UML class is the best adapted concept to represent a TOGAF "business entity" (Phase B), but also a "message," or "data" in phase C. Figure 6.4 shows how these different concepts, all of which are based on the UML class concept, are distinguished by particular extensions. Figure 6.5 shows the representation of other TOGAF objects supported by the EAP.

The use of UML with the EAP and of BPMN therefore enables us to reuse the standards shown in Figure 6.3 by bringing them together in a language dedicated to TOGAF. The open source Modelio tool is used to represent the TOGAF models presented in this book. However, since UML, BPMN, and profile implementation are standard techniques, other modeling tools available in the marketplace can also be used.

This also has the advantage of reusing modeling techniques referred to by TOGAF and are explicitly covered by these standards, such as Use Cases (UML) or BPMN.

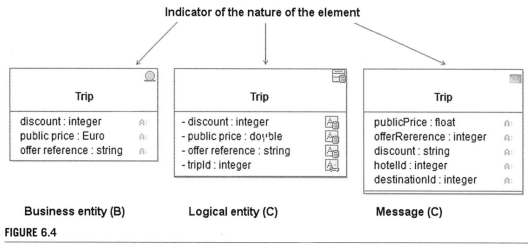

FIGURE 6.4

The UML profile for TOGAF distinguishes TOGAF concepts. (For color version of this figure, the reader is referred to the online version of this chapter.)

---

[4]The EAP profile can be freely downloaded from www.togaf-modeling.org/togaf-en-pratique/. Documentation on this profile can also be found here.

FIGURE 6.5

TOGAF objects represented using the EAP. (For color version of this figure, the reader is referred to the online version of this chapter.)

6.3 THE "DISCOUNT TRAVEL" ENTERPRISE

Throughout our entire presentation of artifacts, we use the same enterprise example, that of the "Discount Travel" enterprise. We based this example on specifications provided by Ceisar.[5]

Discount Travel is a service provider that provides the public with a list of trips that have not been sold by travel agencies.

Different trip/holiday formats are proposed at reduced prices. Discounts can reach 50% of the published price applied by travel agencies.

The prices offered by Discount Travel are explained by the fact that the departure and return dates are fixed, and are often imminent. The future client must therefore be willing to depart within 2 weeks of making his or her reservation.

Until now, Discount Travel has provided a telephone service open to the public from 8 am to 8 pm from Monday to Friday. The potential client selects the trip that is of interest to him or her with the help of a customer advisor. The processes of the enterprise are not formalized and the information used by customer advisers to respond to clients takes the form of paper documents, updated daily by the marketing department according to the evolution of the stock of available products.

A website exists that currently enables order elements to be entered. These order elements are then processed manually by an agent. Orders are recorded using an application accessed by sales representatives.

Discount Travel is considering the possibility of providing a reservation service online. Moreover, the enterprise wishes to improve its customer service. The design of the information system must therefore be reviewed.

---

[5]http://www.ceisar.fr/: Center of excellence in enterprise architecture, affiliated with the Ecole Centrale in Paris.

A trip corresponds to a format (combination of flight, hotel, and car rental), a destination, and an accommodation service.

Destinations are identified by the continent (North Africa, Africa (except North Africa), Europe, Asia, and America) and the country.

The trip takes place in one country only.

The relationship with travel agencies is managed by the marketing department, who defines priority products to search for among the range of trips available in travel agencies. The goal of the marketing department is to develop the most attractive range of trips possible for the clients of Discount Travel.

In our work on this example, we go into detail on the organization of the enterprise, in particular clarifying the enterprise's goals and business processes. We also describe business entities (what a trip is, a client file, etc.), geographical locations, the enterprise's business and IS requirements, application architectures, and technology architectures.

6.4 FUNDAMENTAL CONCEPTS

The following fundamental concepts were introduced in this chapter:

- EAP: Profile that adapts and filters UML in conjunction with BPMN to map it to TOGAF enterprise architecture modeling.

Models for Phase A: Vision

7

Based on the Discount Travel company example, we identify which models and diagrams are useful during the Vision phase. Goals and objectives are key elements developed during the Vision phase. Modeling activity starts at this point.

7.1 PHASE A ARTIFACTS

7.1.1 Nature of phase A artifacts: Vision

The *vision* phase prepares the following phases through a general representation of the baseline and target architectures (see Section 2.2.2). To provide a wide vision that can be used to scope all the work, the vision phase uses initial schemas of an essentially informal nature. These artifacts are very high level and do not yet involve detailed modeling activities. They will be developed "free hand," in the form of images or matrices, in order to prepare later phases of the ADM. However, certain artifacts can still be translated in the form of models, and where this is the case, we show their correspondence. Translation into models, which is very quick to carry out based on initial schemas, is used to initiate future modeling work and to provide the first elements that will be used to trace decisions during the following phases.

Certain artifacts are clearly not part of any modeling phase, such as the stakeholder map matrix, defined by TOGAF as being "sensitive information which does not require any specific metamodel (therefore model) entities."

One of the tasks of the vision phase is to prepare the ADM cycle. Essential business goals must also be prepared and validated.

Artifacts linked to business goals are often initiated during the preliminary phase or earlier before being reworked during the vision phase (phase A). They provide a framework for work to be carried out during the architectural cycle to come and will essentially be consolidated during the business architecture phase (phase B).

A general plan of the complete architecture cycle must be defined. For this reason, the first sketches of the envisaged solutions, which have their place for the most part in phases B and application architecture phase (phase C), must be established during phase A. Solution concept diagrams will notably be used to this end (Table 7.1).

The modeling techniques presented also use goals and formalize the different links possible between architecture models and goals. The goal diagram, which is an extension of TOGAF, provides added value by representing these links.

7.1.2 Essential concepts used in models

Phase A sketches models that will be reworked during the development phases. To this end, it implements a number of concepts clarified in phases B and C. Essential concepts are presented in detail in the paragraphs on model-focused phases.

Here we present "goals," which are heavily reworked during phase A, and also requirements, since these are initiated at this stage and are closely linked to goals. TOGAF places requirement analysis at the heart of the ADM (see Figure 3.2). Thus, requirements concern all ADM phases.

Table 7.1 Phase A Artifacts

TOGAF Artifacts	Models Presented	Remarks
Stakeholder map matrix	Stakeholder matrix	
Value chain diagram	Value chain diagram	
Solution concept diagram	Solution concept diagram	
Driver/Goal/Objectives catalog	Goal diagram	The goal diagram is an extension to TOGAF allowing it to be formalized more precisely
Driver/Goal/Objectives catalog	Goal catalog	The catalog and the diagram are two different ways of representing the same goals
Requirements catalog	Requirements diagram, requirements catalog	Initial requirements are initiated in phase A, and developed throughout the entire ADM cycle
Process/Event/Control/Product catalog	Business process catalog	
Event diagram	Event diagram	Event diagrams are used to produce business process catalogs and map processes

- Goal or objective of the enterprise: Determines the orientations of the enterprise.

- Requirement: Required aptitude at enterprise or IS level.

- Internal actors, who participate in the functioning of the enterprise (for example,

  "Marketing manager").

- External actors, who are external to the enterprise but who interact with it (here, "Clients"

  and "Partners").

- Business process (for example, "Reserve Trip").

- Business event, such as the cancellation of an order or the end of the marketing season.

- Entity component: Autonomous component of the IS, which is configured and deployed.

  Entity components can be physical or logical components. We provide a service component
  typology for SOA architectures, indicated by the character associated with the icon (here,
  "E" for "Entity" component). This is explained fully in Chapter 9.

- Application: Form of application component that designates an application in the

  traditional sense of the term. It is used widely to represent existing applications, for example, to
  carry out application mapping. It allows applications to be designated as having been bought off-
  the-shelf, such as ERPs or custom-developed applications.

Note: Like those presented earlier, these notations are provided by the EAP profile used in this book.

7.2 STAKEHOLDER MATRIX

Name	Stakeholder matrix
Experts	General management, organization unit directors, business managers
Designers	Business analysts
Recipients	All participants in enterprise architecture
Aim	To define the different actors participating in the construction of the enterprise architecture in order to facilitate the organization of the ADM cycle and to determine which artifacts are to be produced by whom
Useful preliminary information	Actors and human resources of the enterprise

Table 7.2 Stakeholder Matrix

Participant	Skill	Decision-Making Power	Level of Interest
CEO	Goal orientation, decisions	High	High
Organization unit director	Requirements orientation, decisions	Quite high	Medium
Business analyst	Business, analysis techniques	Low	High
Business architect	Business, architecture	Medium	High
Application architect	Application architecture	Medium	High
CIO	Project management, IS	Quite high	High
Business manager	Business	Quite high	High
Business expert	Business	Low	High
Data architect	Data architecture	Low	Quite high
Software designer	Software design	Low	Medium
Technical architect	Technology architecture	Low	Quite high
User	Use mode	Low	Low
Security expert	Software security	High	Medium
Operational manager	Deployment and functioning of applications, management of the application park	High	Medium
System and network engineer	Hardware, systems, network	Low	Medium

Section 1.2.5 described the importance of stakeholder management when setting up an ADM cycle. All those participating in enterprise architecture work must be identified, along with their influence on commitments and their main concerns that must be addressed through enterprise architecture work. The stakeholder matrix influences the ADM cycle and the organization of participants since it indicates who is involved in the work, who must be informed, and who has a significant influence on requirements, goals, and the priority given to them.

The role of participants and their tasks in the ADM cycle must be determined. Knowledge of the different participants' concerns guides the choice of artifacts that it will be useful to produce and the way in which they will be produced. In particular, models will be selected so as to be easily understood by participants. For each of the artifacts described in this book, we find the list of participants concerned.

Table 7.2 provides an example of a stakeholder matrix. The level of interest designates the interest of the stakeholder in question for enterprise architecture. The name and the attributions of actors vary greatly from one enterprise to the next. It is certain that for the "Discount Travel" company, this list is too rich. Thus, a single person will probably carry out the tasks of several actors.

7.3 ARTIFACTS LINKED TO GOALS

7.3.1 Goal analysis

Goals: A company's reason for being

TOGAF defines an enterprise as being a collection of organizations with a common set of goals. This shows just how important *goals* are within an enterprise; they are its reason for being. An enterprise has a history, which is translated notably by its organization, the locations where it is present, and its information system. An enterprise operates in one or several business domains, where its skill lies. The transformations required to guide the enterprise architecture are defined by the enterprise's goals. Goals provide direction, the place we want to get to. As far as possible, all enterprise architecture tasks will refer to goals to define what the desired results or outcome are and hence to decide what must be done. Goals will justify the work to be done, the reorganizations to be carried out, the orientation of the activity toward businesses to be put in place, and the evolution of the IS to support everything by rationalizing choices.

Goals in phase A

Goals are often known before phase A. By deciding on the start of an ADM cycle, the preliminary phase has already identified goals. Goals are reworked in phase A, for example, by using the techniques described below, before being finalized in phase B. The development of business architecture in phase B identifies architecture elements that are recognized as being necessary, which also enables goals forgotten during phase A to be identified later.

Goals and objectives

TOGAF distinguishes between goals and objectives. An objective breaks down a goal in order to set a time-specific milestone which corresponds to the progress made with regard to the goal. Objectives set the targets for goals in order to monitor whether or not they are met. Goals are the "what," in other words, the desired results, while objectives are the "how," that is to say, the courses of action that will lead to goals being achieved.

For example,

*   "increase the use of our transport capabilities by 30% by the end of next year" is an objective
*   "be one of the global top five in our activity sector in 5 years" is a goal.

The definition of goals is particularly based on the estimation of the enterprise's capacity to progress, as well as on how well business drivers are taken into account. Business drivers or influencers are conditions outside the enterprise and linked to the sector of activity, such as competitive constraints (reduction in costs, competitor growth, etc.) or legal constraints (bank capital, travel agency insurance, etc.). Goals are always center-stage when an ADM cycle is triggered. Prior definition of goals therefore exists, often in an informal form.

One of the first enterprise architecture activities during phase A consists in formalizing, structuring, hierarchically organizing, and rationalizing goals with the help of the techniques presented earlier. Goals are completed and clarified by driver analysis and knowledge of the business and the IS.

Identifying goals

Identifying and selecting goals and giving them a priority level are not easy tasks. The definition of goals is a discipline in itself.

TOGAF reminds us that an objective must be SMART:

*   *S*pecific, by determining what must be done in the business
*   *M*easurable, by implementing clear metrics for success
*   *A*ttainable, by:

- Clearly breaking down the problem
- Providing the basis for determining elements and plans for the solution
- *R*ealistic, by indicating deadlines and conditions that can be met by the enterprise's capabilities within stipulated time and cost limitations
- *T*imely, by explicitly indicating when interest in the solution will disappear

An essential point is that architectural choices must be aligned with the organization's business goals. By constantly referring to goals, everyone is faced with his or her responsibilities, only asking the IS for the most fundamental things, defining priorities, allocating the necessary budget where the stakes are high, and identifying who is responsible for which goal.

Assigning goals and objectives

Assigning responsibility is a key step in the finalization of goal definition, as it implies negotiation on the feasibility of goals and agreement between stakeholders. By designating who will be responsible for reaching an objective, negotiation must take place with the people responsible, which therefore leads to communication on and validation of the objective in question. Goals and objectives are by no means just a list of pious wishes, but rather strategic choices that will guide the future activity of the enterprise. Responsibility for each objective must therefore be assigned to a person who will be in charge of attaining it.

Most of the time, goals are corporate-level goals, in other words, goals are frequently assigned to the entire enterprise, while objectives are allocated more specifically to people. Where they are assigned to organization units or business processes, the responsible element is always clearly identified (the process owner, the organization unit manager).

Goal graph

Goals are constructed hierarchically. Goals constitute the roots of the goal/objective tree. For every high-level goal, the question, How can we reach this goal? is used to identify lower-level goals, which are generally objectives. Conversely, identifying a low-level objective leads to the question, Which objective or goal will this help us reach? Finally, for every breakdown of a high-level goal, it is useful to think about alternative breakdowns: Do any obstacles exist that will hinder the realization of current goals? What other paths can be envisaged to reach higher-level goals?

This breakdown continues until a set of elementary objectives has been identified, whose allocation is clear and whose feasibility is confirmed.

We will see that the goal diagrams presented here go beyond a simple breakdown hierarchy. Analysis of the goal graph also looks at consistency and conflicts between goals: some goals contradict others (negative influence) or reinforce them (positive influence).

For example, the goal of improving customer service, which requires more staff, is in conflict with the goal of reducing costs. This is not an absolute contradiction, but it does require analysis to determine the exact quantification required and the right balance between the two goals.

Defining priorities for goals

Objectives must be measurable. This enables us to check that they really have been attained. Measuring facilitates the quantification of the advantages expected for the business once the objective has been met. These advantages have to be weighed against the effort required to obtain them. Thus, if the

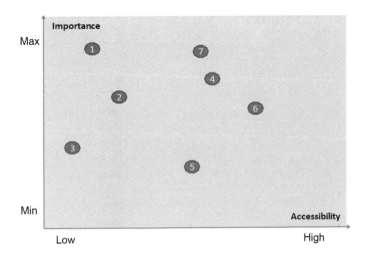

FIGURE 7.1

Evaluating goal/objective priorities. (For color version of this figure, the reader is referred to the online version of this chapter.)

objective is "We want to give a full and immediate response to clients placing orders over the telephone," then we must ask ourselves what advantage this objective brings to the organization. If it is a question of increasing client satisfaction, then it is necessary to measure the increase in satisfaction. For the enterprise, this can have the advantage of generating consistently higher turnover, a better image, increased revenue, and so on.

Goal/objective determination comes up against priority definition, which leads to the postponement of certain goals/objectives and the promotion of others. A common technique consists in evaluating the importance of goals/objectives, as well as their accessibility (how difficult it is for the enterprise to attain them).

Figure 7.1 thus provides a more rational basis for assigning priorities to goals. This exercise can also be useful during phase E when analyzing opportunities and solutions. While it is easy to decide to retain "7," "6," and "4" (they are accessible and extremely important) and to defer "3" and "5" (they are not easily accessible and have limited importance), it will be more difficult to decide about goal "1," which is important but difficult to attain.

Summary of best practices for defining goals

Define the following:

- Subgoals/objectives, by asking how a goal can or should be implemented.
- Supergoals, by asking why a goal is necessary or needed.
- Alternatives, by asking what different ways of satisfying the supergoal exist.
- Conflicting goals, by asking what goals may conflict with each other.
- Allocation/assignment to individual parts of the business.
- Means of measuring their fulfillment.

7.3.2 The "Goal diagram" artifact
Description of the artifact

Name	Goal diagram
Experts	General management, organization unit directors
Designers	Business analysts
Recipients	Architecture cycle stakeholders, general management and business architects, application architects, CIOs
Aim	To define the goals/objectives that will guide the changes that are to be made to the enterprise and its IS. To quantify objectives and allocate them. To provide a rational basis for the assignment of priority levels to goals/objectives
Useful preliminary information	Previously identified goals, enterprise drivers, "SWOT"[a] analyses, earlier marketing studies

[a]SWOT: Strategic planning method based on evaluating strengths, weaknesses, opportunities, and threats with regard to one or several of the enterprise's activities.

 Goal

- - - - -> <<part>> Hierarchical breakdown of goals

- - - - - - - -> <<+ influence>> Indicates that the source goal will make it easier to attain the destination goal.

- - - - - - - -> <<- influence>> Indicates that the source goal will make it more difficult to attain the destination goal.

The goal diagram is an extension to TOGAF, which only provides the goal catalog. The goal diagram provides useful complementary information, notably through the different types of links represented.

Goal diagrams are used to summarize goals, represent them in the form of a hierarchy, and present the links that exist between goals and other model elements. Goals are situated at the top of the diagram, with the operational objectives that constitute them appearing lower down, via the "Part" link.

Goals are broken down hierarchically using the "part" link. Thus, in Figure 7.2, "Increase turnover and profits" is a strategic goal, which is broken down into operational objectives such as "Increase number of trips reserved per day," which itself is broken down into "Increase sales presence," "Optimize client transformation rate," and "Render products more attractive." Objectives orient the strategies used to achieve goals. They start to express what must be done. The "why" is expressed by the goals they break down. We can see that the "Reservation via the Internet" goal breaks down the "Increase sales presence" goal, since the capability of selling via the Internet is a new form of sales presence ensuring wide geographical coverage and availability. This goal has a positive influence on the "Optimize client transformation rate," "Improve business process management," and "Reduce file processing times" goals.

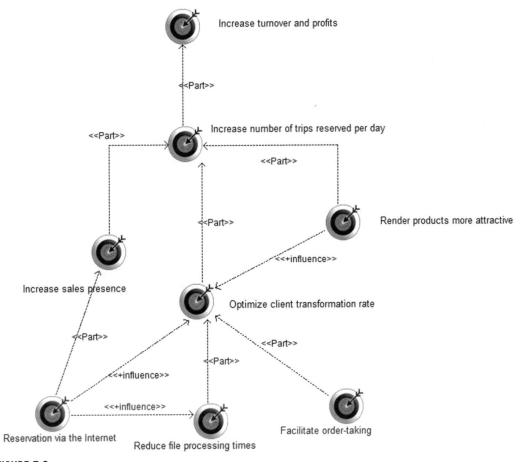

Increase turnover and profits

<<Part>>

Increase number of trips reserved per day

<<Part>>

<<Part>>

Render products more attractive

<<Part>>

<<+influence>>

Increase sales presence

Optimize client transformation rate

<<Part>>

<<Part>>

<<+influence>>

<<Part>>

<<+influence>>

Reservation via the Internet

Reduce file processing times

Facilitate order-taking

FIGURE 7.2

Goal diagram. (For color version of this figure, the reader is referred to the online version of this chapter.)

The existence of drivers imposes the creation of associated goals. This is the case for the "Reservation via the Internet" goal. In a competitive environment where most travel agencies provide access to their services on the Internet, the marketing management team can identify this capability as being a driver: providing this access modernizes the company image and contributes to increasing sales. This capability therefore has the status of a strategic goal, which conditions how the company is organized, notably for the marketing, sales, and accounts departments.

During phase A and then phase B (business architecture), goals are reworked in order to make sure that they meet SMART criteria as closely as possible. Thus, a goal such as "Improve business process management" can be called into question: it is nonspecific, difficult to measure and act upon, and has no time limit. No one within the enterprise will accept responsibility for this goal, and the monitoring of its realization will only be a vague, overall evaluation at the enterprise level. It is preferable to focus on more factual and operational goals, such as specific points on how to improve certain identified processes.

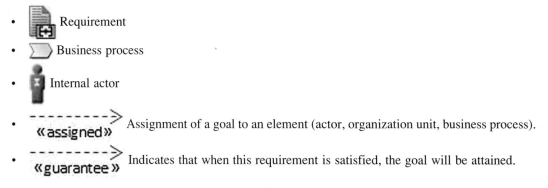

- ![Requirement icon] Requirement
- ![Business process icon] Business process
- ![Internal actor icon] Internal actor

- ----------> 《assigned》 Assignment of a goal to an element (actor, organization unit, business process).

- ----------> 《guarantee》 Indicates that when this requirement is satisfied, the goal will be attained.

Figure 7.3 provides complementary information. Links assigning goals are represented (《assigned》). In the example in Figure 7.3, the "Optimize client transformation rate" goal is assigned to the "Sales director" internal actor, while the "Render products more attractive" goal is assigned to the "Marketing director" internal actor.

7.3.3 The "Goal catalog" artifact

The goal catalog is the equivalent of the goal diagram. It presents the same elements, is realized by the same designers, and has the same experts and the same objective.

Goal analysis is essentially carried out using tables, which present values for the properties of each goal.

The properties assigned to a goal depend on enterprise practices. The preliminary phase must define which attributes will be used to evaluate goals.

Here is a typical example of goal properties:

- *Name*
- *Description*
- *Kind* (*goal* or *objective*)
- *Global*: Determines whether or not the goal concerns the entire enterprise or if it should be assigned more precisely. Goals are often global, whereas objectives are often not.
- *Type: qualitative or quantitative*. Quantitative goals (most often objectives) have a clear unit of measurement (for example, "turnover"). Qualitative goals (most often goals) require human evaluation of whether or not they have been attained.
- *Required level of satisfaction*: *evaluated* or *firm*. An evaluated goal is based on the fact that many goals are never totally met. For example, "improve employee well-being" is an "evaluated" goal. Because of this, evaluated goals are achieved when evaluation estimates that satisfaction factors are greater than failure factors. Firm goals can be judged in a more binary fashion: either the value has been reached or not.

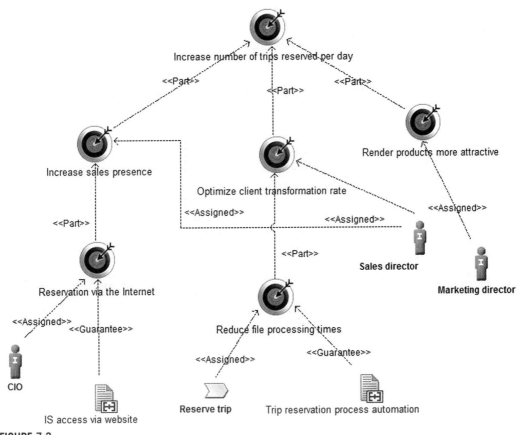

FIGURE 7.3

Assigning goals and links to requirements. (For color version of this figure, the reader is referred to the online version of this chapter.)

- *Unit of measurement*: Determines the unit of measurement used to measure objectives.
- *Target value*: Value to attain in order to satisfy the objective.
- *Current value*: Value measured on the date on which the objective is defined.
- *Problems*: Obstacles that can get in the way of the goal being met.
- *Source*: Determines the origin of the definition of the goal.

Table 7.3 presents a simplified version of a goal catalog, with the scope and the values indicated for each goal.

In Table 7.3, "drivers" are not shown. For the example of a travel agency, we can imagine that pressure from competitors is increasing, notably with regard to prices. We can also imagine that consulting and ordering trips online is becoming more and more widespread in the field. These constitute two "drivers," which will guide the enterprise's strategic goals.

Table 7.3 (Partial) Example of a Goal Catalog

Name	Description	Scope	Type/Target Value
Internet access	Propose a reservation service on the Internet	Strategic	Qualitative
Improve quality image	Improve the image of the quality of both products and services (support, sales)	Strategic	Qualitative
Financial optimization	Manage the company's accounts by optimizing the company's cash flow and margins	Strategic	Quantitative: net margin = 8%
Improve payment management	Payment times must be reduced and payments secured; the implementation of remote payment mechanisms through credit cards must be systematized	Operational	Qualitative
Improve clientele follow-up	Better understand clients, their tastes and preferences, and their loyalty; inform them of the status of their order, and/or new offers and promotions	Operational	Qualitative
Increase number of trips reserved per day	The average volume of trips sold per day must be increased; this volume will be measured for a full year. This increase must take place based on average prices and margins, which are either constant or growing	Operational	Quantitative: number of purchase per day = 90 in the next 1.5 years
Optimize client transformation rate	When a prospect consults our offers, the rate of clients proceeding with a purchase must be increased	Operational	Quantitative: number of purchases/number of consultations = 0.4
Reduce file processing times	Client order-taking processing times must be as short as possible	Operational	Quantitative: duration (min) = 30

7.4 ARTIFACTS LINKED TO REQUIREMENTS

Requirements management is at the center of the TOGAF ADM. In practical terms, this means that requirements management is constantly being carried out during each phase. This work begins in phase A and continues throughout the entire cycle.

7.4.1 The "Requirements catalog" artifact
Description of the artifact

Name	Requirements analysis diagram; requirements catalog
Experts	Business experts, business managers, application architects
Designers	Business analysts, application architects (nonfunctional requirements)
Recipients	Business architects, application architects, software designers
Aim	To define the specifications for evolutions to the business architecture and the IS. To translate goals into detailed requirements on enterprise architecture components
Useful preliminary information	Goals of the enterprise, business architecture, application mapping

Table 7.4 Functional Requirements: Example of a Catalog

Name	Description	Benefit	Cost	Risk	Target Version
Internet access	The information system must allow the client to consult available trips and to place his orders via a dedicated Internet site	Critical	200	Medium	1
Client autonomy	The client must be able to place his orders in an autonomous manner (without the involvement of salespeople) in at least 95% of cases	High	10	Low	1
Process automation	Order placement and monitoring processes must be able to run with no human intervention	High	120	Low	1
Purchase automation	This activity will be automated on the new website by direct connection to the "GIE" credit card server	Critical	10	Low	1

Requirements analysis often takes place by constructing tables such as Tables 7.4 and 7.5. Requirements have a name, a description, and a set of associated properties (which vary according to the enterprise approach). The benefit/cost/risk ratio produced by this example is used to decide on the priority level to be assigned to each requirement: the decision (target version) is therefore indicated in one of the properties of each requirement. The use of tables to support requirements analysis limits the ability to link requirements to goals, work items, test cases, and other artifacts and model elements of the EA and its lifecycle. Requirements should also be managed in the model repository.

Thus, a high risk on a requirement that is not particularly important will certainly lead to the assignment of lower priority to the requirement in question.

It is not easy to place a limit on the number of requirements formulated. The criteria and attributes presented above enable us to rationalize the process of defining priorities and choosing requirements to take into account. Finally, budgetary constraints will intervene to limit them.

Table 7.5 Nonfunctional Requirements: Example of a Catalog

Name	Description	Benefit	Cost	Risk	Target Version
Site availability	The trip reservation site must have an availability rate of 99.4%, that is, less than one hour of unavailability per week	High	100	Medium	1
Reliability	The IS must operate 24 hours a day, 7 days a week, with a maximum interruption rate of 2/1000; redundancy and hot standby mechanisms must guarantee the continuity of the system	Critical	60	Low	1

Characteristics of a requirement

The definition of requirements in the ADM cycle was presented in Section 2.2.6. A requirement specifies a capability or a condition that must (or should) be provided by a system. A requirement can concern the enterprise in general, one of its processes, one of its functions or organization units (for example, "the sales department must manage order cancellations"), or the information system more specifically (for example, the nonfunctional requirements in Table 7.5). Requirements must be satisfied by the business architecture (meaning that business processes, business services, actors, and organization units must be defined or adapted to handle order cancellations), or by application and technology architectures (for example, we will see that the application architecture includes a "CreditCard" component to implement the "purchase automation" requirement). Requirements concerning the IS will then be sent to projects and will constitute their specifications.

Functional requirements present a complete description of the way in which the system will operate. They should enable actors (users or technical actors) to have a realistic image of the system and to see all aspects of its functioning, before its construction.

Using Table 7.5, nonfunctional requirements will primarily interest technical architects, who will use them to deduce the needs of the infrastructure. Security experts, operations managers, and system and network engineers are also concerned.

Properties that must be verified by a requirement

The "business book of knowledge" (BABoK)[a] defines the properties that must be respected by the requirements in Table 7.6.

In practice, requirement analysis is an extremely difficult task. The following are some of the issues involved:

- Customers often don't know the requirements.
- Analysts and designers need to have a thorough understanding of the essence of the requirements, and what it means to match them.
- Requirements are not stable between the time they were analyzed and the time the solution is delivered.

Good requirements management has to address these realities. This is why TOGAF puts them in the center of the ADM circle, and why requirements analysis is a continuous activity throughout the ADM.

Goals and requirements

Goals constitute one of the starting points for the development of requirements, and help make requirements clearer for stakeholders. Goals focus on the "why" (strategic questions) and the "what" (the results we want to achieve), whereas objectives clarify the "how" (operational questions), before using

---

[a]BABoK is a guide to good practices in business analysis, published by the International Institute of Business Analysis. Among other things, it develops best practices for analyzing requirements (www.iiba.org/imis15/IIBA/Home/IIBA_Website/home.aspx).

Table 7.6 Useful Properties for Requirements (BaBoK)

Criteria	Description
Assignable	This requirement can be assigned to a component of the system, where it can be implemented
Attainable	The requirement is technically feasible, in the context of budgetary and time constraints
Complete	All known requirements are documented and all the conditions under which the requirement applies are identical. Requirements must contain the information necessary to design a solution and to check that a solution satisfies them
Consistent	A requirement must be able to be satisfied without coming into conflict with another requirement
Correct	A requirement must precisely describe the expected function or condition. Only the initiator of the requirement (client, user, stakeholder) can judge this
Not solution-oriented	The requirement must be expressed in such a way as to leave the widest possible range of implementation options
Measurable and testable	Requirements must be designed to check whether or not the solution satisfies them
Necessary	A necessary requirement is a requirement that is essential to the satisfaction of business goals. Requirements must be traced to goals to check their necessity
Ranked	A priority is assigned to each functional requirement in order to indicate whether or not it is essential for a particular version of the system. These priority levels are used to make choices with regard to budgetary constraints
Traced	The source of the requirement must be known: a person, a business rule, a use case, and so on. Requirements must have a unique identifier
Not ambiguous	All readers must interpret the requirement in the same way. It is preferable to use simple, concise terms when writing requirements. The use of terms featuring in a previously defined business glossary helps ensure that requirements are not ambiguous
Understandable	Solution designers must be able to easily understand requirements

requirements to broach the question of the detailed functional and nonfunctional characteristics of the solutions that realize the strategies used to achieve the goals. Requirements introduce the "what" at the solution level (which developments to carry out, which system to put in place, etc.).

The breakdown of goals often helps identify initial requirements. Respecting these requirements will then help *guarantee* (using the "guarantee" link) that goals are reached (see Figure 7.4). Thus, when the "Trip reservation process automation" requirement on the IS is satisfied, this will facilitate the guarantee that the "Reduce file processing times" goal be reached.

It is not always easy to distinguish between goals and requirements. In the example mentioned in this section, we can see that the goal has a general scope, whereas the requirement appears as a solution to the goal.

Operational objectives are *assigned* (using the "assigned" link) to an actor, an organization unit, a business process, a business function, or a business service. They are never assigned to an IS

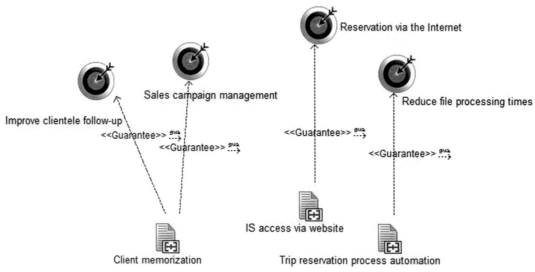

FIGURE 7.4

A requirement can "guarantee" that a goal is reached. (For color version of this figure, the reader is referred to the online version of this chapter.)

component; this level of detail corresponds to requirements that can be *satisfied* (using the "satisfy" link) by an IS component.

Requirements are written like behavioral specifications rather than goals to be reached (the system will carry out..., access will be limited to...).

7.4.2 The "Requirement diagram" artifact
Description of the artifact
The requirement diagram presented here is based on the SysML[b] standard.

- ![] Requirement

- ![] Goal

- ![] Interaction component

---

[b]System Modeling Language: An OMG standard dedicated to complex system modeling. The field of system engineering has a strong focus and lengthy experience in requirement engineering.

-  Use case

- ----➤
  <<part>> Breaks a requirement down into more elementary requirements.

- ---------➤
  «refine» Describes the manner in which a model element or a set of model elements
  can be used to refine a requirement.

- ---------➤
  «satisfy» Determines that a model element is used to satisfy a requirement by supporting
  the requested function or by responding to the formulated constraint. Very often an application
  component satisfies a requirement.

- ---------➤
  «verify» Defines the manner in which a test case (which can be a use case) verifies a
  requirement. For example, a use case can express test sequences, which check whether or not a
  requirement is satisfied.

Requirements can be presented in graphical form. Here, requirement modeling enables requirements to
be positioned and several types of links to be defined between requirements and the rest of the model.
Requirements often appear in architecture models, to remind us which requirements refer to which
represented model elements. Matrices can be used instead of diagrams.

These links between requirements and the architecture model are used to measure:

- Whether or not each requirement is satisfied by at least a part of the system
- Whether or not at least one test case is planned for each requirement
- Which model elements satisfy no requirements

Thus, requirements are justified through their links to goals, and the model itself is justified through its
links to requirements. Moreover, requirements enable us to closely monitor how well the model
respects the specifications.

In Figure 7.5, the "IS access via website" requirement guarantees the "Reservation via the Internet"
goal. It is satisfied by the "TripReservationSite" component, and will be verified by the "Reserve trip"
and "Cancel trip" use cases.

7.5 ARTIFACTS LINKED TO BUSINESS PROCESSES
7.5.1 Modeling business processes in phase A

Phase A is mainly concerned with the high-level identification of *business processes* (see Sections 2.2.2
and 12.2), in order to help establish the vision. Business process modeling is carried out by business
analysts, who use their knowledge of the organization of the enterprise (roles and actors) and the business functions of the enterprise.

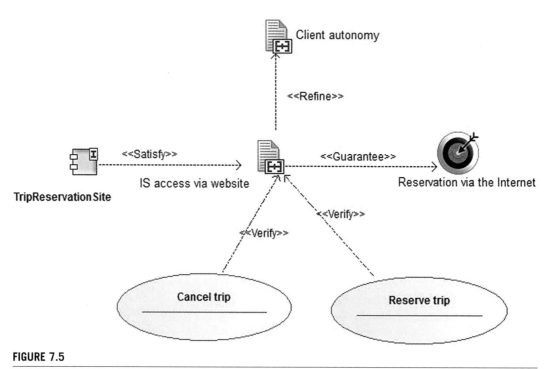

FIGURE 7.5

Example of a requirement diagram with different types of links. (For color version of this figure, the reader is referred to the online version of this chapter.)

The TOGAF event diagram particularly describes the links between events and business processes. It is used to obtain a "macro" vision of business processes by mapping them, while detailed information on business processes is defined by process flow diagrams (see phase B artifacts).

7.5.2 The "Event diagram" artifact
Description of the artifact

Name	Event diagram
Experts	Business analysts, organization unit managers
Designers	Business process analysts
Recipients	Business analysts, application architects, organization managers
Aim	To identify processes, characterize them, and provide general mapping. To decide on priority optimization lines
Useful preliminary information	Definition of actors, functions

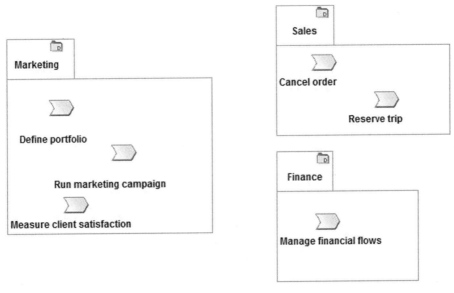

FIGURE 7.6

Process map of the travel agency. (For color version of this figure, the reader is referred to the online version of this chapter.)

Event diagrams present business events, but also and above all provide a macroscopic view of processes. They cover what is traditionally referred to as a "process map," and can be implemented with several levels of detail. Three different views are presented here. The most macroscopic level is used to carry out general mapping of business processes (Figure 7.6); an intermediate level presents events, participants, and data linked to a group of processes (Figure 7.7); the most detailed level focuses on one given process and provides details on the process' external environment.

- Organization domain
- Business process

Figure 7.6 presents organization domains (for example, "Marketing") which structure processes (for example, "Define portfolio"). It provides a macroscopic view of processes that is useful when mapping them; in other words, when producing an inventory of processes that can then be organized.

The enterprise's key business processes

Phase A and then business architecture must identify the key business processes linked to the enterprise transformation targeted by the ADM cycle. These key business processes must therefore be listed, classified, and their respective positions specified, while providing information on the context. These business processes will constitute determining reference elements for application architecture, which will

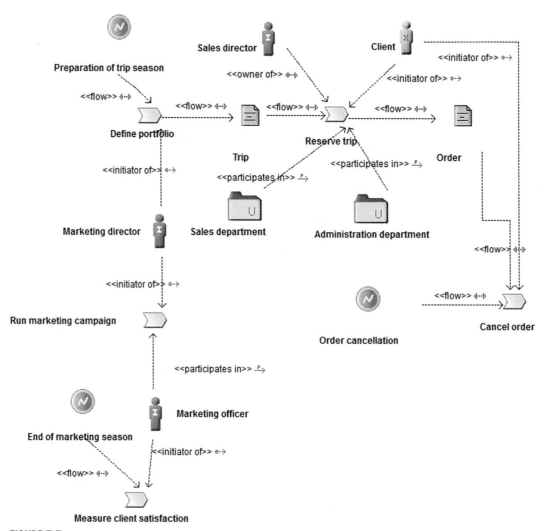

FIGURE 7.7

Event diagrams provide an overview of business processes. (For color version of this figure, the reader is referred to the online version of this chapter.)

have to provide services to support some of them. Their definition will be used for business governance, which will make sure that they run correctly, that results are efficiently produced, and that enterprise functioning rules are respected.

The event diagram provides an overview of processes and their connections to other processes and to other business architecture elements. The most general event diagram view, presented in Figure 7.6, is used to establish the business process map by classifying them (in business domains as shown in

Figure 7.6) and by providing information on their context. This map will be completed by process files similar to those presented in Section 12.2.2.

Based on this business process map, business managers and analysts can define priorities with regard to processes that must be overhauled or optimized. They identify critical zones, think about processes impacted by new enterprise goals, and may begin more detailed studies of certain processes, which involve additional business process modeling and analysis work.

Business events and processes

Business events represent any event that can arise during the functioning of the enterprise and which necessitates management work on the part of the enterprise. A "request for information" from a client or a "cancellation" are examples of business events. Events can be of different types, for example:

- External events, initiated by an entity outside the enterprise (for example, "order from a client").
- Temporal events, initiated by a time-linked condition (for example, "month end" or "fiscal year end").
- Internal events, initiated within the enterprise (for example, "current stock level lower than stock renewal level").

Most events require action to be taken within the enterprise, and this action will be described in business processes. When a business event occurs, this can also trigger a process that will produce a business result or response.

The "Event diagram" artifact (intermediate view)

-  Business event

- Product

- Business process

- Internal actor

- External actor

-  Link indicating a flow of data (input or output) on an active element (here, <<flow>> processes).

- «initiator of» The origin actor is the initiator of the process.

- «participates in» The origin actor or organization unit participates in the running of the process.
- «owner of» The origin actor is the owner of the process.

Event diagrams provide an overview of processes, trigger events or sent events, participating actors, roles or organization units, and products received or sent. At this intermediate macroscopic level, there is no sequence between processes, even if we can see that products sent by a process can be reused by another process. This intermediate level of detail cannot be presented for all company processes in a single diagram. For reasons of size, several diagrams of this type must be created and then classified, for example, by process domain (identified in the map).

The event diagram, shown in Figure 7.7, presents support processes (see Section 12.2.4) linked to marketing and financial services and production processes linked to trip reservation. It associates trigger events or sent events to these processes, as well as input or output products.

It associates actors to these processes, actors who initiate or participate in processes, events that trigger or that are generated by processes and input or output products on processes.

The "Event diagram" artifact (view focused on a process)

-  Product
- Goal
- External actor
- Internal actor
- Business event
- Organization unit
- Business process
-  Function
-  <<flow>> Link expressing incoming and outgoing information between an event and a

process, or between a product and a process. This kind of link exists between the "Order" product and the "Reserve trip" process, or between the "Order cancellation" event and the "Cancel order" process.

- ---------------> A "participates in" link from a role or organization unit to a process.
  «participates in»
  Thus, the sales department and the administration department participate in the realization of the "Reserve trip" process.

- ----------> An "initiator of" link from a role or organization unit to a process. Thus,
  «initiator of»
  the client is the initiator of the "Reserve trip" process.

- ----------> An "owner of" link between an actor and a process. Every process must
  «owner of»
  have an owner whose role is to guarantee the correct functioning of processes by supervising them and by applying corrective measures when they are run. Here, the sales director is the owner of the "Reserve trip" process.

Event diagrams can focus on a particular process in order to determine its context in greater detail. For a given process (here, "Reserve trip"), the actors and organization units that initiate or participate in the process will be expressed, as well as the owner of the process, the trigger events or events sent by the process, and the incoming/outgoing information flows. Goals assigned to the process also appear in this diagram. They are used to identify priority processes that must be modeled, as well as to orient modeling and planned improvements in performance, automation, better synchronization with information systems, and so on. Key performance indicators (KPIs) can be partially deduced from goals assigned to processes.

For reference purposes, TOGAF indicates the characteristic operational objectives that can be assigned to a process:

- Increase process production rate (for example, "Optimize trip reservation times")
- Ensure consistent process production quality (for example, "Reduce reservation failure or error rates")
- Obtain a foreseeable process execution cost
- Increase existing process reuse
- Reduce interprocess information provision times

Figure 7.8 focuses on a process and is a graphical view of the process file (see below).

Business process catalog

TOGAF defines the process/event/control/product catalog. This kind of catalog will be produced as a result of process mapping. Macroscopic diagrams (Figure 7.6) and intermediate diagrams (Figure 7.7) can be referenced in this catalog. In Table 7.7, we show the information resulting from identification. Qualification generally happens during phase B and provides other defined properties (frequency, complexity, etc.), as shown in Table 7.8.

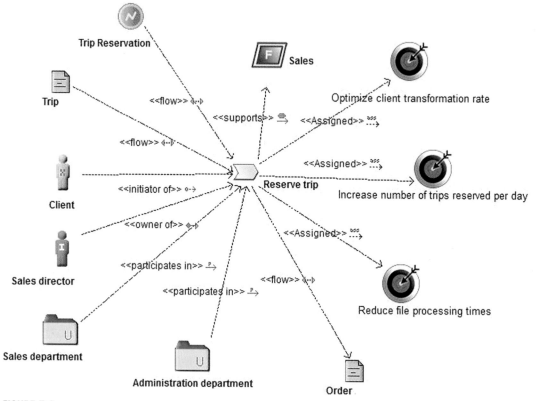

Trip Reservation

Sales

Trip

Optimize client transformation rate

<<flow>>

<<supports>>   <<Assigned>>

<<flow>>

<<Assigned>>

Client

<<initiator of>>   Reserve trip

Increase number of trips reserved per day

<<owner of>>

<<Assigned>>

Sales director

<<participates in>>

<<flow>>

<<participates in>>

Reduce file processing times

Sales department

Administration department

Order

FIGURE 7.8

An event diagram focused on a single business process. (For color version of this figure, the reader is referred to the online version of this chapter.)

Table 7.7 Business Process Catalog

Process	Description
Reserve trip	Proceed with the reservation request for the client's trip, including payment aspects and availability checking
Define portfolio	Constitute the trip catalog for the following season
Cancel order	Manage the cancellation of a client's order

Table 7.8 Detailed File on a Business Process

Process	Reserve Trip
Finality	Proceed with the reservation request for the client's trip, including payment aspects and availability checking
Trigger events	Reservation request
Input	Trip catalog (Trip)
Output	Order
Key performance indicators (KPIs)	File processing time <10 minutes; abort rates during order <30%; "Discount Travel" employee intervention <5%
Governance	Sales director
Resources used	Website, IS, partners ISs
Main actors	Client, sales department, administration department
Work underway	Opportunity study

7.6 THE "SOLUTION CONCEPT DIAGRAM" ARTIFACT
7.6.1 Definition of the artifact

Name	Solution concept diagram
Experts	Business and application architects
Designers	Business architects, functional architects
Recipients	General management, analysts, architects, CIOs
Aim	To share a preliminary vision with all stakeholders by providing general information on the changes that are going to be implemented
Useful preliminary information	Goals, organization, existing application and business architectures

Figure 7.9 presents an overview of the target architecture: a website destined for clients and sales representatives will be built. Work will concentrate on the trip reservation process, which will be implemented by a set of new application components linked to the accounting management application (ERP).

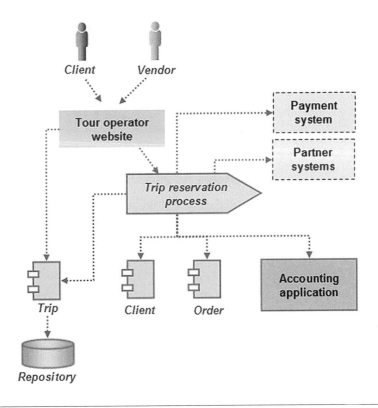

FIGURE 7.9

Sketch of the solution: "Solution concept diagram." (For color version of this figure, the reader is referred to the online version of this chapter.)

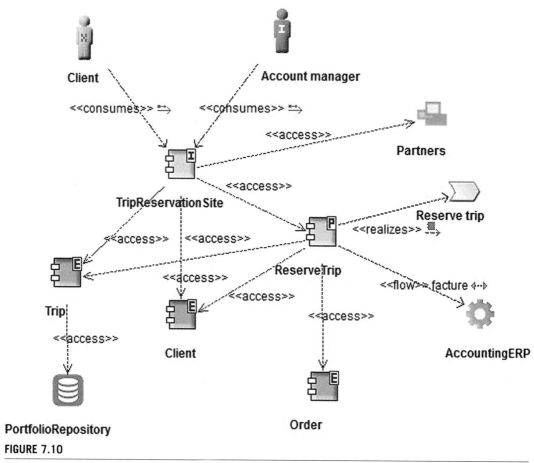

FIGURE 7.10

Solution concept diagram. (For color version of this figure, the reader is referred to the online version of this chapter.)

Once consensus has been obtained, this type of model can then be reentered more formally in the modeling tool and used to begin systematic modeling work in the different architecture domains concerned. Figure 7.10 presents the same model slightly more developed in the modeling tool.

The central elements represented in Figure 7.10 are application components with their interdependency (access) links. The links between the information system and functions, business services, or business processes are indicated ("realizes" implementation links).

The "TripReservationSite" component provides clients and sales representatives with Internet access. The "ReserveTrip" process component implements the "Reserve trip" business process. It uses the "Order," "Client," and "Trip" entity components. It interacts with the accounting ERP application by transmitting invoices to send out.

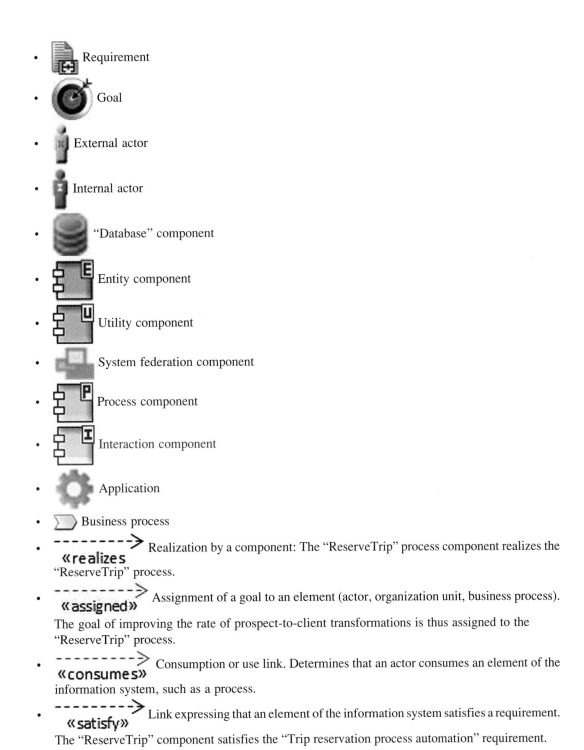

- Requirement

- Goal

- External actor

- Internal actor

- "Database" component

- Entity component

- Utility component

- System federation component

- Process component

- Interaction component

- Application

- Business process

- «realizes» Realization by a component: The "ReserveTrip" process component realizes the "ReserveTrip" process.

- «assigned» Assignment of a goal to an element (actor, organization unit, business process). The goal of improving the rate of prospect-to-client transformations is thus assigned to the "ReserveTrip" process.

- «consumes» Consumption or use link. Determines that an actor consumes an element of the information system, such as a process.

- «satisfy» Link expressing that an element of the information system satisfies a requirement. The "ReserveTrip" component satisfies the "Trip reservation process automation" requirement.

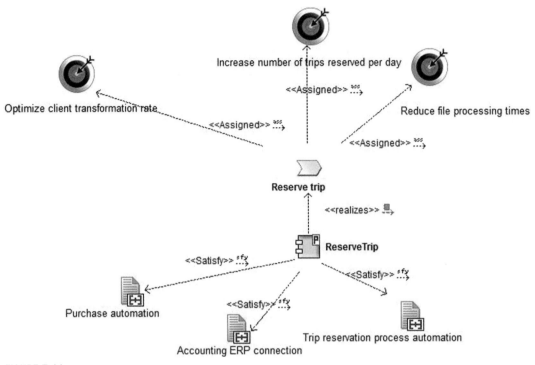

FIGURE 7.11

Solution concepts, links to goals and requirements. (For color version of this figure, the reader is referred to the online version of this chapter.)

We must refer to goals to remind ourselves why we have decided to make the IS evolve and why we have to introduce or further develop such and such an application component. In Figure 7.11, the "ReserveTrip" business process is linked to the assigned goals. The "ReserveTrip" component satisfies the "Accounting ERP connection," "Trip reservation process automation," and "Purchase automation" requirements.

Assignment is generally about accountability of organization units or their members. Assigning a goal to a process means that the process owner will be accountable for the goal, or in practice to the KPI inferred from the goal or objective.

7.6.2 Providing the envisaged solution with an orientation

A solution concept diagram provides a high-level orientation of the solution that is envisaged to achieve the goals of the enterprise architecture. Unlike the more formal and detailed architecture diagrams developed in later phases, solution concepts represent a sketch of the expected solution without going into any detail.

In a broader EA context, a solution concept diagram would include different opportunities and solutions, investment strategies, change initiatives, and their impact on a broad range of architecture building blocks. Solution concept diagrams can contain key goals, requirements, and constraints for the engagement, and can also highlight main work areas that will have to be investigated in more detail using more formal architecture modeling. The goal of this diagram is to share an early vision with all stakeholders by giving them an idea of the changes that are to be put in place. Each participant then understands the envisaged architectural engagements, and the way in which these will produce a solution that will achieve the enterprise's goals.

We recommend that only essential application components be presented and that their interconnections be summarized using dependencies (without considering service assembly). New components to be introduced must be linked to existing applications where necessary. They must be linked to requirements, processes, or functions, which themselves are linked to goals. It is also useful to use "consumes" links to show which actors use which components.

The model has the benefit of being understood by everyone, but this does not mean it is frozen in terms of its elements. It will have to undergo several iterations and improvements during subsequent phases in order to take into account all business constraints and the more elaborate application architecture. It is generally not elaborated using "formal" modeling tools, and will be built using simple graphical tools such as PowerPoint.

7.7 THE "VALUE CHAIN DIAGRAM" ARTIFACT
7.7.1 Definition of the artifact

Name	Value chain diagram
Experts	General management, business organization unit managers
Designers	Business analysts
Recipients	Business analysts, architects, general management, business managers
Aim	To identify the source of values brought to the client, values that must be preserved or improved. To identify the capabilities necessary to achieving new business opportunities
Useful preliminary information	Knowledge of the organization and the business; business functions and capabilities

Value chain diagram representation is often informal, as in Figure 7.12. Different enterprise functions involved in the chain are grouped together with support functions (Marketing and Advertising) distinguished from the main activities involved in value production (for example, "Sales"). The margin is provided as a result of the chain.

- Function

- Sequence between functions

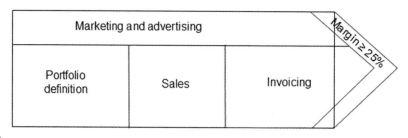

FIGURE 7.12

Value chain diagram—standard representation.

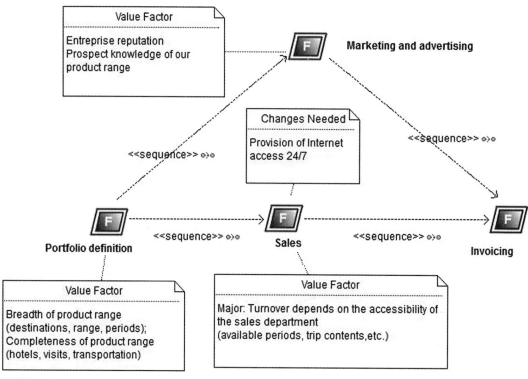

FIGURE 7.13

Value chain of the Discount Travel company. (For color version of this figure, the reader is referred to the online version of this chapter.)

With a modeling tool, this can also be represented using functions defined in the enterprise architecture. In the example in Figure 7.13, sequence links express the usual order of sequencing (this order is informal and not inflexible) in order to illustrate the chain between valued functions. "Value factor" and "Changes needed" notes indicate value factors and required changes.

7.7.2 **Contribution of business functions to value**

Value chain diagrams[c] provide a high-level orientation view of an enterprise and how it interacts with the outside world. They do not provide an exhaustive or formal view of the enterprise, but rather concentrate on the impact of certain orientations and on the relative importance of certain decisions. The aim is to quickly align decision-maker views on priorities and the relative importance of components. All participants must quickly understand the organizational and functional context of an architectural engagement.

Value chain diagrams are used to identify the source of values provided to the client, values that must be preserved or improved. They make it easier to measure the impact of investments on the value provided, and summarize factors such as production times, cost, and quality. Value chain diagrams allow alternative configurations to be compared and vulnerabilities and nonessential activities to be identified. They also enable the capabilities necessary to achieving new business opportunities to be identified. Finally, they constitute an entry point that can be used to center business process improvement work.

7.8 **FUNDAMENTAL CONCEPTS**

The following fundamental concepts were introduced in this chapter:

- Goal: Determines the orientations of the enterprise.
- Objective: Breaks down a goal in order to set a time-specific milestone that corresponds to the progress made with regard to the goal.
- Requirement: Required aptitude at the enterprise or IS level.
- Application component: Encapsulation of application functionality aligned to implementation structure.

---

[c]Michael Porter's theory of competitive advantage.

Models for Phase B: Business Architecture

8

Enterprise architecture puts very strong emphasis on business architecture, which will then shape the entire ADM cycle. Goals, objectives, organization, business processes, functions and capacities, and business entities are some of the most important aspects modeled during the business architecture phase.

8.1 PHASE B ARTIFACTS

8.1.1 Nature of Phase B artifacts: Business architecture

Phase B is dedicated to defining business architecture (see the definition in Section 2.2.3). TOGAF defines a very rich set of artifacts related to phase B (Table 8.1). In particular, it focuses on the following elements:

- The organization of the enterprise, which will be described through its organization units, actors, and roles. Its geographical distribution (sites, location) will also be presented.
- The enterprise's capabilities, which are described in greater detail through its functions and business services.
- The enterprise's activities, represented by its business processes.
- The essential concepts of the business, through a business dictionary and conceptual models of business entities (Table 8.2).
- Business architecture will be optimally defined to satisfy the goals of the enterprise. Phase B participates in the definition and consolidation of goals, already presented in Section 7.3.

8.1.2 Essential concepts used in business architecture models

- Function: Produces one of the enterprise's capabilities. For example, "marketing," "client contract management," and "telemarketing" are functions.

- Business service: Represents a service provided by the business. A business service can be realized by one or several IT services, or by other constituents of the enterprise.

- Role

- Location: Enterprise site.

- Headquarters: A specific location, the company headquarters.

- Organization units: Units that group the functions and capacities of the enterprise. They have resources (personnel, material), missions, and a certain degree of autonomy (for example, the sales department, the administration department).

- Products, such as the trip or the order.

- Business events.

Table 8.1 TOGAF Artifacts and Artifacts Presented in This Chapter

TOGAF Artifacts	Models Presented	Comments
Organization/Actor catalog	Actor organization diagram	This diagram is an extension to TOGAF. It is used to produce the TOGAF catalog. The benefit of this diagram is that it represents the organization of actors through several types of link.
Driver/Goal/Objectives catalog	Goal diagram and catalog	Seen in phase A; phase B consolidates them.
Role catalog	Organization decomposition diagram—role allocation	The diagram can produce the catalog; it represents the links of the roles played by the actors.
Service/Function catalog		Deduced from the model.
Location catalog	Location diagram	
Contract/Measure catalog		Deduced from the model; contracts are associated with business services.
Business interaction matrix		Information is provided by "Organization decomposition diagram—role allocation" diagrams and by flow diagrams.
Actor/Role matrix	Organization decomposition diagram—role allocation	The diagram can produce the catalog; it represents the links of the roles played by the actors.
Business footprint diagram	Business footprint diagram	
Service/Information diagram	Business service information diagram	
Functional decomposition diagram	Functional decomposition diagram	
Product lifecycle diagram	Product lifecycle diagram	
Goal/Objective/Service diagram	Goal/Objective/Service diagram	
Business use case diagram	Business use case diagram	
Organization decomposition diagram	Location organization diagram	
	Flow diagram	Very general view of the organization as a system; an extension of TOGAF.
Process flow diagram	Process flow diagram	
	Business dictionary	Extension to TOGAF; a useful addition for defining business terminology.
Conceptual data diagram	Conceptual data diagram	Pertains to data architecture; conceptual data diagrams are defined here in phase B.
Data dissemination diagram	Data dissemination diagram	Pertains to data architecture.
Data security diagram	Data security diagram	Pertains to data architecture.
Data migration diagram	Data migration diagram	

Table 8.2 Extract from the Dictionary of the Discount Travel Travel Agency

Name	Definition
Trip	Corresponds to a formula defined by the agency and includes a destination and an accommodation service.
Destination	Identified by the continent (North Africa, Africa [except North Africa], Europe, Asia, North America) and the country.
Marketing department	The relationship with travel agencies is handled by the Marketing department. The Marketing department defines priority offers to look for among the trips proposed by travel agencies. The aim of the Marketing department is to draw up the most attractive range of trips for Discount Travel's clients.
Agency	Designates partner travel agencies.
Participant	The person taking the trip.
Client	The person who has ordered a trip, or the person taking a trip.
Accompanying person	A participant who is not the person who placed the order.
Accounting department	Keeps the companies accounts up to date and establishes the annual balance sheet and results. It also checks client solvency.
Flight	Also incorrectly called "plane"; identifies the airline, flight number, date and time of the flight, departure, and arrival of the client's air transportation.
Holiday	Trip service provided for one or several participants, corresponding to the trip offer, with allocated accommodation and transportation.

- Business process (for example, "Reserve Trip").

- Use case: Represents an interaction between actors and the system in order to meet a functional need.

- Business entity: Describes the semantics of business entities, independently of any organizational or IS-related considerations (storage, technology, etc.).

- Business entity (expanded form): Enables an entity's attributes and operations (specific services operated by this entity) to be presented.

- Association between classes: An association has a name, and provides each end with a role name and cardinality (number interval indicating the number of possible linked entity occurrences).

- Information domain: Unit that structures business entities into coherent subdomains.

- State: Represents one of the stable situations of a business entity or product.

8.2 THE "BUSINESS DICTIONARY" ARTIFACT
8.2.1 Description of the artifact

Name	Business dictionary
Experts	Business experts
Designers	Business analysts or business experts
Recipients	Business analysts, business experts, application architects
Aim	To stabilize and specify business terminology in order to obtain a reference for all participants
Useful preliminary information	Business terms

Table 8.2 is a simplified example of a dictionary. According to different enterprise preferences, several attributes can be used to complete terms (lines in the table), such as an attribute indicating the origin of the term. Several types of links can also be used, such as synonym or homonym links. In this example, the dictionary clarifies what a "Trip" is; in this context, it is used as the definition of a trip such as those managed in the product range. However, the trip that a client actually takes is called a "holiday" here, and corresponds to an instance of a trip defined in the product range.

The terms of a dictionary can appear in different diagrams (Figure 8.1) in order to link model elements to the definitions to which they refer. In this figure, we can see class links to terms, as well as association and role links (UML) to terms.

- Business entity

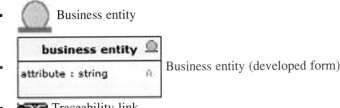

- Business entity (developed form)

-  Traceability link

- Dictionary term

8.2.2 Terminology: The cornerstone of business knowledge

Business knowledge requires clearly defined terminology. There is a normative need for the same meaning to be assigned to a given term by all participants, as well as a need to share knowledge by establishing a dictionary. A dictionary also aims to clarify synonyms, while limiting their number. Homonyms should be avoided in order to assign a single definition to each work, thereby avoiding confusion.

Businesses very often use norms linked to their domain, which provide an extremely useful initial dictionary. This dictionary then has to be completed by terms used within the enterprise itself. The difficulty of this task consists in finding consensus where the terms are not used in the same way by all participants. Terminological ambiguity is omnipresent within enterprises. Enterprise

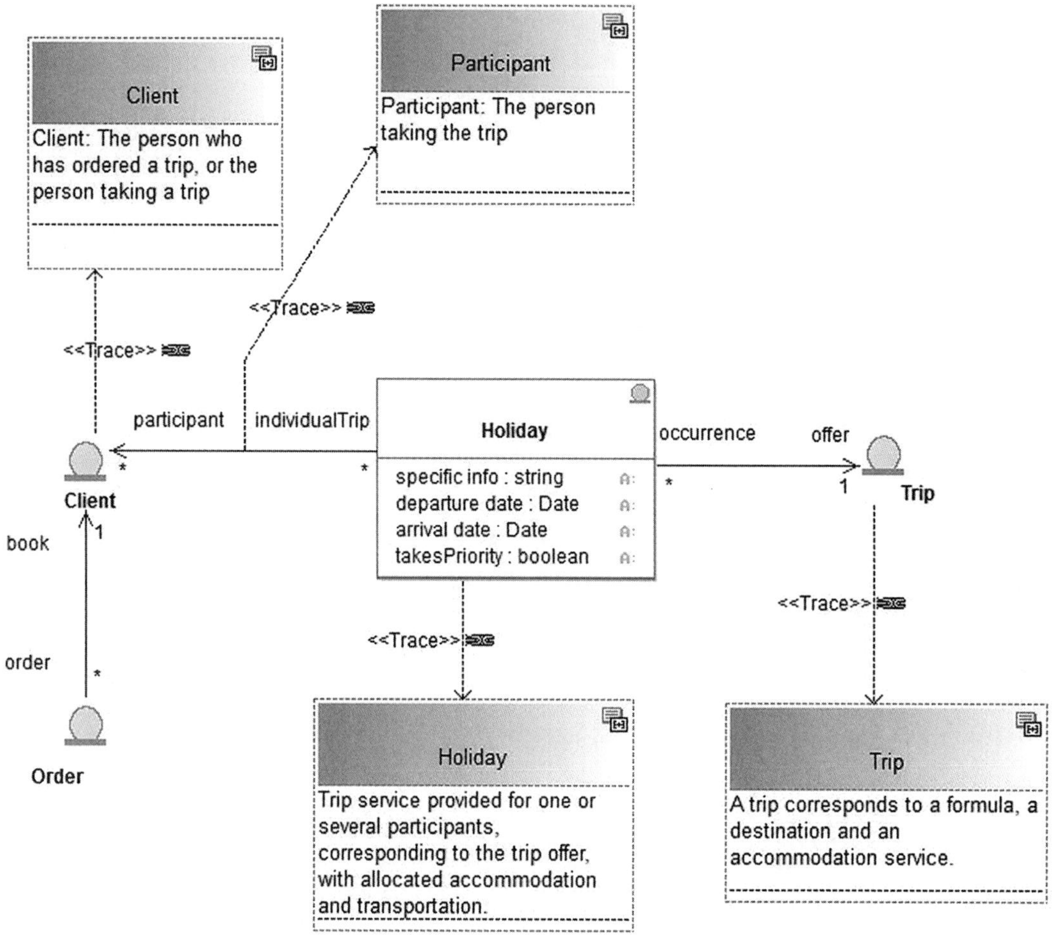

FIGURE 8.1

Business entity diagram traced to associated terms. (For color version of this figure, the reader is referred to the online version of this chapter.)

architecture models are then clouded by these ambiguities and unclear terminologies. Communication between participants and the quality of the results produced can be compromised. This confusion must therefore be resolved by defining a dictionary.

The existence of a dictionary is a significant asset when building an enterprise model; in particular, business entity and business process definition will make massive use of the information contained in the dictionary. For example, the dictionary contains concepts that are essential to the business, and which we also find in business entities.

The dictionary will essentially take the form of a catalog (name, definition). It can be structured into several domains, according to the range of the enterprise's business. It is then up to analysts to decide if and how terms will subsequently be represented as more formal model elements, such as business entities. Terms can be formalized by one or several business entities, attributes, states, events, actors, and so on.

The integration of the dictionary into the model is used to manage traceability to the rest of the model. For example, the definition of a business entity can be linked to a dictionary term, thereby indicating its semantic and terminological reference.

8.3 ARTIFACTS LINKED TO ENTERPRISE ORGANIZATION

8.3.1 Concepts that support enterprise organization

Diagrams supporting enterprise organization modeling are used to establish the mapping of the organization. Roles within the enterprise are determined and positioned with regard to the organization and the different enterprise locations. Organization units, actors, roles, and locations are the key concepts used to represent the organization.

8.3.2 Actors and roles

TOGAF clearly distinguishes the two concepts of actor and role in an enterprise.

An *actor* is an active enterprise participant (person, system, organization) who takes part in the activities of the enterprise. For example, an "account manager" who carries out sales operations with clients is an enterprise actor. A "board of directors," which makes decisions regarding the orientation of the enterprise is also an enterprise actor. An actor is never a physical person. It designates a category of function that participants can carry out, as well as a type of skill required. A physical person can represent several actors. This is typically the case in small to medium-sized companies, where the same person can, for example, be the "receptionist" and the "executive secretary," or where the "sales director" can also assume the role of "marketing director." An actor can designate a group of people (such as a "decision-making committee") or any active entity participating in the functioning of the enterprise. In this way, it can also designate external organizations (a "partner"), or information or technical systems that play a particular role within the organization. An actor frequently designates several people who perform similar functions, such as the "account manager," the "accountant," and the "client."

Identifying actors outside the enterprise helps clarify how these actors are positioned with regard to the organization: who interacts with them. They enable the enterprise to be represented as it is seen from the outside. The "client" or the "partner" are examples of typical external actors.

The *role* represents one of an actor's usual or expected functions. Roles are often described as responsibilities. They establish accountability and are the foundation for enterprise governance. The role is the function that an actor performs in a particular situation. It corresponds to a certain skill domain of the actor and to the contribution the actor makes within the enterprise through the implementation of his or her skills, knowledge, experience, and capabilities. For example, a sales director performs the function of managing sales, as well as managing commercial resources. Several different actors can play identical roles. For example, the sales director, marketing director, and administrative director all play the role of managing the human resources for which they are responsible.

8.3.3 The "actor organization diagram" artifact
Description of the artifact

Name	Actor organization diagram, actor catalog
Experts	Management, organization unit managers
Designers	Business analysts, business experts
Recipients	Business architects, management, organization unit managers, business process analysts
Aim	To define the types of positions with the enterprise, to describe their responsibilities and prerogatives. To identify participants outside the enterprise
Useful preliminary information	Knowledge of the enterprise, organization charts

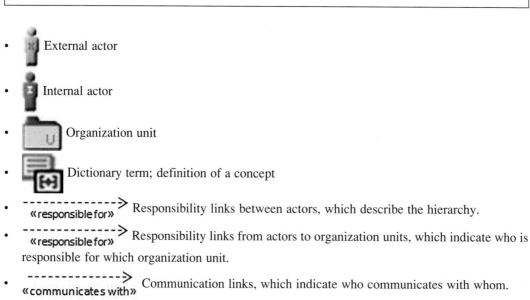

- External actor

- Internal actor

- Organization unit

- Dictionary term; definition of a concept

- «responsible for» Responsibility links between actors, which describe the hierarchy.

- «responsible for» Responsibility links from actors to organization units, which indicate who is responsible for which organization unit.

- «communicates with» Communication links, which indicate who communicates with whom.

- «composed of» Composition links, which define the constitution of composite actors.

Figure 8.2 indicates that the client communicates with the account manager. The account manager reports to the sales director, who is responsible for the entire sales department and who is a member of the enterprise's board of directors.

The actor model clarifies enterprise functioning
The definition of actors and their prerogatives, hierarchical links, and responsibilities provides valuable information on the functioning of the enterprise. Clarifying current responsibilities and roles and determining how these will evolve in the changes to come has a significant impact on enterprise architecture stakeholders, and is a key element in change management. Changes to actors, roles, responsibilities, and the nature of participants' work are thus determined.

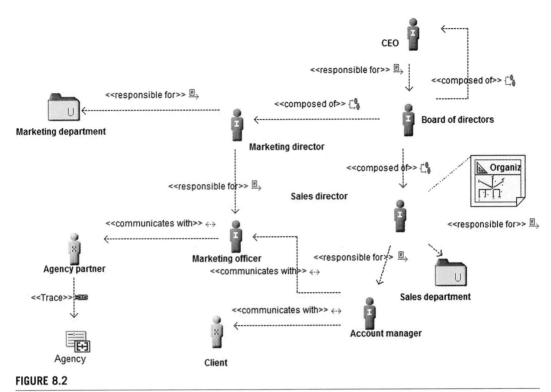

FIGURE 8.2

Actor organization diagram showing responsibility and communication links. (For color version of this figure, the reader is referred to the online version of this chapter.)

Defining and positioning the enterprise's actors constitutes a good basis for defining the organization of the enterprise by providing an overview of the organization. We will also see that these models provide a very useful foundation upon which to define not only the enterprise's business processes and use cases but also models linked to the security of and access rights to enterprise data. We know who communicates with whom, who manages what, and who is responsible for what.

Actor-centric view: Definition of positions

This model also provides precious information used to clarify the definition of positions within the enterprise.

As is the case for all diagrams, it is possible to develop views focused on each element—here, each actor. These views are useful additions to job descriptions. Furthermore, each actor is described by providing information on the skills required of him or her within the enterprise. Here we can see that in addition to the responsibilities already described, the sales manager has two enterprise goals assigned to him, is located in Paris, and is the "owner" of the "Reserve Trip" business process. Being responsible for a process implies that the actor will have to monitor the smooth progress of the process, as well as the value of performance indicators. An actor can have participation links in a business process, which will describe the tasks for which he is responsible. He can also initiate a process. Roles assigned to the actor can also be represented (see Figure 8.3), further specifying the skills expected from this actor.

Actor catalog

The actor catalog uses the elements of this model (assigned goals, responsibilities, locations, participation in processes), as well as description elements such as required skills. Allocated roles can also be presented in organization diagrams or in organization decomposition diagrams (see Figure 8.3).

- Actor: Sales director
- Roles: Team management, sales forecasts, reporting
- Responsibilities: Account manager(actor), sales department
- Managed processes: Reserve Trip
- Location: Paris
- Goals: Optimize client transformation rate, improve client follow-up
- Required skills: Sales management, management, sales

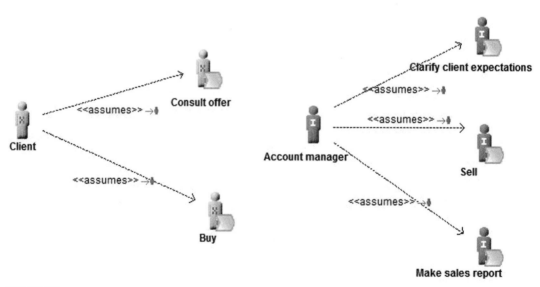

FIGURE 8.3

Roles played by actors. (For color version of this figure, the reader is referred to the online version of this chapter.)

8.3.4 The "organization decomposition diagram—flows" artifact

Name	Organization decomposition diagram—flows
Experts	Executive managers, organization unit directors
Designers	Business analysts
Recipients	Executive managers and directors, analysts
Aim	To provide an overview of the enterprise and essential information exchanges
Useful preliminary information	Knowledge of the enterprise and its organization

-  External actor

- Organization unit

-  Link showing the circulation of data between active enterprise entities (actors, organization units, etc.).

The tasks and responsibilities of actors and organization units can also be represented in terms of the information flows that circulate between them. This type of representation describes the information received, processed, or sent by each participant in the organization. Presenting the information handled by participants illustrates what they need to know to perform their responsibilities within the enterprise.

In Figure 8.4, the marketing department receives information on availability from agency partners. It sends the description of the trip portfolio to both clients and account managers. This diagram therefore presents the essential information flows that are in transition within the enterprise. These are received by or sent to actors or organization units. This example focuses on the flows sent or received by external actors and processed by the enterprise's essential organization units. This type of diagram provides a very useful first glimpse of how the enterprise functions. Its generality means that it can be understood by everyone, while providing elements that facilitate the identification of business processes and managed business entities.

This model does not show how, when, or in what order flows are exchanged and gives no indication of the nature of the flows. Other models will have to provide this information.

The flows exchanged provide interesting information on the responsibilities of the entities involved in the exchanges. For example, the marketing department must provide the portfolio of available trips, while taking into account availability and partner product ranges. Figure 8.5 shows a diagram focused on an actor (Sales Director) that is a useful summary of the responsibilities, goals and connections of the actor. Skills can be added to get a complete actor definition.

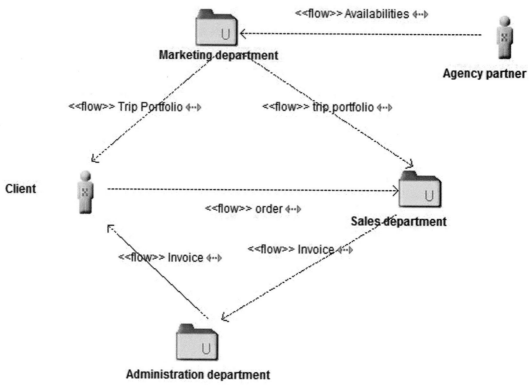

FIGURE 8.4

Essential flows exchanged between the enterprise and external actors. (For color version of this figure, the reader is referred to the online version of this chapter.)

8.3.5 The "organization decomposition diagram—role allocation" artifact

Name	Organization decomposition diagram—role allocation
Experts	Management, organization unit managers
Designers	Business analysts, business experts
Recipients	Business architects, organization unit managers, business process analysts
Aim	To define each of the functions of the different posts in the enterprise
Useful preliminary information	Knowledge of the enterprise, organization charts

-  External role

-  Internal role

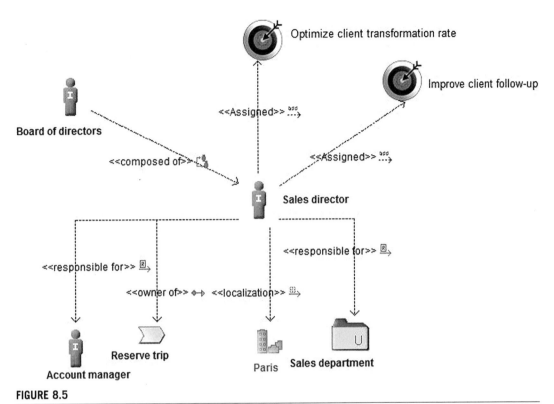

FIGURE 8.5

Organization role diagram focusing on the "Sales director" actor. (For color version of this figure, the reader is referred to the online version of this chapter.)

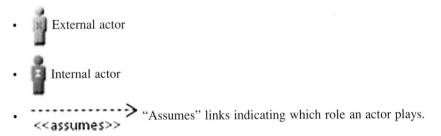

- External actor

- Internal actor

- "Assumes" links indicating which role an actor plays.

Figure 8.3 shows which roles are played by which actors. As we can see, the account manager clarifies client expectations, sells products, and makes sales reports.

An actor plays a role in order to carry out a task in a business process. This is one of the usual or expected functions of an actor, or the part that someone or something plays in a particular situation.

Here, the "assumes" link shows which roles are played by which actors.

For example, a smaller enterprise can have the same roles as a larger enterprise in the same business, but these roles will be distributed across a smaller number of actors.

Information on which roles an actor can assume can be produced in detailed diagrams on actors (Figure 8.3) by adding "assumes" links. It can also be summarized in matrices.

8.3.6 The "location organization diagram" artifact

Name	Location organization diagram
Experts	Executive managers, organization unit managers
Designers	Business analysts, business experts
Recipients	Executive managers, analysts, organization unit managers
Aim	To define the geographical distribution of the enterprise organization
Useful preliminary information	Enterprise organization

- Locations: enterprise sites

- Internal actor

- Locations: enterprise headquarters

- Deployed instance of an organization unit

- 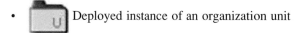 Links determining the location of actors and roles, where this is not implicit.

TOGAF defines the location organization diagram as being the description of the links that exist between actors, roles, and locations within an organizational structure. Organizational mapping procures the executive manager and decision-maker chain of command within the organization. Although this type of diagram does not focus on goal modeling, it can also link goals to associated participants.

The example in Figure 8.6 represents locations and actors. The headquarters are in Paris, and there are three branches in Nantes, Toulouse, and Lyon. In this image, organization units are shown in specific locations to illustrate their deployment; the IT department is thus situated in Toulouse. These are not organization units themselves, but rather instances that appear in deployment locations. In this way, several occurrences of the same kind of organization unit can appear in different locations. Thus, the sales department is present in Toulouse, Paris, Nantes, and Lyon. We can see therefore that the majority of services are concentrated in Paris. The sales department is divided between each of the branches.

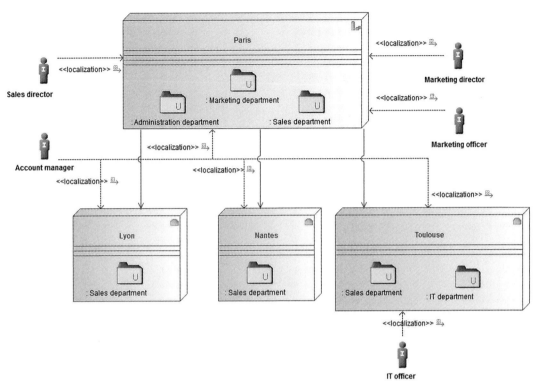

FIGURE 8.6

Representation of actors, locations, and organization units in a location organization diagram. (For color version of this figure, the reader is referred to the online version of this chapter.)

The same technique can be used to localize roles. As in Figure 8.6, we can also use the "location" dependency to represent this. However, the geographical location of roles is often implicit through their responsibility links (role to role or role to organization unit).

8.3.7 The "location diagram" artifact

Name	Location diagram
Experts	Executive managers, organization unit managers
Designers	Business analysts, business experts
Recipients	Business analysts, business process analysts
Aim	To list the company's sites and headquarters
Useful preliminary information	Organization of the enterprise

- Location: enterprise headquarters

- Location: enterprise site

The location diagram can be used as an alternative to the TOGAF location catalog. Once established, location diagrams then enable us to represent the location of organization units and roles (phase B), and then in phase D to represent the geographical deployment of hardware and applications. Locations are used to take into account geographical constraints during the definition of enterprise architecture. Figure 8.7 shows that the headquarters of the company are in Paris, with three associated branches situated in Nantes, Toulouse, and Lyon.

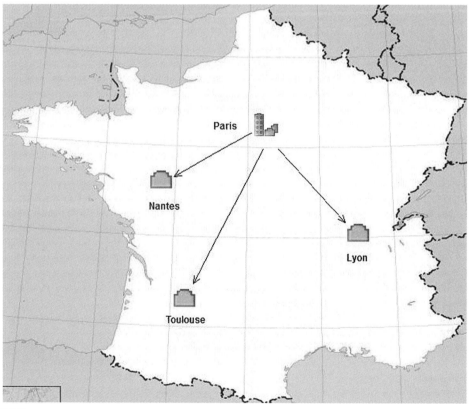

FIGURE 8.7

Location diagram. (For color version of this figure, the reader is referred to the online version of this chapter.)

8.4 ARTIFACTS LINKED TO ENTERPRISE FUNCTIONS AND SERVICES

8.4.1 The "functional decomposition diagram" artifact

Description of the artifact

Name	Functional decomposition diagram
Experts	Executive managers, organizational unit managers
Designers	Business analysts, business experts
Recipients	Business analysts, business process analysts
Aim	To determine the enterprise's essential functions. To be able to subsequently define how these functions can best be carried out
Useful preliminary information	Organization of the enterprise; goals requiring evolutions or new functions

- Function: Continually takes care of one of the enterprise's missions.

The elements present in this diagram are *functions*, which can be hierarchically embedded.

In Figure 8.8, functions are organized into layers. Enterprise management, which orients strategy, is found on the top level. Next come operational functions essentially linked to marketing and sales, and finally we have support functions, such as administration and IT.

Functional decomposition is represented here through the graphical embedding of functions. The "Marketing management" function is thus broken down into the "Offer management" function (and other functions), which itself is broken down into the "Portfolio definition" function (and other functions).

Business function

A business function takes care of carrying out one of the enterprise's capacities. The enterprise is described through all its capacities and the services that deliver them. A business function is carried out continuously in order to guarantee one of the enterprise's missions. Unlike a business process, a business function has no specific temporal nature—no identified start or finish, no precisely defined incoming or outgoing products, no trigger events, and so on.

Summarized representation of the enterprise's capacities

Functions are graphically represented through a hierarchical structure. The aim of the functional decomposition diagram is thus to represent, on a single page, all the capacities of an organization that are relevant to the definition of an enterprise architecture. The functional decomposition diagram is not concerned with the "how" (in other words, with the way in which the enterprise carries out its functions). It thus provides a useful abstraction, focusing on what the enterprise must do and not on how it does it.

The construction of a functional decomposition diagram requires knowledge of the enterprise and its missions. Business functions can be demarcated by the business services participating in the function, as well as with the business processes.

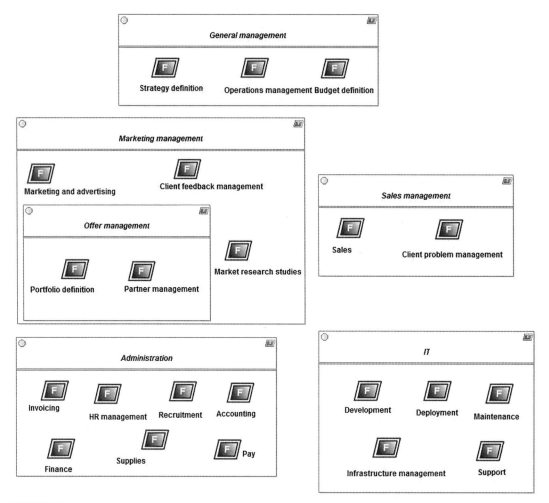

FIGURE 8.8

Essential functions of the Discount Travel company. (For color version of this figure, the reader is referred to the online version of this chapter.)

Initial models indicating major directions for solutions, designed to help enterprise capacities evolve, can then be constructed to clarify the scope of enterprise architecture work and to orient decisions. For example, a plan for the progressive addition of new capacities can be defined.

The functional decomposition model can be enriched by adding specific links to orient future choices and decisions. For example, these links can indicate which application component supports which function, or which role participates in which function, and so on (see business footprint diagram in Figure 8.9).

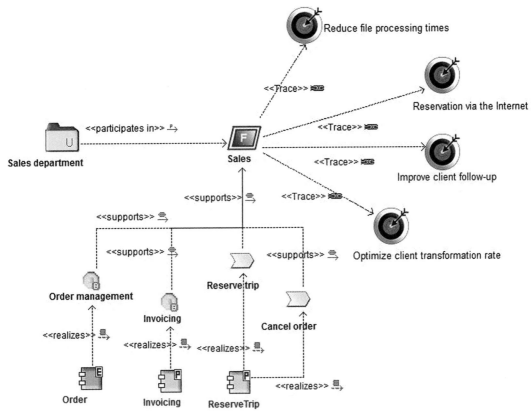

FIGURE 8.9

Business footprint diagram focused on the "Sales" function. (For color version of this figure, the reader is referred to the online version of this chapter.)

8.4.2 The "Goal/Objective/Service diagram" artifact
Description of the artifact

Name	Goal/Objective/Service diagram
Experts	Business experts
Designers	Business analysts
Recipients	Business analysts, application architects
Aim	To present the services that contribute to the realization of goals
Useful preliminary information	Functional decomposition of the enterprise, identified services, goals

- Business service

- Goal

-  Allocation of a goal to a business service.

The aim of Goal/Objective/Service diagrams is to define the way in which a business service contributes to achieving a business vision or one of the enterprise's strategies.

Services are associated with strategic or operational goals, as well as with associated measures, in order to enable enterprises to understand which services contribute to which aspects of business performance. The Goal/Objective/Service diagram also provides a strong indication of performance indicators for a given service.

"Assigned" links between services and goals are used to associate them. In the example shown in Figure 8.10, the "Order management" service is thus associated with the "Reduce file processing times," "Reservation via the Internet," and "Optimize client transformation rate" goals.

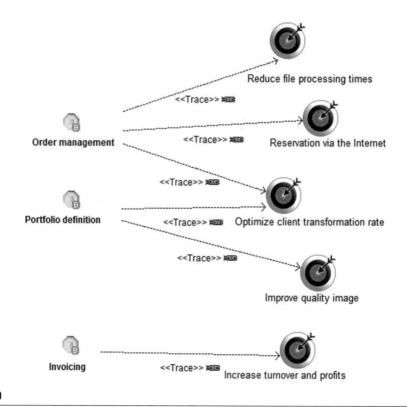

FIGURE 8.10

Goal/Objective/Service diagram. (For color version of this figure, the reader is referred to the online version of this chapter.)

Business service

A business service is a service that the enterprise or one of its business units provides to its internal or external clients. Business services are linked to business functions, with clearly defined boundaries and explicit governance. For example, a "pay" function, which describes the ability of an enterprise to manage and pay its employees' salaries, can be associated with more precise services, such as calculate pay, calculate bonuses, transfer salaries, or modify salary. Business services have a service interface and a service contract interface that determines their usage conditions. A business service will be associated with the incoming and outgoing business entities that it handles.

A business service can be carried out through manual or automated operations. It can also be sub-contracted outside the enterprise.

8.5 ARTIFACTS LINKED TO BUSINESS PROCESSES

8.5.1 Key business processes of the enterprise

Business architecture endeavors to identify the key business processes linked to the ADM cycle. It goes back to the process mapping initiated in phase A in order to complete it, notably by qualifying processes (see Section 12.2.2).

Based on business process maps, business managers and analysts can define priorities related to the processes that are to be revamped or optimized. They identify critical zones, consider processes impacted by new enterprise goals, and launch more detailed studies of certain processes, which involve additional business process analysis and modeling tasks.

Phase B updates and produces event diagrams (presented in Chapter 7 in phase A), which present an overview of processes by mapping them and by identifying contextual information (trigger events, participants, incoming and outgoing products) that will be used in process flow diagrams.

8.5.2 The "process flow diagram" artifact

Description of the artifact

Name	Process flow diagram
Experts	Business experts, functional managers
Designers	Business process analysts
Recipients	Analysts, application architects, business managers, business experts
Aim	To detail how business processes work (evolution, optimization, automation, etc.)
Useful preliminary information	Actors, event diagrams, products, and business entities

BPMN notation is very rich and only essential elements are presented here.

- Pool and lane: Determine who carries out the tasks they contain. Pools are autonomous and are not constrained by ordering sequence (such as here, the client and the organization).

- ☐ Activities carried out within a process. BPMN defines two types of activity: the task and the subprocess. A task is an atomic activity, while a subprocess is an activity that can be further broken down.

- ▤ Data object: Describes the data exchanged between different activities.

- ⬤ Event: Describes the occurrence of an event (for example, the arrival of a message or signal) sent or received by the process.

- ◆ Gate: Control structure used to define choices or synchronizations within the process. Where a cross appears in the diamond (as in Figure 8.11), this is a "parallel gateway" indicating that parallel branches are executed and synchronized.

- ✉ Messages and message flows: Elements sent and received between different *pools*.

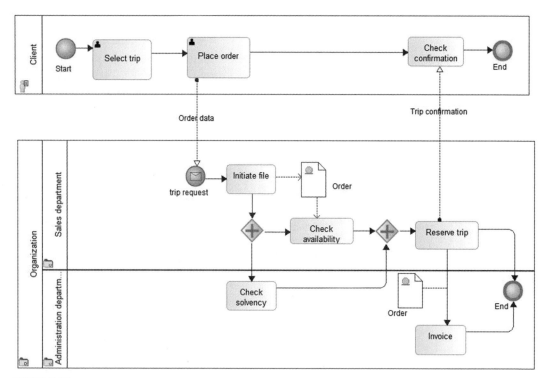

FIGURE 8.11

Model of the "Reserve Trip" BPMN process. (For color version of this figure, the reader is referred to the online version of this chapter.)

The example shown in Figure 8.11 presents two level-one BPMN pools representing client actions and actions carried out within the Discount Travel company (the organization). For each of these autonomous areas of responsibility, which should be considered as independent processes, different activities are represented ("Select trip," "Initiate file," etc.) and linked through sequencing links. The "Order" element, called "data object" in BPMN, represents a piece of TOGAF information handled by the process. Here, these are occurrences of business entities within a process.

In this example, the process we are interested in is the one described by the "Organization" pool (we do not control the ordering of client actions). The "lanes" ("Administration department," "Sales department") indicate who or what is responsible for different activities, even if the activities are automated by the information system.

Modeling the behavior of business processes

Process diagrams, called "flow diagrams" by TOGAF, are used to model the sequence of activities within a process. Process modeling formalizes practices and describes the manner in which they should take place.

Flow diagrams represent process participants, activity sequences, information exchanged during a process, and trigger events. Processes can also detail the different checks, choices, and coordinations that exist within a sequence of activities.

Processes can be modeled to different degrees of detail according to the goal of the model in question. In the example shown in Figure 8.11, the model is extremely general. Chapter 12 goes into more detail on the techniques used to model business processes.

8.5.3 The "business use case diagram" artifact
Business use cases and application use cases

TOGAF distinguishes business use cases (phase B) and system use cases (phase C). *Business use cases* present the relationships between the producers and consumers of business services. They provide additional depth when describing the enterprise's capabilities by illustrating how and when they are implemented. They help clarify actors and roles with regard to processes and functions. They can be reused to define system use cases. *System use cases* describe the relationships between the consumers and providers of application services. Application services are consumed by actors or application components. System use cases help describe and clarify the requirements for the interactions between actors and their roles with applications.

Description of the artifact

Name	Business use case diagram
Experts	Business process experts, functional managers
Designers	Business analysts, business process analysts
Recipients	Analysts, business process experts, application architects
Aim	To describe the different use cases of the main actors, with regard to the enterprise's services
Useful preliminary information	Actors, business processes, functions

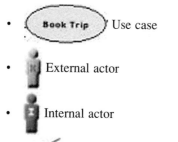 Use case

- External actor

- Internal actor

- Communication link between an actor and a use case.

In the example shown in Figure 8.12, the use cases focus on three actors: the "Account manager," the "Invoicing officer," and the "Client." Communication links link the actors to the use cases and detail who participates in which use cases.

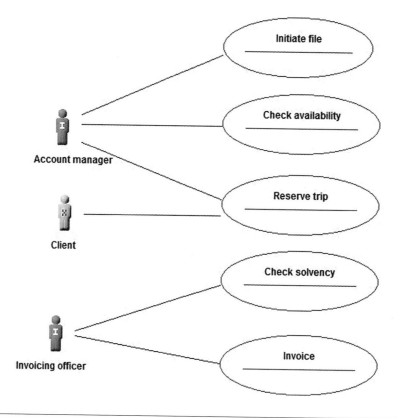

FIGURE 8.12

Use cases resulting from the "Reserve Trip" process. (For color version of this figure, the reader is referred to the online version of this chapter.)

Implementing business use case diagrams

A business use case diagram will detail the actions carried out by an actor or a role to complete a particular task. It will enable the interactions between the enterprise's actors or with the enterprise's business services to be described and validated.

Business use case diagrams are used in conjunction with business processes. For example, Figure 8.12 presents the use cases linked to the activities of the business process presented in Figure 8.11. The use cases focus on the main actors (for example, the "Account manager") and their essential activities ("Initiate file," "Reserve Trip," etc.).

A use case represents a requirement for an interaction between actors and the rest of the enterprise (IS, business services), in the aim of meeting a fundamental need. Each of these use cases can then be detailed to describe the typical sequence of tasks that the main actor must carry out in order to accomplish the use case (scenario). This level of detail is rarely used during phase B.

The use case can be completed in order to provide information on application conditions and exceptional cases.

In practice, use cases will be used to provide more details on parts of process models or to summarize the essential attributions of certain actors or roles.

8.5.4 The "service/information diagram" artifact

Name	Service/Information diagram
Experts	Business experts, business analysts
Designers	Business analysts
Recipients	Application architects
Aim	To describe the information necessary to business services. To prepare the data architecture and application architecture
Useful preliminary information	Business entities, business services, functions, and business processes

The Service/Information diagram presents the information used to support one or several business services. This type of diagram defines which type of data is consumed or produced by a business service. It can also present the source of the information. It provides an initial representation of the information used within an architecture. In this way, it will provide a basis for detailing data architecture during phase C.

"Data flow" type links (flows) between business services and business entities represent which type of entity is used as input or produced as output by services.

- Business entity

- Business service

- - - - - - - - - - -> Data flow between data (business entity, event, product) and active elements of the
  <<flow>> system (business process, service).

8.5.5 The "business footprint diagram" artifact

Name	Business footprint diagram
Experts	Functional experts and business process experts, application architects
Designers	Business analysts
Recipients	General management, analysts, and application architects
Aim	To provide an overview that traces essential elements to be built or revised from goals through to components
Useful preliminary information	Goals, organization, business functions, processes, business services, initial application architecture elements

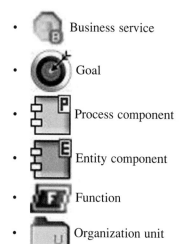

-    Business service

-    Goal

-    Process component

-    Entity component

-    Function

-    Organization unit

-    Business process

- «supports» Determines that a function, service, or process is supported by finer-grain business elements.

- «participates in» Determines that a participant participates in an enterprise activity or part of an enterprise activity.

- «trace» General traceability link: The origin of the traceability link has its foundation in the destination of the link.

- «realizes Realization by a component: Realizes an element identified at business level.

A business footprint diagram describes the links between business goals, organization units, business functions, and business services. These functions and services are also traced with technical components producing the required capabilities. By following these links, the business footprint diagram enables us to obtain traceability between a technical component and the business goals that it satisfies, while also revealing the owners and managers of the identified services.

A business footprint diagram is only interested in essential elements that show the connection between organization units and functions to produce services. It is used to communicate with the management of the enterprise.

Business footprint diagrams focus on the current concerns of the business. Depending on these concerns, they can concentrate on one or several application components requiring further development, as well as on one or several business functions. Thus, we select the goals that we judge to be the most important to the subject, and create or reuse application components, business functions, and business services that we trace to these goals. The diagram then defines what has to be worked on, enabling all participants to understand that a more detailed analysis for each architectural domain will develop these previously identified elements.

This type of diagram positions identified elements with regard to goals and traces them to each other using specialized dependencies.

8.6 ARTIFACTS LINKED TO DATA

8.6.1 The "conceptual data diagram" artifact

TOGAF considers data architecture to be a subphase of phase C. However, data architecture also contributes to phase B, notably where business entities are handled (Figure 8.13).

Three different views are presented here, showing specific levels of detail. At the highest level, we find the information domain diagram (Figure 8.14), which presents the structuring of entities into different domains. Next, Figure 8.15 presents the main business entities that appear in "undeveloped" form, in other words, without showing details on their attributes and properties. Finally, Figure 8.16 presents the most detailed view of entities, where these are developed and their attributes defined.

Description of the artifact

Name	Conceptual data diagram
Experts	Business experts
Designers	Business analysts
Recipients	Business analysts, data architects, application architects
Aim	To identify and formalize business objects
Useful preliminary information	Existing data, dictionary, business process messages

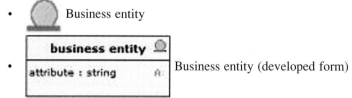

- Business entity

- Business entity (developed form)

- Association between classes

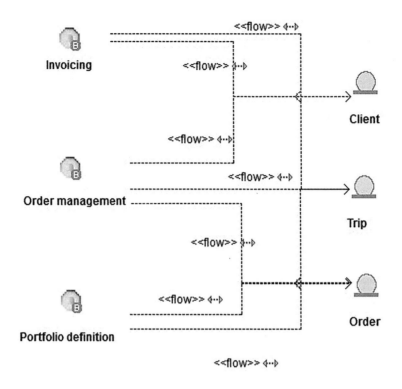

FIGURE 8.13

Business entities used by business services. (For color version of this figure, the reader is referred to the online version of this chapter.)

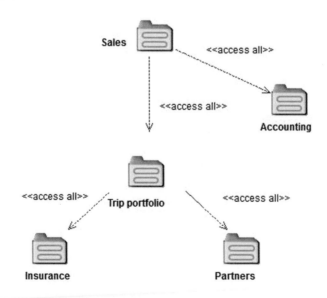

FIGURE 8.14

Discount Travel's business information domains. (For color version of this figure, the reader is referred to the online version of this chapter.)

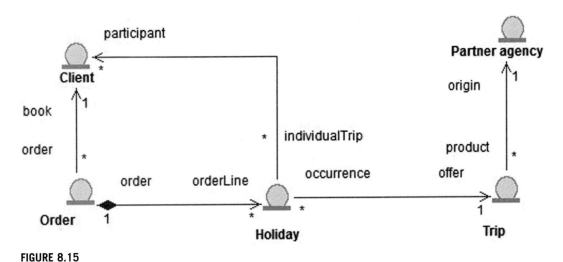

FIGURE 8.15

Main business entities and associations of the Discount Travel domain. (For color version of this figure, the reader is referred to the online version of this chapter.)

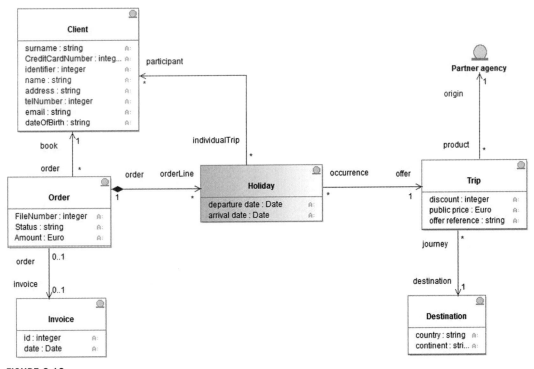

FIGURE 8.16

A more detailed view of certain key concepts. (For color version of this figure, the reader is referred to the online version of this chapter.)

The model shown in Figure 8.15 shows the key concepts of client and trip. The separation between "Holiday" and "Trip" is clearly presented. A trip is defined at product range level. It includes its destination and the hotel providing the accommodation, and indicates who the partner agency is. A holiday is an instance of a trip for a set of participants. It includes information on the date, as well as information specific to the trip in question (room reserved, flight, insurance, etc.). This additional information is presented in more detail in Figure 8.16.

Modeling business concepts

Conceptual data diagrams represent essential business concepts together with their properties, and show their associations. Within business architecture, conceptual data diagrams represent entities at the conceptual level, without taking into account any technological location and realization issues. At this stage, we are not interested in whether or not entities are persistent, whether they are transferred via messages between services, or in any other application questions. The focus here is to define all the essential concepts that will enable the business to be described in the most general way possible in the enterprise's application domain.

This business formalization work can be undertaken very early in the enterprise architecture cycle. As for all other models, the presence of a dictionary that establishes terminology will greatly facilitate this modeling: it helps make sure that relevant names are used and enables us to check the completeness of the concepts and properties used.

Defining this high-level conceptual model lets us define the essential concepts of the business without being distracted by organizational or historic considerations specific to the enterprise. This allows us to leave the business and to think about the best possible organization of the enterprise and the IS for the realization of the enterprise's functions on its business according to the goals assigned.

For example, the Praxeme enterprise method[1] encourages significant development of conceptual models through its concept of semantic models.

Further details brought to the model

The business data model will be used as a tool to identify and describe key entities. We see that Figure 8.16 develops certain classes in order to show the attached attributes.

The model can add useful semantic constraints and details as a complement to the class diagram. For example, we can see that the client has a "CreditCardNumber" property, which poses a set of questions. Is a client obliged to have a credit card? Does a client only ever have one credit card? Is the last credit card used the only one to be memorized? Would it not be more relevant to associate the credit card number with the order? Should we not rather create an entity linked to the means of payment, which details the different options available? Should we not retain a transaction number rather than a credit card number?

It quickly becomes apparent after this kind of critical review that knowledge of payment modes is not sufficient. This exercise shows that many business questions arise, necessitating detailed expertise.

However, as far as phase B is concerned, this level of detail is rarely used. Models that have identified the main concepts can be summarized as shown in Figures 8.15 or 8.16.

---

[1]Praxeme—public enterprise method, www.praxeme.org.

Using conceptual data diagrams

A pertinent conceptual data model is a legacy of knowledge upon which many enterprise architecture models can be based:

- Data models obviously derive from the conceptual data diagram.
- Service data diagrams will be based on this model.
- "Entity" application components[2] will be derived from the most important key business entities of this model, as well as their access interfaces.
- Business processes can share the definition of their information flows or products exchanged with the business entities defined in conceptual data diagrams.

The use of a modeling tool based on a central repository provides great consistency to all diagrams, some of whose model elements are shared and others derived (Figure 8.17).

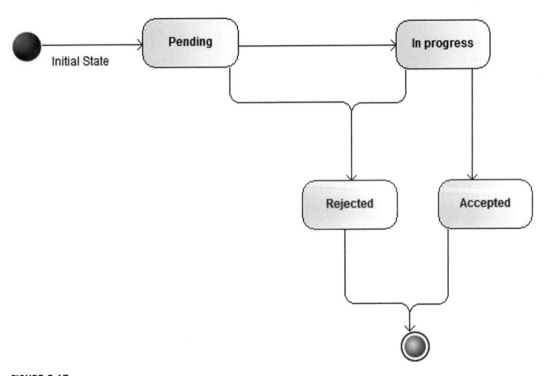

FIGURE 8.17

Lifecycle diagram for the "Order" business entity.

[2]See Chapter 9.

Structure in business information domains

Very often, the number of entities requires that they be structured into business information domains. A general view of domains is then presented, where each domain can present the local model of the entities that belong to it.

- Information domain

- ‑‑➤ Dependency link between information domains, summarizing the dependencies between the business entities of the different domains.

8.6.2 The "product lifecycle diagram" artifact

Name	Product lifecycle diagram
Experts	Business experts
Designers	Business analysts
Recipients	Business analysts, business process analysts
Aim	To define the possible states and essential transitions of business entities
Useful preliminary information	Class diagram, business entities

The product lifecycle diagram defines the main states of a given entity, and the possible transitions between these states. In this way, it presents the possible changes in state for an entity. This entity is considered as being an autonomous element that reacts to the operations and processing that can be applied to it, independently of the definition of the business processes and applications that can use it.

Each change in state is represented in the diagram. These can include events, conditions, or rules that provoke transitions between states. Product lifecycle diagrams then constrain the business process involving these entities, forcing them to respect defined transitions.

Several processes can act on identical entities: the definition of rules at entity level enables them to be shared at a higher level.

To identify states, we must imagine the different "stable" situations in which an entity can find itself, in other words, the situations where the entity does not undergo any transformation or processing. For example, a document can be in the following states: "created," "under review," "approved," and so on. Next, the possible transitions between these states must be defined. For example, it is not possible to pass directly from the "created" state to the "approved" state, and the logical transition goes from "created" to "under review." When an entity is not undergoing any processing, it is in a defined state.

Defining the business entity lifecycle ensures better formalization of entities and provides an indication of the stages that are essential to their management. This state model can be linked to the process model. Thus, the BPMN diagram can show that an entity is in a specific state at certain stages of the process.

- State

- ⊢➤⦗ Transition: Describes the change in state from an original state to a destination state, following an operation being carried out on the entity, a particular condition being met, or an event occurring.

8.7 FUNDAMENTAL CONCEPTS

The following fundamental concepts were introduced in this chapter:

- Business architecture: Defines the business strategy, governance, organization, and key business processes.
- Business function: Produces one of the enterprise's capabilities. For example, "marketing," "client contract management," and "telemarketing" are functions.
- Business entity: Describes the semantics of business entities, independently of any organizational or IS-related considerations.
- Business dictionary: Specifies the business terminology in order to obtain a reference for the enterprise.
- Actor: Active enterprise participant (a person, system, or organization) who takes part in the activities of the enterprise.
- Role: One of an actor's usual or expected functions.

Models for Phase C: Information System Architecture

9

Business architecture has defined the way in which the enterprise must be organized and must function. It has initiated data architecture at a conceptual level. It defines requirements on the information system and a context enabling expected IS evolutions to be determined. Application architecture identifies IS components and their interactions in order to meet business architecture expectations, while guaranteeing overall consistency and respecting the rules of an architectural framework. The application component is the key concept for application architecture. Here, we put particular emphasis on an SOA-oriented architecture where application components cooperate through "services," but we also have to cope with the legacy system, which is often simply expressed in terms of applications and flows.

9.1 PHASE C ARTIFACTS

9.1.1 Nature of phase C artifacts: Information system architecture

As presented in Section 2.2.3, information system architecture takes into account the existing IS, which often has to be mapped in order to be properly understood in detail, and then determines the changes that must be made to evolve to a target IS, according to a defined path. At each identified step of the path, we have to establish how the IS will be used in the enterprise and how migration from the previous step to the current step will be achieved.

The aim here is not to design software applications, but rather to provide a logical view of them. Logical capability groups must be identified, groups that manage system data, support business functions and business processes, and interact with other logical groups and with users. At this stage, no reference is made to particular realization technologies. This subject is discussed during phase D (technological architecture), before being dealt with in detail during software design, which happens downstream (project progress).

We recommend an SOA-type (service-oriented architecture) approach when defining application architectures. As far as architecture is concerned, TOGAF is independent, although it does mention the SOA approach and takes inspiration from it in its application component concepts. We encourage this approach and most often consider TOGAF application components as service components in an SOA architecture. Of course, existing architecture is not often SOA-oriented, and taking this existing architecture into account imposes hybrid architecture, which mixes the traditional concepts of application and repository with the concept of service components.

The central artifact of phase C is the application communication diagram, which presents the architecture and positioning of application components from which components and applications are identified and their interfaces and interconnections defined (Figure 9.3).

Although matrices can frequently be deduced from models and diagrams (Table 9.1), they are useful since they often present a complete portfolio list while diagrams show partial views. Matrices are useful for establishing and reasoning about relationships.

SOA architecture: Typology of application components

Literature dedicated to SOA architectures recommends that a component typology be defined, and that components be structured into levels.[a] For this reason, we use the typology detailed in the "Architecture Logique: Principes, structures et bonnes pratiques" white paper,[b] and distinguish four types of

---

[a]For example, Enterprise SOA, Dirk Krafzig, Karl Banke, Dirk Slama, The Coad Series, 2005, Peter Herzum & Oliver Sims.
[b]SOA: Architecture Logique: Principes, structure et bonnes pratiques, Gilbert Raymond, Softeam 2007, 2011, www.softeam.fr.

Table 9.1 Phase C Artifacts

TOGAF Artifacts	Models Presented	Comments
Application portfolio catalog		Artifact useful to application mapping; can be deduced from application communication diagrams
Interface catalog		Can be deduced from application communication diagrams
Application/organization matrix		Can be deduced from use links established between organization units and application components
Role/application matrix		Can be deduced from use links established between roles and application components
Application/function matrix		Can be deduced from realization links between functions and application components
Application interaction matrix		Can be produced from application communication diagrams
Application communication diagram	Application communication diagram	
Application and user location diagram	Application and user location diagram	
Application use case diagram	System use case diagram	
Enterprise manageability diagram	Enterprise manageability diagram	
Process/application realization diagram	Process system realization diagram	
Software engineering diagram		Provided by the UML standard, sometimes with extensions (profiles) dedicated to the technical target
Application migration diagram	Application migration diagram	
Software distribution diagram		See "Networked computing diagram" in phase D, which covers this requirement
	Service data diagram	Clarifies messages exchanged in an SOA architecture; an extension of TOGAF
Logical data diagram	Logical data diagram	It is important to distinguish between the persistent data required to implement applications and services, and the service data exchanged between them. Service data diagrams and logical data diagrams serve very different purposes, and each has to be modeled

components, interaction, process, function, and entity, organized into four logical levels of increasing stability (as shown in Figure 9.1). To these, we add the utility and public components, which handle cross-organizational functions and exchange with external systems.

Logical levels of increasing stability establish the basic rule of dependency: a component cannot use a higher level component (for example, an entity component cannot use a function component or a process component).

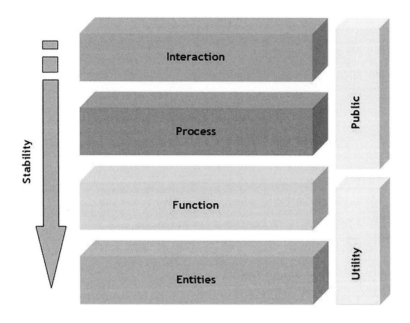

FIGURE 9.1

Different layers in an SOA architecture. (For the color version of this figure, the reader is referred to the online version of this chapter.)

Each type of component plays a specific role:

- *Interaction* components manage the dialog between the system and external actors. In particular, they take care of managing graphical user interfaces and maintaining the user's session context.
- *Process* components handle the automation of business processes: task sequencing, connections to services, event management. We are in the field of BPM here, with its dedicated techniques and tools (BPMS), adapted description languages (BPMN), or process supervision (BAM) (see Sections 12.2.5 and 12.2).
- *Function* components play an intermediary role between process components and entity components by handling certain business processing, validation, or message adaptation.
- *Entity* components focus on a key business entity of the system (for example, client, contract, or order). Their role is to allow access to information related to this entity, most often associated with a database. Typically, we find, read, write, and query operations. Entity components can also take on problems concerning the distribution and duplication of the associated repositories.
- *Utility* components provide cross-organizational services, which are relatively independent of the enterprise's business, such as directories, messaging, or electronic publishing. These components, which are generally stable, are often implemented by widely used, low-risk software packages.
- *Public* components are dedicated to services that can be accessed from outside the IS (B2B, partner relationships).

Architecture components are always layered as in Figure 9.1, which corresponds to a typical dependency graph, as in Figure 9.2.

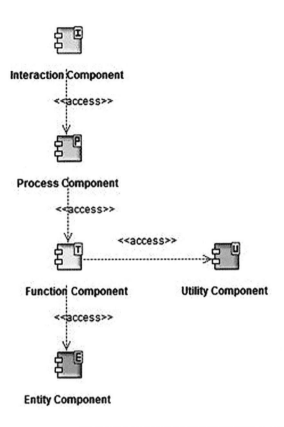

FIGURE 9.2

Typical dependency graph between different kinds of components. (For the color version of this figure, the reader is referred to the online version of this chapter.)

Essential concepts used in models

- Entity service component

- Interaction component: In the example above, the interaction component is the web interface

- Process service component

- Utility component

- Database component: Represents a database or repository.

- Application component: Represents one of the existing or target system's applications.

- System: An organized set of application components with autonomous functioning.

This often represents the enterprise's IS. A very large IS can be broken down into several (sub) systems.

- System federation: Highest application level, containing all other application components.

It assembles systems in order to federate them, as in the case of cooperation between different information systems in different enterprises.

- Provided service: Access point to service components, via services defined at this point.

- Required service: Services required by a service component. Must be connected to provided services (other components) that have the same interface.

- Persistent entity: Entities are considered at a logical level during phase C. They are represented as persistent entities, used by applications.

- Message: Flow of information exchanged between applications (the IS's services in an SOA architecture) (sometimes called *data object* or *business data type* in certain approaches).

9.2 THE "APPLICATION COMMUNICATION DIAGRAM" ARTIFACT
9.2.1 Description of the artifact

Name	Application communication diagram
Experts	Application architects, technical architects
Designers	Application architects
Recipients	Analysts, technical architects, CIOs
Aim	To present interconnections and communications between applications and the system's application components
Useful preliminary information	Business processes, requirements, existing application architecture, class diagrams, business use cases

- Provided or required service

- External actor

- Internal actor

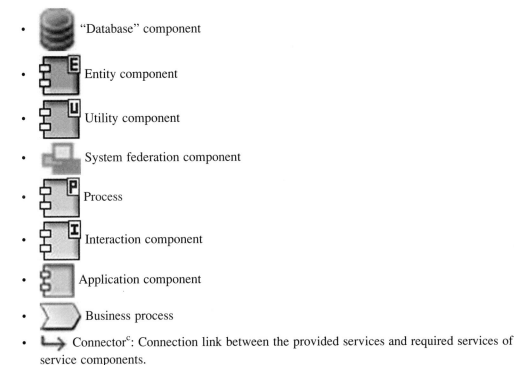

- "Database" component
- Entity component
- Utility component
- System federation component
- Process
- Interaction component
- Application component
- Business process
- Connector[c]: Connection link between the provided services and required services of service components.
- <<flow>> Sent or received flow between data (business entity, event, product) and an active element of the IS (business process, service).
- «consumes» Link between a participant (for example, an actor) and an element of the studied system. Expresses that the participant consumes the IS element.

In Figure 9.3, we can see a hybrid architecture, which presents both applications and service components. This model focuses on the trip reservation site, which is based on a central process component, "ReserveTrip." Three entity components provide fundamental site data: "Client," "Trip," and "Order." Certain components simply constitute a front used to handle communication with existing applications. The "Trip" entity component must access the preexisting repository, while the "Invoicing" process component interacts with the existing accounting ERP. These components can prepare a migration strategy, for example, the constitution of a unified repository, the development of a service component dedicated to invoicing, or migration to a new accounting ERP.

Here, the "Partners" component represents a system federation. The federated systems are external partner systems. The "CreditCard" component is a utility component provided by the credit card providers.

Service components, which have SOA architecture, are linked by connectors between the required services of certain components and the provided services of others. When the connection is made with

---

[c]This is an extension of UML, which restricts the use of connectors only between "parts" assembled within components.

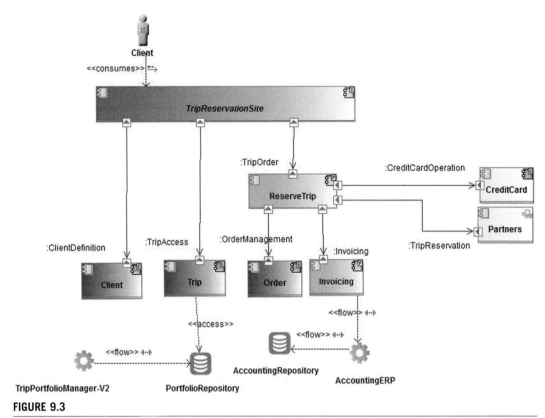

FIGURE 9.3

The architecture is structured in layers, with "interaction" components at the top and "entity" components at the bottom. (For the color version of this figure, the reader is referred to the online version of this chapter.)

applications, this connection (which is less structured than the SOA approach) is represented by data flows (flow links; for example, between "Invoicing" and "Accounting ERP").

9.2.2 Modeling application architecture

The aim of application communication diagrams is to present the interconnections and communications that exist between the applications and application components of the system. The TOGAF concept of the *application component* is at the heart of these models. These components will frequently have services that enable exchanges between components. These information services can be a realization of business services. They will exchange messages that contain data from business entities. Here, we can see that business architecture elements are used heavily when constituting application architecture.

The elements presented in application communication diagrams are defined at a logical level. The aim is not to define software components nor to determine the means of software or physical communication used (for example, web service, http, LAN). These models therefore focus on the functional level, concentrating on the identification of components that will play a specific role in the IS and on communication requirements between components. In practice, and particularly where existing architecture must be taken into account, there can be a mix of pure logical components and existing applications or off-the-shelf applications, such as ERPs. The logical level is particularly important for the parts of the architecture that are to be reformed or for new extensions.

TOGAF recommends the use of an SOA-oriented architecture where possible. We advocate the construction of an SOA-oriented architecture whenever the model is developed at the logical level, notably by defining application components as service components in an SOA architecture.

We have seen that we have a service component typology enabling service components to be structured into layers, three key layers being "interaction," "process," and "entity."

Application architecture will often be hybrid, through the introduction of existing or off-the-shelf applications, or the localization of repositories. For this, certain application components will be of an "application[d]" or "database" nature.

Service components will be interconnected via the services they require and provide. "Connectors" are links connecting these services. In general, services are modeled in more detail in specific diagrams. Similarly, messages, which are types of information exchanged by services, have to be modeled in detailed elsewhere (see Figure 9.14). The services, service operations, inputs and outputs, exceptions, and protocols need to be specified.

Application communication diagrams can be dedicated to describing current architecture, target architecture, or intermediate architecture. Models can thus evolve from hybrid architecture (containing many applications and few service components) into reformed, SOA-oriented architecture, which will have reorganized applications by extracting and combining new service components.

9.3 THE "APPLICATION MIGRATION DIAGRAM" ARTIFACT
9.3.1 Description of the artifact

Name	Application migration diagram
Experts	Application architects, technical architects
Designers	Application architects
Recipients	Technical architects, CIOs, users, and business directors
Aim	To build an application migration strategy by defining a path consisting of different steps
Useful preliminary information	Baseline architecture, target architecture

- 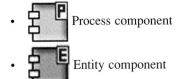 Process component

- Entity component

- Application component

---

[d]The notion of "application" has no formal definition. It is mainly a "unit of deployment" concern. However, this is how the legacy IS is identified and structured, and what IS bricks are often called.

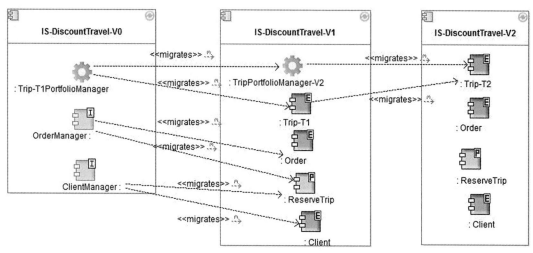

FIGURE 9.4

Migration strategy in three steps. (For the color version of this figure, the reader is referred to the online version of this chapter.)

-  System

- ╌╌╌╌╌> «migrates» Migration of elements between two versions of the IS; frequently used between application components.

Figure 9.4 shows us that the "Trip" application component will be developed over three versions. The first version will be based on the "TripPortfolioManager" application (which already exists), while the following version will run autonomously with direct access to the repository.

Each version of the IS is represented by a different "System" component ("IS-DiscountTravelV0...2"), in which instances of application components are deployed. We can see which application components are retained, and which are migrated to one or several new application components.

This can also be done using traditional lifecycle management techniques for versions and variants. That is, change over time can be handled as an orthogonal concern not built into the diagram itself. Diagrams help elicit technical details.

9.3.2 Building the migration strategy in accordance with the application evolution path

Application migration diagrams identify application migrations, from the current situation right through the application components of the target application. This migration is broken down into steps in order to describe the migrations between each intermediate situation. This type of diagram enables a more precise estimation of migration costs by presenting exactly which applications and interfaces must be mapped between each migration step.

An efficient practice consists in representing the system as a component that contains all application components. These are deployed as instances of the component they represent. Each instance can then be specifically configured in each version of the system. Thus, an instance a1 of a component A can be connected to an instance b of a component B in a version of the system, while an instance a2 of the same component A can be linked to an instance c of a component C, which is different to B, in another version of the system.

In this way, instances of identical components configured specifically for each version of the system are presented. We indicate which components are retained, which are replaced, and which are retained but isolated by other components that act as interfaces, and so on.

Migration links are defined between these instances of components.

It is important to make sure that continuity of service is guaranteed at every step. Furthermore, scenario modeling (for example, using sequence diagrams) highlights the order in which different architecture elements are used. This often varies according to the different steps.

9.4 THE "APPLICATION AND USER LOCATION DIAGRAM" ARTIFACT
9.4.1 Description of the artifact

Name	Application and user location diagram
Experts	Business experts, application architects
Designers	Business analysts
Recipients	Application architects, business managers, operational managers and engineers, system and network engineers
Aim	To define the geographical deployment of applications. To define who uses which applications where
Useful preliminary information	Application architecture, location definition, actors

- Headquarters (location)

- Site (location)

- External actor

- Internal actor

- Application component

- Interaction component

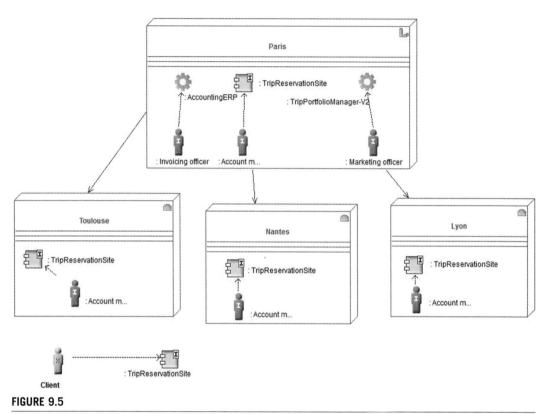

FIGURE 9.5

Model showing who uses which application on which site. (For the color version of this figure, the reader is referred to the online version of this chapter.)

Like actors and roles, application components are deployed in locations in the form of instances.

In the example in Figure 9.5, the account application is located in Paris, and used locally by an invoicing officer. The location of the "Client" is not defined, since his Internet access provides him or her with generalized access. The actor him- or herself is used, rather than a deployed instance.

9.4.2 Study of the geographical distribution of users and applications

Application and user location diagrams present the geographical distribution of applications. They can be used to show where applications are used, and by which types of users. They can indicate where applications are implemented, tested, and deployed. Analysis can reveal opportunities for rationalization, as well as duplications or omissions. The aim of application and user location diagrams is to clearly present the business locations where users and applications interact, as well as application infrastructure locations.

This type of diagram is used to:

- Identify the amount of hardware and software necessary to support the population of geographically distributed users.
- Estimate the number of user licenses necessary for software purchased off-the-shelf.
- Evaluate user support needs and define the locations of support centers.
- Select the necessary system administration tools to support users, partners, and clients, both locally and remotely.
- Define schedules for setting up technological components for the business: server sizing, network bandwidth, storage and saving capacities, and so on.
- Obtain initial indications of performance when applications and technological architectural solutions are implemented.

Users interact with the IS in different ways. For example:

- To support daily business operations
- To participate in the running of a business process
- To access information (consultation, update)
- To develop applications
- To administrate and maintain the application

Application and user location diagrams typically show where servers are located and where applications are run. This deployment model is developed by creating instances of application components inside instances of IT hardware, which are themselves inside geographical locations. In cloud computing systems, this type of diagram is very useful for identifying and positioning the services and applications deployed in the cloud.

9.5 THE "SYSTEM USE CASE DIAGRAM" ARTIFACT
9.5.1 Description of the artifact

Name	System use case diagram
Experts	Business analysts, application architects
Designers	Application architects or business analysts
Recipients	Application architects, technical architects
Aim	To define the functions expected from application components and the different usage modes
Useful preliminary information	Business use cases, actors, business processes, business services

-  Use case

- External actor (TOGAF)

- Internal actor (TOGAF)

- Process component

- Entity component

- Communication link between actors (UML) and the use cases in which they are involved.

- «realizes» Component realization: Link between an application component and a use case implemented by the application component in question.

In the example shown in Figure 9.6, the "Account manager" and the "Client" can be associated with certain identical use cases. The "Account manager" can carry out these actions when instructed to do so by the "Client." The "Account manager" and the "Invoicing officer" also take part in use cases that are specific to them. The use cases presented summarize how certain application components are used. A detailed description of these use cases will then enable the definition of the services that the components must provide, and of the typical situations in which they provide them.

9.5.2 Application use cases: Principles

A UML use case model describes and formalizes the relationship between an application component to be developed and the outside world. This description is based on the external perspective (black box) without taking into consideration the internal structure of the component. The aim is to specify the boundaries of the component and the different interactions implemented during the realization of business requirements. In the context of TOGAF, the system has been broken down into application components, which themselves carry services. Information services are consumed by other application components or, for higher level components, by actors identified in the business architecture. When the application component is of "interaction" type, the outside of the system will generally be the actors or the roles these actors can play. Use case modeling will probably lead to the identification of new roles, which will be assigned to actors.

System use case diagrams provide additional depth by describing the functionalities of application components or their services, and by illustrating how and when these are implemented. The aim of system use case diagrams is to help describe and validate interactions between consumers (actors or components) and providers (application components). Use cases can be further detailed to provide information on application conditions and exceptional cases. Use case diagrams are precious tools when preparing application component validation scenarios, since they contain the description of how the component is used.

Communication links are used to link actors to use cases by showing who takes part in which use case.

We recommend that use cases be described for the most important components. On a one-page diagram, the use case diagram of a component provides a good overview of its functional scope.

"Realization" links specify which component realizes which use case.

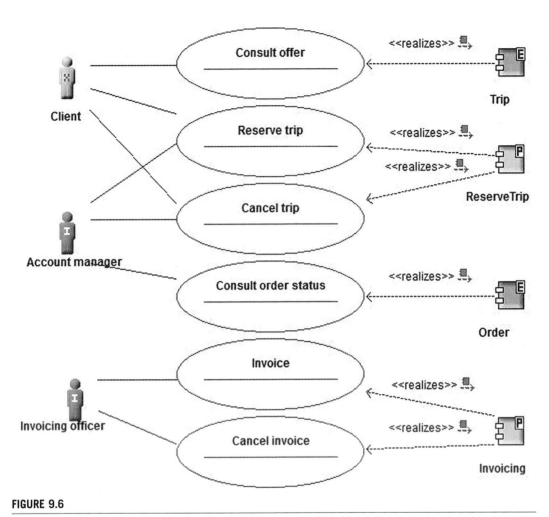

FIGURE 9.6

Example of a system use case diagram. (For the color version of this figure, the reader is referred to the online version of this chapter.)

9.6 THE "PROCESS SYSTEM REALIZATION DIAGRAM" ARTIFACT

9.6.1 Description of the artifact

Name	Process system realization diagram
Experts	Business experts, application architects
Designers	Application architects
Recipients	Business analysts, technical architects
Aim	To consolidate application communication diagrams by providing additional information on constraints illustrated by detailed process realizations
Useful preliminary information	Application architecture, business process

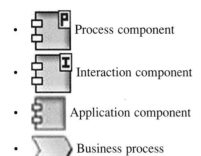

- Process component

- Interaction component

- Application component

- Business process

- - - - - - - - -> Realization by a component: An application component realizes the designated
  «realizes element (for example, a business process).

- ··········> Information flow: Defines the flow of any type of information (business entity,
  <<flow>> event, product, informal element, etc.) between active entities of the enterprise.

In particular, Figure 9.7 illustrates that the "Reserve trip" process is realized by one interaction component and one process component.

Figure 9.8 shows an alternative approach to model interaction scenarios between application components. UML interaction diagrams (frequently called "sequence diagrams") are used in this example. In this diagram, we see sequences of messages exchanged between occurrences of application components. This model shows how the business process defined in Figure 8.10 can be executed by the application components presented in the model in Figure 9.2.

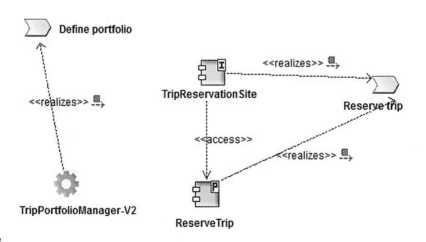

FIGURE 9.7

Two processes are realized by an application and two application components. (For the color version of this figure, the reader is referred to the online version of this chapter.)

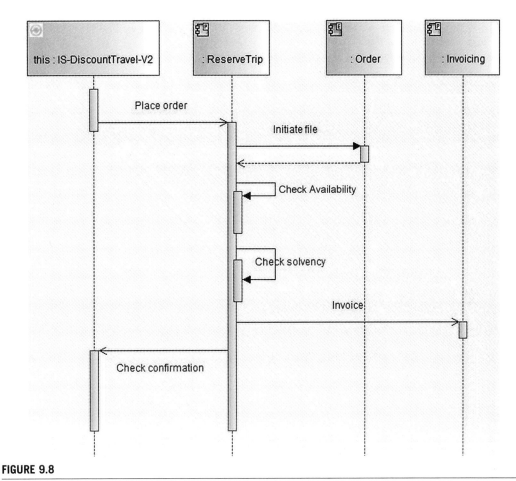

FIGURE 9.8

Modeling application component cooperation through interactions. (For the color version of this figure, the reader is referred to the online version of this chapter.)

9.6.2 Strengthening application communication diagrams: Sequences and synchronizations

The aim of the process system realization diagram is to highlight the sequence of events that take place when several components are involved in the execution of a business process. Process system realization diagrams consolidate application communication diagrams by adding sequencing constraints and synchronization points between real-time and batch processing. They are used to identify complex sequences that can be simplified, as well as possible rationalization points in the architecture. They also enable improvements in process efficiency to be identified by reducing the volume of traffic and interactions between applications.

In these models, information on roles or order can be presented using information flows (as in the example) or textual notes attached to elements. UML tools (sequence diagrams, collaboration diagrams) enable more detailed sequencing information to be provided.

9.7 THE "ENTERPRISE MANAGEABILITY DIAGRAM" ARTIFACT

Name	Enterprise manageability diagram
Experts	Business experts, application architects
Designers	Application architects
Recipients	Business experts, technical architects
Aim	To illustrate cooperation between components and applications to support the management of a solution
Useful preliminary information	Application architecture, business processes, functions

- Provided service
- Required service
- Interaction component
- Entity component
- Application component
- "Database" component
- «migrates» Migration of elements between two versions of the information system; used here between two versions of application components.
- <<flow>> Information flow: Defines flows of any kind of information (business entity, event, product, message, etc.) between the active entities of the enterprise and its IS.
- Connector: Used between provided or required services, or with instances of application components.

The enterprise manageability diagram shows how one or several applications interact with application and technical components to support the operational management of a solution. In actual fact, this schema is a filter on the application communication diagram, specially designed for software dealing with enterprise management. Analysis can reveal overlaps, omissions, and optimization possibilities with regard to the functioning of organization management IT services. It can identify temporary applications, unused applications, and the infrastructure necessary to ensure migration operations (for example, parallel execution environments). UML collaboration diagrams provide a more complete means of expressing sequencing.

The "migrates" dependency is frequently used in this type of model.

In the example shown in Figure 9.9, an enterprise manageability schema shows how a part of the system will evolve to progressively switch from a hybrid situation (where the "Trip" component (T1) uses the current "TravelPortfolioManager" application, which manages access to data) to a situation without this earlier application, where the "Trip" component (T2) uses the new central repository. The use of "migrates" links highlights which older parts of the IS will be replaced by which new parts. We must also document which business requirements are being met and which performance gaps are being closed by the migration.

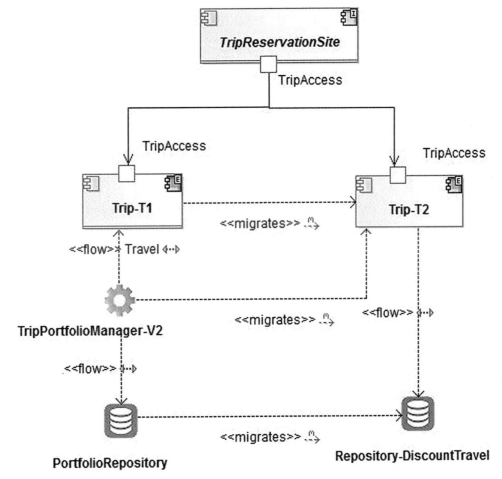

FIGURE 9.9

Enterprise manageability diagram focused on the migration steps of the "Trip" application component. (For the color version of this figure, the reader is referred to the online version of this chapter.)

9.8 DATA ARCHITECTURE

9.8.1 The "logical data diagram" artifact

Name	Logical data diagram
Experts	Application architects, data architects, technical architects
Designers	Data architects
Recipients	Technical architects, software designers
Aim	To present a logical view of the relationships between critical logical entities. To prepare the design of databases
Useful preliminary information	Application architecture, business entity diagrams, existing database schemas

- ▥ Persistent entity
- ▤ Persistent attribute
- ▣ Identifier attribute
- ↳ Association

The logical data model is based on the conceptual data diagram (see Figure 8.15), which it further defines in order to target the logical exploitation of the data by the IS. The design of this model concentrates on data that will be persistent (generally stored in relational databases), and adapts this model to later facilitate storage. The model is standardized (relational normal forms) and existing data schemas are studied in order to take into account aspects linked to the reuse or migration of what already exists. The diagram shown in Figure 9.10 was obtained by automatically transforming the diagram shown in Figure 8.15 and manually editing it. It should be noted that identifier attributes have systematically been added.

9.8.2 The "data dissemination diagram" artifact (Figure 9.11)

Name	Data dissemination diagram
Experts	Application architects, data architects
Designers	Application architects
Recipients	Application architects, technical architects, software designers
Aim	To define how entities will be physically managed and distributed according to application components
Useful preliminary information	Data architecture, class diagrams, application architecture

- ▥ Persistent entity

-  "Database" component

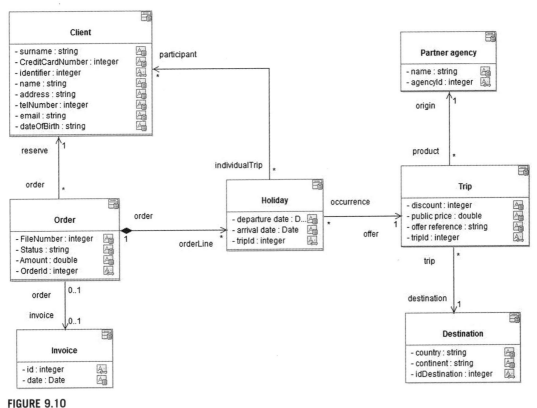

FIGURE 9.10

Logical data model focused on "Holiday." (For the color version of this figure, the reader is referred to the online version of this chapter.)

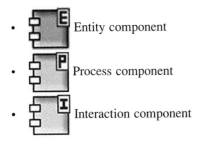

- Entity component

- Process component

- Interaction component

The aim of data dissemination diagrams is to define the way in which data will be distributed and managed between services and application components.[e] The relationships between business services, application components, and business entities are used to formalize this distribution. Data dissemination diagrams show how business entities will be physically managed and handled by application

---

[e]Component typology has been defined in chapter 9.1.1.

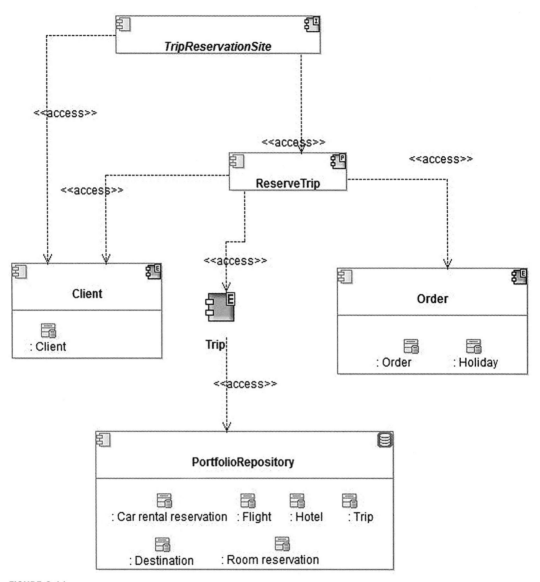

FIGURE 9.11

Data dissemination in application components. (For the color version of this figure, the reader is referred to the online version of this chapter.)

components. This allows applications to be sized and information to be provided on necessary memory and calculation resource capacities. The affectation of business values to handled data gives an indication of criticality to the component applications that support this data.

In the SOA architecture, data dissemination diagrams are directly deduced from application architecture, due to their layer structuring, which specializes the "entity" components responsible for the most important business entities and closely related entities. In non-SOA or hybrid architecture, data dissemination diagrams can reveal data replication issues and problems regarding application responsibility on data.

Data dissemination diagrams can include services that encapsulate data handling and are realized by application components. Once again, in an SOA architecture, these relationships are made easier through their systematization: an entity component manages a business entity, and presents the services enabling other components to handle this entity. This homogeneous architecture identifies who or what is responsible for a business entity and systematizes the way in which entities are managed.

Data dissemination diagrams reuse application architecture models, such as application communication diagrams, by connecting persistent entities (logical data model) to application components. Data dissemination can be presented either by deploying an instance of an entity in a component, which will be visualized as being graphically embedded (as in Figure 9.9 where the "Flight" data is embedded inside "PortfolioRepository"), or by linking the entity to the component via a specific dependency (flow). In the example presented, data is located either in a dedicated repository ("portfolio repository" or "accounting repository") or in dedicated entity components (for example, the "Client" component). We can see that the "Trip" entity is managed in the "PortfolioRepository" repository (the hybrid nature of the SOA architecture), while the "Order" entity is managed by the "Order" entity component.

9.8.3 The "data security diagram" artifact

Name	Data security diagram
Experts	Security experts
Designers	Analysts
Recipients	Analysts, security experts, application architects
Aim	To define and control data access security
Useful preliminary information	Class diagrams, business entities, business processes, organization, and actors

- External actor

- Internal actor

- Persistent entity

- «flow-{habilitation· CRUD}» Dataflow: Links an active element (actor, process, etc.) to an element carrying data (entity, event, etc.). Habilitations can be expressed on these flows, thereby indicating which access rights the active element has to which data.

Figure 9.12 shows who is authorized to access which data, and with which access rights. Thus, the account manager can create (C) or delete (D) a holiday.

Data constitutes an essential element of the enterprise's heritage. Guaranteeing data security and understanding data access rights is a vital part of security analysis. Ensuring data security means that data integrity will not be compromised and that access authorization will be controlled. Data security

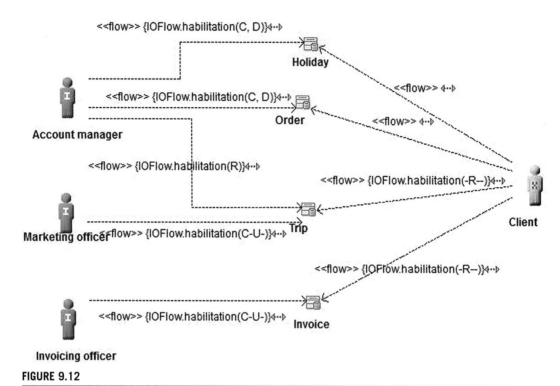

FIGURE 9.12

Representation of access to data. (For the color version of this figure, the reader is referred to the online version of this chapter.)

diagrams determine which actors (people, organization, or system) can access which enterprise data. This can be graphically represented in a specialized diagram or via dedicated matrices, such as RACI matrices. Diagrams can be used to show conformity with standards or privacy laws (HIPAA, SOX, etc.). Data security diagrams are also used to analyze the level of confidence or risk when other enterprises (subcontractors, partners) can access the enterprise's IS, or when data is hosted in other locations outside the enterprise (an example of cloud computing).

Diagrams that are too extensive quickly become illegible. We recommend that one security diagram be created per organization unit, or even per actor of the enterprise. In this way, when a diagram is focused on an actor, it can model his or her habilitations. These diagrams can also focus on access from outside the system, in other words data that can be accessed by actors outside the system.

Table 9.2 presents an example of a data security table that can be produced.

The commonly used "CRUD" acronym determines create, read, update, and delete rights. The characters corresponding to the rights provided are highlighted.

However, links must be created in the modeling repository, since these can appear in all types of diagrams to illustrate access right problems in several contexts.

Identified business entities and actors must therefore be reused to indicate who can access what subject to which conditions.

Table 9.2 Data Security Table

	Client	Holiday	Order	Trip	Invoice
Account manager	C..D	C..D	C..D	...D	C..D
Marketing officer				C..D	
Invoicing officer					C..D
Client	C...	C..D	C..D	.R..	.R..

C, Create; D, Delete; R, Read; W, Write.

9.8.4 The "data migration diagram" artifact

Name	Data migration diagram
Experts	Data architects, analysts
Designers	Analysts (at business level)
Recipients	Data architects, application architects, analysts
Aim	To define the migration of data between two stages of information system change
Useful preliminary information	Class models, business entity/conceptual data models, data models

- ⊞ Persistent entity

- - - - - - - ≻ Element migration between two versions of the information system; most often «migrates» presented between two business entities or application components.

In Figure 9.13, we can see that several attributes from the original data model have been promoted to the status of persistent entities in the target data model. This reveals a more complete target model, which requires a more extensive breakdown of system data.

The data migration diagram presents data transformation flows between the source application and the target application. It provides a visual presentation of the differences between the source and the target, and is used to carry out data audits and to check that no information has been lost. This type of diagram can be developed and improved in as detailed a way as possible. For example, a data migration diagram can show a general overview of the data to transform, or it can go into great detail, showing all attribute and data type transformations.

The presence of a logical model of source data makes work easier, since this data can be used to define what is transformed into what at a high level of abstraction. This exercise must be carried out on physical data, but can be delegated when transformations are realized.

The "migrates" dependency is the key element in formalizing migrations.

Source data models and target data models will generally be arranged in separate information domains.

To avoid too much complexity in diagrams, we recommend focusing on each important entity, either source entities or destination entities.

As with any traceability-oriented diagram, tables can be used as an alternative (Table 9.3).

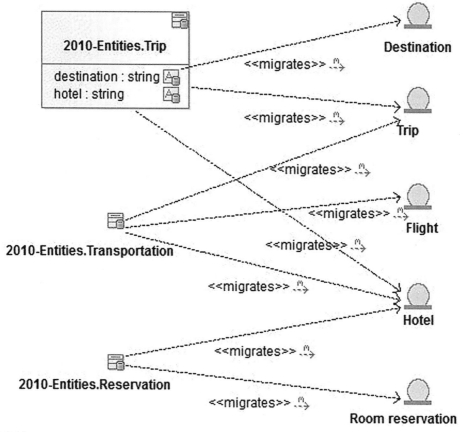

FIGURE 9.13

Migration dependencies can exist between business entities or can be defined more precisely at the attribute level. (For the color version of this figure, the reader is referred to the online version of this chapter.)

Table 9.3 Data Migration Matrix			
Source		**Migrates to**	
Element	**Nature**	**Element**	**Nature**
Transportation	Class	Trip	Class
		Hotel	Class
		Flight	Class
Trip	Class	Trip	Class
Trip.destination	Attribute	Destination	Class
Trip.hotel	Attribute	Hotel	Class
Reservation	Class	Room reservation	Class
		Hotel	Class

In this example, we see that the new model is better structured, since it groups previously dispersed attributes into new entities. It has been normalized.

9.9 THE "SERVICE DATA DIAGRAM" ARTIFACT (FIGURE 9.14)

Name	Service data diagram
Experts	Application architects, technical architects
Designers	Application architects
Recipients	Technical architects
Aim	To define exchanges of information between application components
Useful preliminary information	Application architecture

- 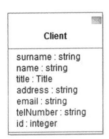 Message
- ↳ Association between messages: In service data models, these associations are composition links between a message and its submessages.

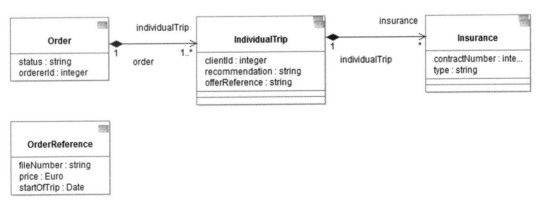

FIGURE 9.14

Three messages: Order, OrderReference, and Client. (For the color version of this figure, the reader is referred to the online version of this chapter.)

Service data or "messages" (sometimes called "business data types" or "Service Data Objects" or "Message Types" in the SoaML[f] standard) need a dedicated definition and model. The constitution of messages is modeled in service data diagrams.

Service data is most often deduced from conceptual data diagrams and the needs of information exchanges between services. It constitutes the parameters of service operations. The service data model is an extract from service data information necessary for the full operation of services. Potential extensibility and reusability needs must be foreseen so that the evolution of a service does not systematically require the redefinition or creation of new service data variants. Service data is very often implemented in the form of XML documents, where a particular message constitutes the root, which is often broken down into message fragments. Service data models "denormalize" conceptual data models (class models) by focusing only on the data that is necessary during exchanges. Thus, there is often a redundancy of information between messages.

9.10 FUNDAMENTAL CONCEPTS

The following fundamental concepts were introduced in this chapter:

- Application architecture: Identifies IS components and their interactions in order to meet business architecture expectations, while guaranteeing overall consistency and respecting the rules of an architectural framework.

---

[f]SOA Modeling Language standardized by the OMG.

Models for Phase D: Technology Architecture

10

CHAPTER OUTLINE

Technology architecture associates application components from application architecture with technology components representing software and hardware components. Its components are generally acquired in the marketplace and can be assembled and configured to constitute the enterprise's technological infrastructure. Technology architecture provides a more concrete view of the way in which application components will be realized and deployed. It enables the migration problems that can arise between the different steps of the IS evolution path to be studied earlier. It provides a more precise means of evaluating responses to constraints (nonfunctional requirements) concerning the IS, notably by estimating hardware and network sizing needs or by setting up server or storage redundancy. Technology architecture concentrates on logistical and location problems related to hardware location, IS management capabilities, and the sites where the different parts of the IS are used. Technology architecture also ensures the delivered application components work together, confirming that the required business integration is supported.

10.1 PHASE D ARTIFACTS

10.1.1 Nature of phase D artifacts: Technology architecture

Among the diagrams presented, network computing hardware diagrams play a central role (Table 10.1). The other diagrams are derived from this type of diagram and provide views that focus on particular aspects. The need to implement a type of diagram also depends on which existing elements are retained (application architecture/technology architecture). If technology architecture is seen as a receptacle for as yet undeveloped application architecture, then the "Platform decomposition diagram" (not presented in this book) is particularly adapted. However, if application architecture is defined to study the best technical platform to host it, then the network computing hardware diagram will quickly be implemented to schematize the best adapted overall configuration (Figure 10.3).

Table 10.1 TOGAF Artifacts and Artifacts Presented in This Chapter

TOGAF Artifacts	Models Presented	Comments
Environment and location diagram	Environment and location diagram	
Processing diagram	Processing diagram	
Networked computing diagram	Network computing hardware diagram	
Platform decomposition diagram		Network computing hardware diagram view focused on technology platforms that support the IS
Communication engineering diagram		Network computing hardware diagram view focused on communication technologies (network, protocols, etc.)
Technology standards catalog		Lists technologies recommended across the enterprise
Technology portfolio catalog		Lists all the technologies used across the enterprise
Application technology matrix		Documents the mapping of applications to technology platforms; can be produced from network computing hardware diagrams

10.1.2 Essential concepts used in technology architecture

- Headquarters (location): Geographically determines where enterprise elements are deployed (organization units, IT hardware, actors, etc.).

- Site (location): Geographically defines where enterprise elements are deployed (organization units, IT hardware, actors, etc.). An enterprise frequently has headquarters and several sites.

- Server: Represents a hardware platform that can be connected to other servers and on which application components will be deployed.

- Workstation: Linked to an information system via network connections. Application components can also be deployed on them.

- Utility component: In the case of technology architecture, physical-level technology components will frequently be utility components. For example, this is how application servers, database servers, or business process servers, which themselves host application components, will be represented.

10.2 THE "ENVIRONMENT AND LOCATION DIAGRAM" ARTIFACT

Name	Environment and location diagram
Experts	Technical architects, business experts
Designers	Technical architects
Recipients	Business experts, technical architects, operations managers
Aim	To define the deployment of hardware and applications on different enterprise sites
Useful preliminary information	Application architecture, existing technical architecture, geographical organization of the enterprise, nonfunctional requirements

-  Headquarter (location)

-  Site (location)

-  Interaction component

-  IT hardware: Server

-  Application component

-  Workstation

- ↳ Association: Here, this describes the connection between a site and its headquarters.

Figure 10.3 shows the definition of several hardware servers (for example, MVS server) and their network connections. In Figure 10.1, we can see that these servers are concentrated in the headquarters (Paris). Three different servers host the accounting ERP, the "TripPortfolioManager" application, and the trip reservation site.

Environment and location diagrams define which locations host which applications. They identify which technologies and/or applications are used in which locations, and can determine which actors interact with these applications in which locations. This type of diagram also shows the existence and position of different deployment environments, including environments not destined for production, such as those destined for development and preproduction.

Because they focus on the representation of deployment on the enterprise's hardware and sites, environment and location diagrams use element embedding. Hardware shown as being embedded inside a location is geographically situated in this location, while an application shown as being

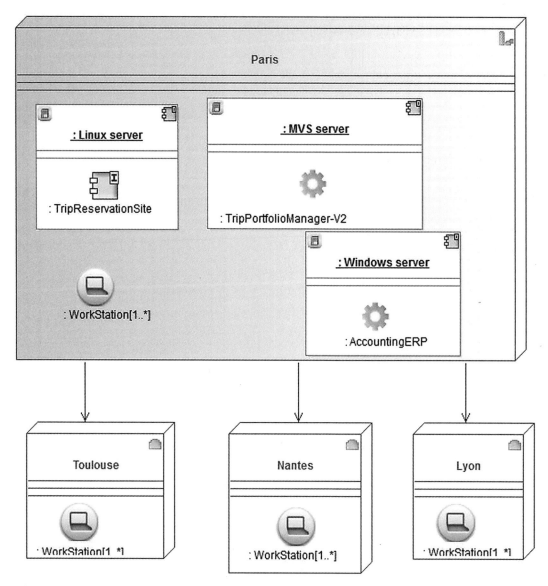

FIGURE 10.1

The main applications and devices are located in Paris. (For color version of this figure, the reader is referred to the online version of this chapter.)

embedded in hardware indicates where it is physically deployed. Shortcuts can be made simply by presenting applications in geographical locations, if the focus is not on the hardware. For example, in the case of cloud computing applications, we can simply express the locations where certain applications are predominantly used. Typically, this type of diagram represents the location where each server is located, and shows the server on which each application is run.

10.3 THE "PROCESSING DIAGRAM" ARTIFACT

Name	Processing diagram
Experts	Technical architects
Designers	Technical architects
Recipients	Operations engineers, developers
Aim	To provide details on the technical components necessary to run application architecture. To define the application architecture deployment mode
Useful preliminary information	Application architecture, existing technical architecture, technological choices

- Utility component: Here, this represents a physical technical component, such as an application server.

- Process component

- Interaction component

- Entity component

- Application component

- Workstation

- Association

- Information flow: Defines the flows exchanged between different servers via their networks.

Figure 10.2 presents three technical components, which act as servers hosting different application components defined by the application architecture: a web server is required for the site and a business process server hosts process components, while the other components are hosted by an application server.

Processing diagrams focus on deployable units of code or application configuration, and on the way in which these are deployed on technical platforms. A deployment unit constitutes a group of business functions, services, or application components. The following questions are dealt with by processing diagrams:

- Which physical groups are implemented to constitute a deployment unit?

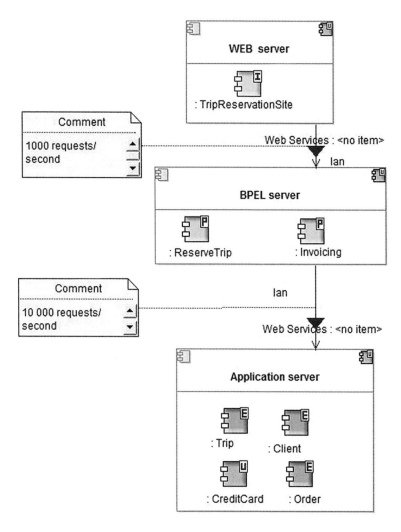

FIGURE 10.2

A processing diagram. Deployment of application components in different types of application servers. (For color version of this figure, the reader is referred to the online version of this chapter.)

- Which deployment units are interconnected (network) using which protocols?
- How do application configuration and usage modes translate into capability or load increase requirements for the different technical components?

Processing diagrams will use deployment in a more generic way than network computing hardware diagrams by focusing on deployment units. Deployment units can be presented in the form of instances of components where application components are deployed, or by utility components, which host the application components deployed. For example, this is the case for an application server, which is a technical utility component in which the application components run by the server are deployed.

In SOA architecture, application components will frequently represent their own deployment units, and this facilitates management and traceability. Sometimes assemblies of application components into a deployment unit may also be defined.

Dedicated links between these deployment units will represent connections, while information flows will be used to indicate the nature of the information exchanged.

Information on hardware and technical component capability requirements will be provided in these diagrams.

However, the deployment configuration presented in the example in Figure 10.2 remains independent of future deployment on physical servers.

10.4 THE "NETWORK COMPUTING HARDWARE DIAGRAM" ARTIFACT

Name	Network computing hardware diagram
Experts	Technical architects, system and network engineers
Designers	Technical architects
Recipients	System and network engineers, developers
Aim	To define the entire network, hardware, and technology architecture to meet functional and nonfunctional requirements
Useful preliminary information	Application architecture, technological choices, existing technical architecture

- Interaction component

- IT material: Server

- Entity component

- Application component

- Workstation

- Database component

-  Process component

- Internal actor

- Internet connection

- External actor

-  Utility component: Here, this represents a physical technical component, such as an application server.
- Association: Here, this describes the network connection between two IT hardware components.

IT systems previously built around "mainframe" architecture evolved into client/server systems before adapting to "eBusiness" and J2EE-type architectures, and then finally migrating to architectures that rely heavily on distributed systems on networks, with secure zones. Most current applications have a "front end" and are based on a multilayer architecture that separates web presentation, business logic, and data management aspects. It is common practice for applications to be based on common technical or software infrastructures. Therefore, it is critically important to document correspondence between logical applications and the technical components (such as servers) that support applications both in development and production environments.

Thus, the aim of network computing hardware diagrams is to present the logical view deployed in a distributed environment on the network of physical and software servers.

Physical servers are represented. In some cases, these will be instances of real servers, and in other cases server typologies. Sometimes these correspond to known, located hardware, while in "cloud computing"-type configurations, the physical servers are not known and can be increased according to load increase needs. In all cases, their typology must be known.

On these "physical" servers, the software used in the infrastructure is presented, for example, web servers or servers for business processes. Finally, application components identified during the definition of application architecture are deployed on physical servers or software infrastructures.

Connections between these hardware or software elements are also modeled, either as physical network connections or software bus connections.

It is useful to link roles and actors identified in business architecture in order to position them with regard to the system and to ensure that the hardware available will suit users.

In the diagram shown in Figure 10.3, deployments (software servers in physical servers, application components in software servers, etc.) are represented through element embedding. Instances of application components are therefore presented in the context of a particular server, and one component can have several instances in different contexts (servers).

This creates a diagram that is highly representative of the future or current configuration of the system.

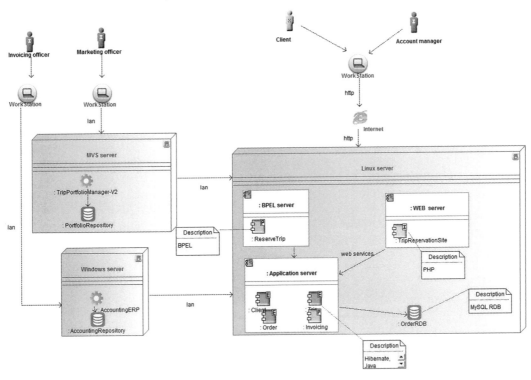

FIGURE 10.3

Diagram showing component deployment, network connections between servers, and the relative position of actors. (For color version of this figure, the reader is referred to the online version of this chapter.)

10.5 FUNDAMENTAL CONCEPTS

The following fundamental concepts were introduced in this chapter:

- Technology architecture: Describes the logical software and hardware capabilities that are required to support the deployment of business, data, and application services.

Models for Phase E: Opportunities and Solutions

11

CHAPTER OUTLINE

Phases B and C are the most demanding phases in terms of models and diagrams. Modeling work subsequently decreases during the following phases. Phase E (described in Section 2.2.4) realizes few models and focuses on the realization strategy. Two diagrams may be used during this phase: the benefits diagram and the project context diagram.

11.1 PHASE E ARTIFACTS

The aim of phase E is to define the realization strategy for the envisaged transformations. In particular, it develops the framework for projects deriving from the results of earlier phases. The result of earlier phases can be seen in terms of gaps, between the as-is and the to-be states, in order to achieve the desired result. Projects then formalize the resources, time horizons, schedules, budgets, and so on, to carry out the work required to close these gaps. Closing a gap has a cost, risk, time to value, benefit, alignment with business and technical objectives, and so on. The gap assessment would generally be to close the lowest cost, lowest risk, highest value gaps to maximize results from available resources/revenue. Phase E prepares project planning, finalizes decisions, and defines the architectural building blocks needed to build the evolutions of the IS.

Phase E reuses models from the development phases and consolidates them. Phase E introduces no new modeling concepts (Table 11.1).

11.2 THE "BENEFITS DIAGRAM" ARTIFACT

Name	Benefits diagram
Experts	Application architects, business architects
Designers	Application architects
Recipients	Business managers
Aim	To identify opportunities for change. To prepare a new ADM cycle
Useful preliminary information	Application architecture, business architecture

207

Table 11.1 Phase E Artifacts

TOGAF Artifacts	Models Presented
Project context diagram	Project context diagram
Benefits diagram	Benefits diagram

- External actor

- Interaction component

- Entity component

- Intermediary component: Implements quite complex business logic.

Benefits diagrams present opportunities identified during architecture definition. These opportunities are classified in terms of their relative size, their benefits, and their complexity. This type of diagram is used by decision-makers to select or assign priorities, or to make decisions regarding the order in which actions should be carried out with regard to opportunities.

Figure 11.1 presents the possibility of creating two new application components and making two others evolve in order to better address visitors who come back to the site, for example, to propose promotions related to previously expressed interests. Thought can be given to this model derived from application communication diagrams in order to answer questions that contribute to the decision-making process:

- What work has been planned for this kind of change?
- What is the associated complexity?
- What are the risks, and in particular, do any migration operations have to be foreseen?
  Are there risks concerning the continued functioning of the IS?
- What is the expected benefit?

This sophisticated evolution was not taken into account in the first iteration of IS change. It was more prudent to first put in place a web infrastructure, which constitutes a major change for the enterprise. Later, once the first step has been successfully completed and changes appear to be managed, then more sophisticated improvements can be envisaged. This evolution can be proposed as an opportunity for change during the next ADM cycle.

Projects can be defined here as a means of organizing the potential changes (opportunities) into units that can be assessed. The projects can also be linked to the goals and assessments of impact.

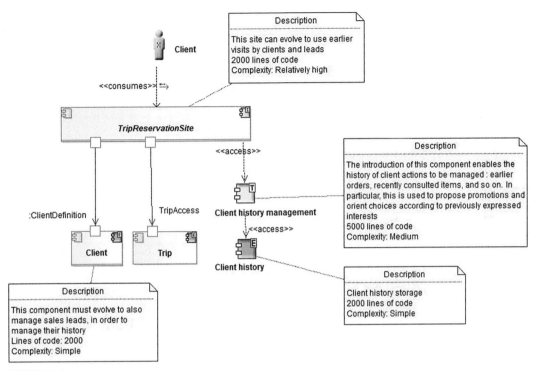

FIGURE 11.1

Benefits diagram. (For color version of this figure, the reader is referred to the online version of this chapter.)

11.3 PROJECT CONTEXT DIAGRAMS

Name	Project context diagram
Experts	Application architects, business experts
Designers	Application architects, business managers
Recipients	Business managers, organization unit directors, CIOs
Aim	To provide a framework for a new project
Useful preliminary information	Application architecture diagrams, business architecture

- External actor

- Internal actor

-  Requirement

- Business process

-  Use case

- "Database" component

- Interaction component

- Application component

- System federation component

- `<<flow>>` Information flow: Indicates a flow of information of any sort (business entity, event, etc.) circulating between active entities of the system.

- «realizes An application component realizes the designated element (for example, a business process).

- «consumes» Link between a participant (for example, an actor) and an element of the system being studied; expresses that the participant consumes the element of the IS.

- «satisfy» Indicates that an element of the IS satisfies a requirement.

A project context diagram presents the scope of a work package, which is realized as part of a change roadmap. The project context diagram links a work package to organizations, functions, services, processes, applications, business or data entities, and technologies that will be added, withdrawn, or modified by the project. The project context diagram is also a useful tool in the management of application portfolios and for initiating a project.

In this type of diagram, the essential application components of the project are presented, along with the main requirements and the linked business elements (business processes, businesses services, business functions). We will express which requirements are satisfied by the project, which business processes are implemented, which business functions are concerned, and which actors or roles will use the targeted application components.

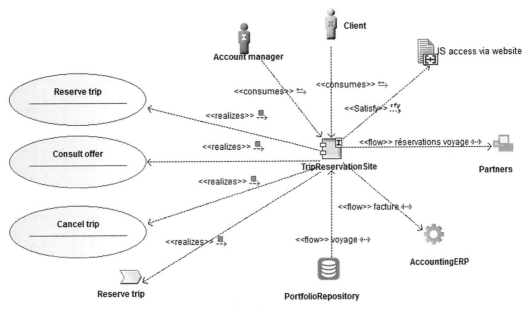

FIGURE 11.2

Project context diagram focused on the "TripReservation" site. (For color version of this figure, the reader is referred to the online version of this chapter.)

Other links to parts of the information system can also be expressed. Figure 11.2 focuses on the trip reservation site. It highlights its connection to the portfolio repository and the accounting ERP (both of which exist in the current system) and recalls the use cases and processes implemented by the site. It indicates that this site accesses partner systems. The client and the account manager are the two actors who use the site. The main requirement satisfied by this site is the request for IS connection to the Internet.

SOA, Processes, and Information

Beyond the context of TOGAF, this chapter looks at three major themes of enterprise architecture and information systems: the SOA approach, business processes, and information.

The first theme concerns information system agility and reuse. Even though Service-Oriented Architecture is no longer perceived today as being the universal solution, it does provide a set of good practices which should be taken into account.

Mastering business processes is a key element in enterprise architecture, at the very heart of changes made within organizations. Identification, modeling, and governance also widely influence architecture work.

Information constitutes the raw material of operations carried out by systems. From databases to messages, from documents to e-mails, the variety of forms of information and information management modes require adapted practices and organization modes in enterprise architecture.

12.1 SERVICE-ORIENTED ARCHITECTURE

12.1.1 SOA in TOGAF

SOA (Service-Oriented Architecture) is a style of architecture organized using common business services that are pooled for a set of business lines or applications.[a] Here we do not discuss so-called technical SOA, which consists of implementing a set of devices and technologies that focus on web services (ESB, UDDI, etc.), since even though these techniques really do facilitate communication between the components of the IS, the structure of the system remains the key architectural question, regardless of the technical means used.

The primary motivation of service-oriented architecture comes from the following observation: The breakdown into independent application silos (monolithic blocks) is one of the major sources of difficulty in system evolution and maintenance work.

Let's not forget that TOGAF does not advocate any particular architectural style. TOGAF presents SOA in the Chapter 22 "Using TOGAF to Define & Govern SOAs" in the ADM Guidelines and techniques part. Furthermore, The Open Group set up a working group dedicated to this subject, who published a specific document[b] alongside the TOGAF publications. Figure 12.1 summarizes the SOA vision developed in this document.

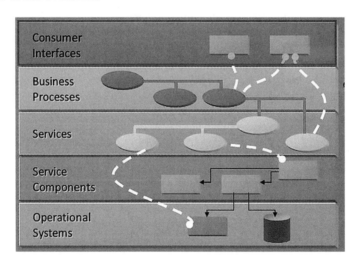

FIGURE 12.1

SOA structure according to "SOA Reference Architecture." (For color version of this figure, the reader is referred to the online version of this chapter.)

---

[a]SOA is an approach to designing software that dissolves business applications into separate "services" that can be used independently of the applications of which they're a part and computing platforms on which they run (Jay DiMare, IBM Global Services, 2006).
[b]"SOA Reference Architecture"—see www.opengroup.org/subjectareas/soa. The work carried out by this working group was integrated into version 9.1 of TOGAF, published in December 2011 (chapter 22).

The system is broken down into five layers:

- The client interface
- Business processes
- Services
- Service components
- The system platform

We can see that the system is no longer broken down into "applications," but rather into components, each positioned in a particular layer that corresponds to a specific role in the system. However, this does not mean that applications disappear: they are built by combining a set of components, which are potentially pooled.

12.1.2 SOA: Not as simple as it seems

This organization aims to encourage system agility and to enable a high degree of service reuse. However, beyond a naive vision, the management of this type of architecture requires a solid understanding of its foundations and its difficulties.

There is a big difference between SOA architecture and the usual structure built from applications (which we can call "application-oriented architecture"). For the latter, the application is the fundamental constituent of the system, and this structure coincides with the organization of teams. We find here a breakdown into application silos, both at the heart of the system and in its management.

With an SOA-type breakdown, things are different. First, the basic constituent of the system (the system component) is much less high level than the application, and this mechanically increases the complexity of the system. For example, we go from managing 100 applications to managing 1000 service components. Second, this breakdown does not cover the historical organization by application, which remains a strong operational unit linked to business demands.

These questions require special, well-managed handling. The proliferation of disorganized services is one of the main pitfalls encountered, often due to overly technically oriented vision. Some people have no hesitation in talking about *spaghetti-oriented architecture*.[c]

12.1.3 Organizing components

One of the best way to control this complexity is to structure components by differents types and levels. We have already seen this kind of approach advocated by TOGAF, which defines five levels (client interface, business processes, services, service components, system platform). This type of structuring is accompanied by rules and best practices. The main rule establishes a norm for dependencies, which forbids, for example, the use of a component by a higher layer (a service component cannot depend on a client interface).

Other typologies exist and are relatively similar, despite variations or different levels of detail. Table 12.1 presents some of these possible typologies:

---

[c]"JBOWS (Just a Bunch of Web Services). An effective, functioning service-oriented architecture requires governance, and the ability to share services across multiple business units and enterprises. It's easy to build Web services. You could build 10 of them in an afternoon. But, then you end up with a JBOWS architecture (Just a Bunch of Web Services), which will grow into a different sort of SOA—a Spaghetti-Oriented Architecture," Joe McKendrick, Seven areas of opportunity around SOA, circa 2007, www.thegreylines.net/2006_12_01_archive.html.

Herzum and Sims[a]	ESOA[b]	Microsoft[c]	IBM[d]
	Front-end application	Presentation layer	Presentation
Process	Process centric	Business process	Business process choreography
	Intermediary	Business service	Composite service
Entity	Basic	Data service	Service
Utility			

Table 12.1 Different SOA Typologies

[a]*Business Component Factory, Peter Herzum and Oliver Sims, Wiley Computing Publishing, 2000.*
[b]*Enterprise SOA, Dirk Krafzig, Karl Banke, and Dirk Slama, The Coad Series, 2005.*
[c]*An Overview of Service-Oriented Architecture in Retail, Moin Moinuddin, Microsoft, January 2007.*
[d]*Bernhard Borges, Kerrie Holley, and Ali Arsanjani, IBM, September 15, 2004, SearchWebServices.com.*

In Chapter 9, we used a typology based on the same principles, which uses the suggestions made in the "Logical Architecture: Principles, structures and best practices" white paper (Architecture Logique: Principes, structures et bonnes pratiques[d]):

- *Interaction component*: Exchange with the outside world
- *Process component*: Process automation
- *Function component or intermediate component*: Business processing and data composition
- *Entity component*: Data access
- *Utility component*: Cross-organizational functionalities (messaging system, address book, etc.)

For the enterprise architect, the exercise consists of identifying and positioning each component within this framework, allocating well-defined services to each component, and specifying the execution conditions for these services in the form of a service-level agreement (SLA).

12.1.4 Encouraging reuse

This objective is not new in the field of software. As we have just seen, it is one of the points highlighted in service-oriented architecture. However, experience shows that it is not always easy to concretely implement this goal. Sharing leads to dependency between different user parts, which creates additional management costs.

The term "reuse" can designate several realities.

Reuse through copying and pooling

Reuse through copying consists of taking what already exists and using it in another context. In the context of software development, this comes down to duplicating a part of the source code from a given example. More generally, it is the widely known mechanism used in design "patterns." A tried and tested practice or structure is reused by adapting it to a specific context. In this case, the reused part

---

[d]SOA: Architecture Logique: Principes, structures et bonnes pratiques, Gilbert Raymond, Softeam 2007, 2011, www.softeam.fr.

is integrated and merged into the target component, which evolves with no direct link to the element used. As discussed in Section 4.1, the TOGAF architecture repository is the ideal place to store this kind of heritage, which must be constantly added to.

Shared reuse or *pooling* is very different. It consists of sharing a component in different contexts; this is the typical schema used in an SOA context, where several applications will use the services provided by a component deployed in the system. To use SOA terminology, users are *consumers*, and the shared component is the service *provider*. This schema develops links between consumers, which must be managed.

The price of pooling

On this issue, TOGAF considers that pooling components multiply costs by at least a factor of two compared with separate development.[e] The main causes of these additional costs are as follows:

- First, pooling requires agreement between consumers regarding the terms of the service provided. This contractualization (SLA) precisely defines the conditions under which the service in question will operate. Moreover, we can see that the nonfunctional part plays its full role here: availability, performance, security, and so on.
- Second, each provider evolution is immediately transmitted to all the user clients of the pooled component. This situation often leads to internal conflicts.

Let's take the example of two applications called A and B, which use the services of a single component named C. For specific reasons, application B needs to quickly modify the interface of component C. The person in charge of application A is forced to resume a test campaign if this component is modified, and to modify his work plan for external reasons.

Thus, we end up with the following paradox: the higher the degree of pooling, the more difficult contractualization becomes. Therefore, if reuse is not managed properly, it can lead to reduced system agility, bogged down by the red tape of contractualization.

Faced with this type of situation, IS managers sometimes decide to temporarily multiply the number of versions of pooled components in order to enable rapid deployment without perturbing other consumers. In Figure 12.2, two versions of component C will be available: version C1 (unchanged) used by application A, and version C2 integrating the modifications requested by application B. This transitional state has to be resolved by the effective pooling of the same version of C by A and B.

This option enables conflicts to be reduced, but leads to a multiplication of versions, which eventually compromises effective reuse and increases the complexity of the system.

For the sake of pragmatism and efficiency, these situations are difficult to forbid entirely. The role of the organization in charge of enterprise architecture consists of avoiding a proliferation of versions. An adapted indicator will facilitate control and management, for example, by fixing a maximum number of simultaneous versions and a limited duration for the coexistence of several versions of a component.

---

[e]TOGAF9 13.4.4.2.

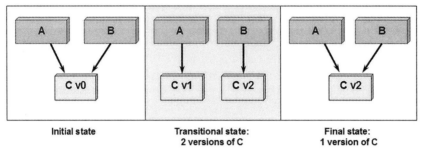

Initial state   Transitional state: Final state:
2 versions of C   1 version of C

FIGURE 12.2

SOA component versioning. (For color version of this figure, the reader is referred to the online version of this chapter.)

> Beware of focusing exclusively on reuse. Many "reusable" components exist, but a lot fewer components are actually "reused." This is one of the most common aspects of "overengineering," which tends to minimize difficulties. We strongly recommend systematically designing reuse in concrete terms (in other words, with at least two uses) and avoiding anticipating potential reuse with no real implementation.

Thus, the work of an enterprise architect consists of finding the best compromise between the advantages of reuse and the disadvantages that we have just discussed.

This choice is based on a set of characteristics:

- The number of consumers
- The stability of the pooled component
- The frequency of use
- The size/complexity of the interface

In other words, for a component used by a large number of consumers, which is very unstable, frequently used, and relatively complex to approach, significant additional costs can be expected.

Stability plays a major role in this type of choice. It is often linked to a certain normalization of the service provided by the provider, which reduces considerably the burden of management. In this category we find many utility components, for example, pooling an e-mail server presents no particular difficulties, despite the fact that it is used by a large number of consumers to automatically send e-mail.

12.1.5 The BPM-SOA couple

Process automation is becoming more and more widespread and constitutes a discipline in itself: BPM (*Business Process Management*),[f] with its community, methods, and tools. This tendency is also found in the main ERPs, which today include the process automation component in their solutions.

---

[f]In actual fact, BPM covers a wider area, from modeling to supervision, but with the aim of increasing business process integration into IT systems.

Two main categories of automated process can be identified: first, processes with a high level of human intervention, in other words, processes in which human actors are in charge of running tasks (using software applications, for example), and second, processes where there is little or no human intervention.

The first category is typically the field of workflows (historically workflow tools). The workflow engine takes charge of sequencing and allocating tasks to different participants, which means that it has to have knowledge of the organization and each person's capabilities. It acts as a "robot" manager which coordinates and manages the progress of the work.

The second category is likely to be simpler to implement, inasmuch as it deals with the sequencing of automatic operations, carried out by defined applications or software components. In this case, the term process "orchestration" is often used.

Figure 12.3 presents a typical architecture change, from an application organization to a BPM/SOA approach.

In the first case (1), each of the three applications is in charge of running a part of the process and then "hands over" to the next. In the second case (2), the process is totally handled by a dedicated

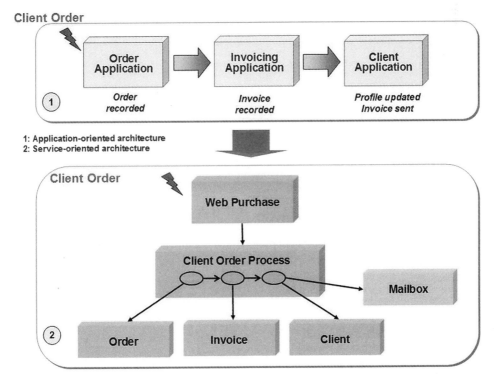

FIGURE 12.3

Application-oriented architecture versus the BPM/SOA approach. (For color version of this figure, the reader is referred to the online version of this chapter.)

component, with one major consequence: *the process itself exists in the system*, while in the previous case it was invisible, masked by the applications. The advantages of this architecture are twofold:

- Evolutions to the process are simpler to implement. The addition of a task or the adjustment of an execution path is handled in a centralized manner, in a framework that is perfectly adapted to this type of operation.
- Process supervision is greatly facilitated. BAM (business activity monitoring) tools fit naturally into a process execution engine, and provide precious assistance (execution reports, logs) in maintenance and improvement work.

From a BPM/SOA perspective, the best practice consists of clearly separating roles: the component in charge of running the process exclusively handles the sequencing and the rules that are directly associated with it. The other functions are delegated to services, such as data access or business processing. This structure, although ideal, is a particularly efficient "pattern," which can be adapted depending on what already exists, for example, by setting up "service mode" interfaces on applications without deploying an architecture that is 100% SOA.

12.2 BUSINESS PROCESSES

12.2.1 The central role of business processes

The day-to-day activity of an enterprise mainly consists of a set of employees participating in the running of business processes. Process management (BPM, Business Process Management) is a key domain, for which a whole series of approaches and techniques have been developed over several years: from process optimization with Six Sigma to the processes and process automation approach. Process management is a critical issue for all actors, CIOs, business owners, and project managers, in terms of system reactivity, activity monitoring, and market positioning.

As representatives of enterprise activity, business processes contribute greatly to the structuring of its architecture. When business processes evolve, architecture change projects are often initiated, with significant consequences for the information system. Moreover, the architecture repository often includes a set of process descriptions, from general mapping to detailed modeling, as a major element in the understanding of the inside functioning of the enterprise.

In the context of the ADM approach, processes mainly participate during phases A (Vision) and B (Business). Along with data entities, they form the core of business architecture. Because of their structuring nature, they also have a significant influence on the development of the information system and the technical foundations. The automation of certain processes accentuates their integration with the system: from the status of descriptive models, they find themselves at the heart of its functioning.

Given the importance of the subject, its contours, difficulties, and pitfalls must be defined. Later in this chapter, we will see that the very definition of a business process can vary, and that there exist a wide variety of types of processes within the enterprise. Add to this the fact that managing processes and their representations is anything but straightforward; the risk of getting lost in the sheer volume of information linked to processes is very real.

12.2.2 **What is a business process?**

This is the first question to ask, even if it seems trivial. All too often, the term "process" is used as a "catch-all," covering very different realities. If you need any convincing of this, just ask each person in a group to give his or her definition of the term "process" and let the debate take place. The diversity of answers is surprising, ranging from the description of screen sequences to the functions of the enterprise, or even the algorithms of IT processing (Figure 12.4).

TOGAF provides the following definition: "A process represents a sequence of activities that together achieve a specified outcome, can be decomposed into sub-processes, and can show operation of a function or service (at next level of detail). Processes may also be used to link or compose organizations, functions, services, and processes."

Fundamentally, a business process is a correlated set of activities producing tangible added value from an initial request (the trigger event). Activities are carried out by actors (human or automatic) using adapted means. The *business* nature of the process is expressed through the nature of the result, which must be meaningful for a client (internal or external) and measurable, where possible.

Here, the term "activity" designates a work unit that brings added value through the transformation or production of information or material. Other terms are also used, such as "task" or "stage."

12.2.3 **Main characteristics of business processes**

Beyond the initial definition, certain characteristics enable the nature of business processes to be more precisely defined: cross-organization, temporality, parallelism, and event processing.

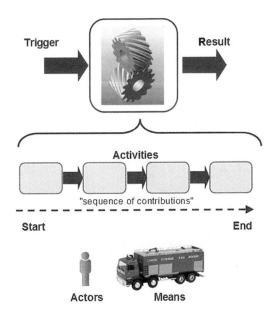

FIGURE 12.4

Business process, trigger, result, actors, means. (For color version of this figure, the reader is referred to the online version of this chapter.)

Cross-organization

A process is inherently *cross-organizational* to the enterprise's functions and entities. It is made up of the different stages that follow one another in a more or less complex manner, from the trigger event until the final result is obtained. We talk about "end to end" processes, with key performance indicators (KPIs) that measure the quality of the final result. Figure 12.5 shows the progress of an order process, which runs across several enterprise entities (sales, invoicing, production, and delivery). Evaluation of this kind of process measures, for example, the time between an order being taken and the actual delivery of the product. Improvement in the quality of the service rendered to the client means working on the entire process (Figure 12.5).

Depending on the complexity of processes, it may be necessary to perform a further breakdown into subprocesses. Some of these subprocesses can be used in several processes, which facilitates simplification through factorization.

Temporality

A process has a beginning and an end, and runs over a given period of time.[g] This statement may appear trite but is worth remembering. For example, "contract management" generally does not represent a process of the enterprise but rather a function or logical group of processes, since "contract management" has no start and no finish. The "contract management" group can include, for example, the "open a new contract" and "amend a contract" processes, which run over a given period of time between the moment they start and the moment the result is obtained.

Parallelism

When a process is run, we often find activities that run simultaneously, notably those that are undertaken by different actors. These parallel branches require that information be exchanged or synchronized. In the previous example, the enterprise can decide to run the invoicing and production activities at the same time. The actual delivery of the product waits for the end of these two activities before starting. This new organization reduces the overall duration of process execution, but requires strict synchronization of the end of the two invoicing and production activities. This is a typical choice

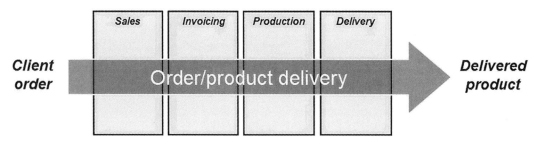

FIGURE 12.5

Process cross-organization. (For color version of this figure, the reader is referred to the online version of this chapter.)

---

[g]This period of time can be long (years), referred to as a "long-term" process.

for process architecture, with greater or lesser repercussions on the other architectural constituents involved, such as business organization or IT elements.

Events

Business processes are rarely isolated. They react to outside events that have a direct influence on their progress. In particular, certain activities will find themselves in the position of waiting for a given event to happen: the process is suspended until this event occurs. For example, when an insurance claim is processed, the investigation will await the results of the evaluation report before continuing. Other events can also interrupt an activity that is underway, such as a cancelation request.

Note that this event aspect is particularly present in BPMN notation, which provides no less than 50 different types of events.

12.2.4 Process typology

In the context of business process descriptions, we are always confronted with the diversity of the situations encountered. This diversity is the expression of the reality of enterprise processes, which exist independently of their representation. Classification of the processes themselves and their internal functioning facilitates their management, both as a qualification tool and as an architecture repository organization tool (business process models are part of business architecture in TOGAF).

Generic typology of business processes

The following classification is fairly widely used,[h] since it provides initial positioning of processes within the enterprise:

- *Operational processes or "core business" processes*, responsible for direct enterprise added value (claims processing, client orders, etc.).
- *Support processes*, which assist operational processes without directly participating in the results (price update, production and update of product catalogs, etc.).
- *Management processes*, linked to the strategies and general management of the enterprise (market studies, general goal definition, supervisions, etc.).

This list can be completed by adding the "internal process" type, which designates processes that are not specific to the business in question, such as recruitment processes or resource management processes.

This typology facilitates the hierarchical organization of processes and enables better definition of their relationships. Operational processes are obviously the most critical for the enterprise, but each process contributes to obtaining defined goals.

Types of sequences

The types of relationships that exist between the activities of a process are variable and define its functioning mode. The sequencing of activities can be strictly determined, or can be left more or less flexible. In the first case, we will talk about deterministic or "mechanistic" processes. Anyone looking at the example in Figure 12.6 will quickly come to the conclusion that the sequence of activities of the

---

[h]Typology from the ISO 9001 norms.

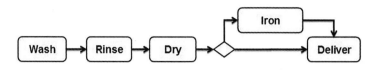

FIGURE 12.6

Simple example of a "deterministic" or "mechanistic" process. (For color version of this figure, the reader is referred to the online version of this chapter.)

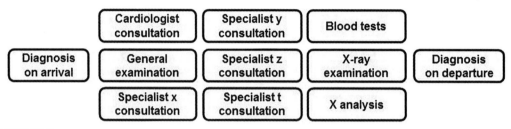

FIGURE 12.7

Nondeterministic process: Example of a medical diagnosis. (For color version of this figure, the reader is referred to the online version of this chapter.)

process in question cannot be different (unless we consider that it is normal to start by ironing and to finish by washing clothes). Different paths can exist, but these are strictly marked out by explicit conditions. In our example, ironing is an option depending on the client's wishes.

In the second case, the sequence of activities is much more random and can be the result of choices made by participating actors (Figure 12.7). This is notably the case with design or diagnosis processes, in which the path to the expected result cannot be described simply, even if the activities themselves are clearly defined.[i]

In the example of the medical diagnosis, we can simplify by stating that each consultation or analysis activity can potentially redirect the patient to one or several other activities according to the practitioner's opinion. The exhaustive description of all possible paths would result in a highly complex, totally unusable graph.

We find a similar distinction in the workflow community between the "procedural" workflow and the "ad hoc" workflow. Procedural workflows (also called production workflows or directive workflows) are business processes known to the enterprise, which are the subject of preestablished procedures, and whose sequence of activities is fixed. Ad hoc workflows are based on a collaborative model in which actors participate in the decisions regarding their sequence of activities.

Knowing which type of sequence of activities is involved (even without going into detail at this level) conditions certain decisions, notably with regard to modeling work and implementation choices.

---

[i]For this type of process, we also talk about "case management."

Most modeling languages such as BPMN are better adapted to describing mechanistic processes, with a fixed sequence of activities.[j] Some approaches advocate representation through event and condition tables in the case of nondeterministic processes.

It is clear that process automation implementation can vary significantly depending on the type of sequence of activities. Once again, process execution history tools facilitate deterministic processes, but the emergence of "case management" solutions[k] provides a more collaborative vision of processes.

Batch processing and desynchronization

We have seen that a process takes place through the sequence of its activities. Activities represent work units, each of which contributes to the final result, as in an industrial production line. Let's take a typical example of a (highly simplified) process concerning order processing. This process (which is deterministic) is broken down into three activities: validation, invoicing, and order delivery (Figure 12.8). It is triggered when the order is received.

But if, as is often the case, the enterprise decides to group several orders into a single delivery that takes place at the beginning of every week, this description becomes incorrect. The "Order delivery" activity does not exist. Furthermore, the real activity of delivery of a batch of orders is not triggered following order invoicing, but rather at a fixed date (at the beginning of the week). A more realistic representation of the process is provided in Figure 12.9.

The process ends up being "decoupled" into two separate processes, each with a different trigger. This is a recurring question with regard to processes and work organization methods: the choice between "just in time" processing and "batch" processing. According to the context, the enterprise

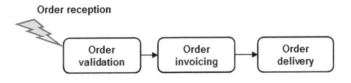

FIGURE 12.8

Simple example of an order process.

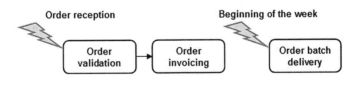

FIGURE 12.9

Example of desynchronization through batch processing.

---

[j]To be exact, BPMN contains the "ad hoc" type of activity to respond to this kind of process. However, this element is little known and little used.
[k]Case Management: A Review of Modeling Approaches, Henk de Man, BP Trends, January 2009.

can choose to manage each order individually right through to delivery, or as we have just seen to deliver batches of orders.[1]

It is easy to imagine that the consequences of this choice on the organization and architecture will be significant: an accumulation of orders over the week, product storage issues, delivery implementation, and so on. Thus, it is essential that desynchronization phenomena be identified in order to properly carry out work on the resulting architecture.

12.2.5 Describing and modeling business processes
Process modeling: A risky business?

All too often, rushing into detailed modeling of processes leads to a paradoxical situation: the proliferation of models that are difficult to use and quickly obsolete. Many enterprises that have undertaken the large-scale modeling of their processes observe that results are poor compared with the investments made: the reality of the situation has evolved while a significant part of the repository has been "treading water."

Note that here we are talking about process models that are intended to last, like architecture repository elements. Descriptions, models, or various representations realized for temporary needs are not concerned. By nature, these are "perishable" and are not subject to the same durability constraints.

Of course, this disconnection between reality and description can be seen for each part of the architecture repository. However, the risk of a break with reality is particularly high for business process models for two essential reasons: first, the elevated cost of investment in process modeling and, second, the frequently changing nature of the subject being dealt with. Modeling a process consists in "dissecting" activities, with all the implicit imprecision and knowledge this includes. The result will only be convincing through the involvement of business resources, which are sometimes difficult to mobilize within a reasonable timeframe. Consequently, the representation of real processes goes beyond simplistic diagrams made up of "boxes" and "arrows," and requires real introspection on the intimate functioning of the enterprise.

How should one proceed faced with this situation? Above all, by starting from the goal in terms of communication and use, and by adapting the form and content of the representation in accordance with this goal: to represent in the repository what we really need and what needs to be maintained over time.

Identification, qualification, and modeling

With this in mind, we suggest the definition of three distinct levels of representation for business processes: identification, qualification, and modeling.

This distinction has two advantages. First, it organizes the process repository into successive layers, by increasing the level of detail, and second, it encourages a more progressive approach, which tends to be quickly beneficial by minimizing investment (both cost and time).

---

[1]Yves Caseau discusses this issue in his book, specifying that the interpretation of process diagrams varies depending on element semantics: the transition arrow between two tasks can represent a strict sequence as in BMPN (these are the semantics implied here) or simply an existing relationship. Urbanisation, SOA et BPM—Le point de vue du DSI, Yves Caseau, Dunod, 2008.

Identification

The *identification* of processes can take several different forms: a simple inventory or an organized mapping. For each process, a set of fundamental information is grouped in the *process identity file*: the trigger event, input and output, participants resources used, key performance indicators (KPIs), and so on. Easily accessible and concise, this file is the entry point to knowledge of the process. The following table gives an example of a process identity file for the order process.

Property	Description
Finality	Delivery of products ordered by the client within set time limits
Trigger event	Receipt of the client's order
Input	Order form
Output	Invoice, product
Key performance indicators (KPIs)	Total duration of the process <3 days
Responsible actor (governance)	Process driver has been designated
Resources used	CRM, delivery management application
Main actors	Client, order manager, delivery service
Work in progress	Optimization study

The Six Sigma method[m] provides a similar tool with the SIPOC (*Supplier, Input, Process Output, Customer*), which macroscopically presents the process in the form of a table or a diagram. TOGAF uses the ICOM acronym: *Inputs, Controls, Outputs, and Mechanisms/resources used.*

Process identification can be widened through the incorporation of *process mapping*. This provides an overview of the enterprise, which enables each process to be positioned in a predefined context (based on business domains, for example). Process mapping positions each process in relation to other processes, and defines the main relationships in the form of interprocess exchanges.[n]

Qualification

The goal of *qualification* is to better define processes in all their diversity and to facilitate decision making. The characteristics grid enables each process to be defined in the same way, using criteria that can be directly used: frequency, complexity, duration, reported malfunction, typology, number of participants, and so on.

> It is not possible to compare a totally automated process that is run 200 times per minute, and another that is managed entirely by human actors and that is run twice a year. The constraints involved, the skills used, and the range of possible solutions vary greatly from one situation to another.

This qualification sometimes requires more in-depth study of the process, for example, by identifying the typologies previously described. Depending on the situation, the use of Six Sigma or

---

[m]Lean Six Sigma: Overview of techniques, http://itil.fr/LEAN-SIX-SIGMA/lean-six-sigma-tour-dhorizon.html.
[n]An example of a process mapping model is presented in Chapter 7.

Lean-type methods will be well suited, such as statistical measurement of errors, blockages, or resource consumption[o] for optimization purposes.

Beyond the information it provides, the result of qualification will guide certain architectural choices, primarily the decision as to whether or not to automate the process, and if so, in what form. This point is discussed later in this chapter.

Modeling

Models based on graphical notation are essential to the detailed representation of business processes, as with the BPMN[p] standard.

Figure 12.10 presents a simple example of a business process described with BPMN. The "Order reception" trigger event starts up the process, which begins with validation of the order. Two parallel branches are then run: dispatch and delivery confirmation on the one hand, and invoicing and payment on the other. The process only ends when both these branches have been completed.

Models have long been used in many sectors to understand, develop, simulate, and communicate (see Chapter 5). Modeling requires particular skills and knowledge: choice of level of detail, gathering and consolidation of information, and communication of results. The type of modeling carried out will vary depending on the goal (general description, detailed information on the process, or support for automation).

Using this principle, Bruce Silver[q] identifies three levels of business process model: the *descriptive* level, the *analytical* level, and the *executable* level. The descriptive level provides the fundamental structure of the process, with its main activities, but without taking exceptions into account. The analytical level establishes the sequence of the process in detail, with all its activities and exchanges. The executable level is used in the context of process automation by integrating links to software elements and technical constraints. Once again, we observe the need to separate viewpoints applied to modeling.

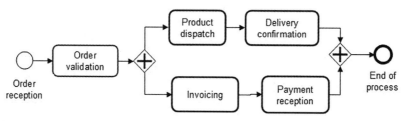

FIGURE 12.10

Example of a BPMN diagram.

---

[o]It is not a question of systematically rolling out the Six Sigma or Lean methods, but rather of using certain tools according to different needs. Intense optimization work is outside the scope of this chapter.

[p]Business Process Modeling Language, standard managed by the OMG consortium (omg.org).

[q]BPMN Method and Style: A Levels-Based Methodology for BPM Process Modeling and Improvement Using BPMN 2.0, Bruce Silver, Cody-Cassidy Press, 2009.

Process description management

Using TOGAF terminology, the breakdown into levels that we have just discussed consists of defining a set of viewpoints dedicated to processes:

- The "identification" viewpoint, which presents high-level views that are simple to use but which provide a summary of the main process-related information.
- The "qualification" viewpoint, which is the result of analysis of the process, its characteristics, and possible improvements.
- The "modeling" viewpoint, which describes process content in a more or less detailed way, using BPMN-type notation.

This structuring in the architecture repository enables more efficient communication and reduces the risk of uncontrolled proliferation of process descriptions.

In practice, the aim is not to define all the enterprise's processes in one "big bang" operation. Priority will be given to "core business" processes or opportunity-driven processes (optimizations, evolutions). Generally speaking, the number of "identified" processes is greater than the number of "qualified" and "modeled" processes. We strongly recommend that the switch from one level to another be clearly justified, notably for modeling, in view of the investment necessary for this type of work.

12.2.6 Process governance

The process driver

The "process driver"[r] function is used in many enterprises to guarantee the quality, monitoring, and continual improvement of business processes. Today, a whole host of publications exist on the subject, as well as sharing communities such as the "Process Driver Club."[s] It has multiple roles and touches on several facets:

- Description and modeling
- Improvement and optimization
- Coordination of the application components involved in the process
- Training and informing of users
- Supervision of execution, key performance indicators
- Feedback from monitoring and information/warnings provided to management
- Maintenance, support, and parameterization
- Study of changes
- Repository update

Furthermore, this function emerged relatively late and is still having difficulty in widely establishing itself. This is paradoxical since everyone is convinced of the critical role played by processes within the enterprise.

---

[r]Or "process owner."
[s]www.pilotesdeprocessus.org.

The main reason for this delay is the cross-organizational nature of business processes. We have already seen that business processes generally run over several functions, managed by distinct organization units. This positioning goes against the historical and sometimes "hierarchical" structure of enterprises. "Traditional" IT applications easily find their place in this type of organization, under the clearly defined responsibility of well-established units. However, installing and stabilizing a cross-organizational-type organization, which plays a real driving role, is a delicate task. That said, this depends on the business context. In fields closely linked to logistics, such as transportation, processes are naturally seen as being at the heart of the business. For other types of activity, the approach by process has only really begun to develop over the past few years.

Role in enterprise architecture

Enterprise architecture, another cross-organizational activity, is an opportunity for process drivers, which are very often found in the frontline during architecture development and transformation work. In this respect, process drivers have to participate in transformation work, throughout all phases of the ADM cycle. In some cases, it is the creation of an architecture project that triggers the implementation of specific process management, which continues beyond the ADM cycle.

12.2.7 BPM, BPMN, standards, and tools

In the context of BPM work, several types of tools are available. In its studies, Gartner® distinguishes BPA (*Business Process Analysis*) tools and BPMS (*Business Process Management Suite*) tools. BPA tools are dedicated to process repository modeling and management, while BPMS tools are positioned as automated process development and deployment platforms. Furthermore, tool publishers are tending to move toward BPMN, which meets the increasing need for a normalized representation language, for both BPA and BPMS tools. BPMN support is available in most UML tools in order to maintain links to other models (such as the class diagram, for example). This proximity of the two standards lends even more weight to BPMN in the context of tool compatibility.

However, the range of process modeling tools is more widely diversified in enterprises. The use of graphical tools (Visio®, PowerPoint®) or office solutions is widespread. This is fine for initial descriptions, which require easy, flexible usage, but quickly turns out to be counterproductive when managing a structured whole over time.

Figure 12.11 shows the evolution of standards linked to BPMN. Three types of standard are represented: modeling languages from which BPMN has resulted, exchange formats, and execution languages (BPEL).

Historically, BPMN was first built as a graphical process notation by the BPMI.org[t] consortium. This consortium merged with the OMG in 2005, resulting in recent versions (2.0) in a more rigorous and formal formulation based on the MOF, XMI, and UML techniques for the definition of the meta-model and the exchange format. The WFMC (WorkFlow Management Coalition) developed XPDL, a process exchange format based on XML and compatible with BPMN. BPEL plays a special role: it is a language and file format that is managed by a process execution engine.

---

[t]http://www.bpmi.org.

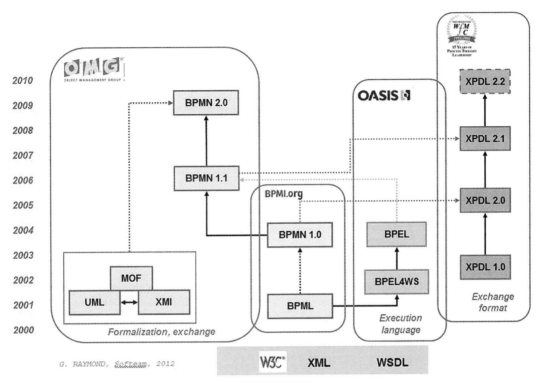

FIGURE 12.11

History of standards linked to BPMN. (For color version of this figure, the reader is referred to the online version of this chapter.)

Even if the BPMN standard defines BPEL mapping rules, the generation of BPEL files from BPMN process models remains a delicate operation,[u,v] BPEL is one way to execute processes, but some runtime platforms can execute BPMN directly, thereby eliminating the need to carry out a transformation.

12.3 INFORMATION

If business processes are at the heart of an enterprise's activity, information constitutes an equally fundamental part. Information systems are primarily built as tools for processing information, and guaranteeing the quality of data remains one of their most critical goals.

Databases are the first image that comes to mind when discussing enterprise information systems. While databases do play a central role, can we really say that they are a unique source of information?

[u]Translating BPMN to BPEL, Chun Ouyang, Wil M.P. van der Aalst, Marlon Dumas, and Arthur H.M. ter Hofstede, 2006, http://eprints.qut.edu.au.
[v]Why BPEL is not the holy grail of the BPM, Pierre Vignéras, 2008, Bull SAS.

In the different activities related to enterprise architecture, we also need to consider the different forms of information handled within a complex organization.

12.3.1 Different types of information in the enterprise
Structured and nonstructured information

In general, we can identify two main categories of information that coexist within an enterprise: structured information and nonstructured information.

- *Structured information* is organized according to a preconceived, defined archetype. Each element of information corresponds to an element that specifies its type and its value domain. These information elements can be handled directly through IT processing. Databases constitute the main support for this type of information.
- *Nonstructured information*, such as textual documents, does not follow a predefined format. It is organized (for example, into chapters), but particular tools are required to process it. This is the field of electronic content management (ECM).

In recent times, two opposing movements have emerged. On the one hand, the transfer of a large amount of nonstructured information to a structured formulation: an order previously transmitted via a paper order form is now directly entered into a form via a website. On the other hand, the multiplication of nonstructured information in all its different forms: electronic messages, videos, forums, and so on. Let's not forget that the number of documents available within an organization is often considerable, and that these documents contain a large proportion of its know-how.[w]

Enterprises (and their employees) have opened up to the outside world, and this has further extended the boundaries of their communication. How can one not regard the web as a gigantic reservoir of nonstructured information?

Consequently, concentrating all efforts on structured information is too restrictive, and does not allow the reality of work modes today to be taken into account. Enterprise architecture also means looking into intranets, document organization, or the efficient management of electronic mail systems.[x]

Resources and messages

Like stocks and flows, information is presented in two different ways:

- *Persistent information*, or resources, which last beyond business activities and processes.
- *Exchanged information*, in the form of messages whose content has a limited duration.

By definition, a client repository or a regulatory document contains persistent information. However, interapplication flows do not last. It is clear that persistent information requires special management in order to guarantee that it remains pertinent throughout its lifecycle. This is typically the field of the MDM (*Master Data Management*), which uses enterprise data synchronization and general management tools. However, the information transmitted during exchanges is more volatile and subject to fewer constraints. We will see that this can lead to some confusion.

---

[w]The TOGAF reference document is part of this nonstructured information.
[x]A study by the Radical Group shows that executives receive an average of 80 e-mails per day, directly impacting their productivity. A French enterprise is even considering withdrawing this type of exchange in the future.

Table 12.2 Examples of Different Types of Information

	Persistent	**Exchange**
Structured	Database	Interapplication flows
Nonstructured	Documents, intranet	E-mail

Table 12.2 summarizes the different types of information that we have just discussed, with examples corresponding to the different possible cases.

> Note: The big issue is that people confuse the schemas for persistent data sources with the schemas for exchanged data, hoping there is some simple automated mapping between the two. There generally isn't and these need to be modeled more or less independently. This point is crucial and must be managed accordingly (see Section 12.3.2).

12.3.2 **Data exchange in the system**

Automatic data exchange is widely used in information systems. This can be synchronous exchanges between two components, or batch processing run at fixed times.

In all cases, automatic processing means that structured data must be used. However, persistent data and exchange data are organized in very different ways.

While persistent data is organized according to strict procedures (by respecting normal forms in relational databases), exchange data is organized in a much less regimented manner. Its content is above all driven by pragmatic, needs-driven considerations: a message[y] will convey the contract and the last 10 orders placed by a client, for example (Figure 12.12).

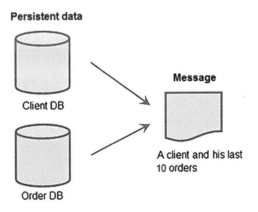

FIGURE 12.12

Persistent data and exchange data.

---

[y]We also see the term business data type (BDT): Business Component Factory, Peter Herzum & Oliver Sims, Wiley Computing Publishing, 2000.

These data exchanges have been present for a long time in information systems. This is the famous "spaghetti" that is presented as the worst possible thing in architecture. The negative nature of this culinary comparison mainly underlines the chaotic aspect when links proliferate between applications. The structure and content of information flows is progressively constituted from localized needs, with no real overall plan. The increase in exchanges goes hand in hand with the multiplication of messages, which in turn leads to an increase in complexity. A colleague recently told us that more than 6000 different types of messages were catalogued in his enterprise, some of which are used in the most basic of ways.

Faced with this type of situation, some enterprises have chosen to undertake normalization and rationalization work through the centralized definition of messages (centralized or common format). The aim of this work is to reduce the number of duplicates (for example, the existence of several, virtually identical "contract" messages), and to facilitate connections between application elements. The use of technologies linked to web services facilitates this rationalization work, notably the use of XML documents to support exchanges; messages are specified using XML schemas,[z] which enable the structure of exchanged information to be automatically checked.

That said, there is a "natural" diversity in the messages exchanged. This diversity, which is well known, is the expression of the sheer number of viewpoints that coexist within an enterprise, just like the "client" type, which is dealt with in different ways by the marketing, invoicing, or delivery departments.

What is the relationship between persistent data and exchange data? In general, a message does not consist of a simple copy of persistent data. Its content can come from several items of data, either as the result of a conglomeration of a set of properties or as a value calculated from a set of properties.

Work on harmonizing and industrializing messages is confronted with two paradoxical stumbling blocks: on the one hand, imposing too much proximity between exchange data and persistent data (in other words, between messages and database tables) and, on the other hand, allowing uncontrolled structures to proliferate, resulting in unmanaged situations.

In any case, the search for a balance between these two extremes is one of the main aspects of enterprise architecture work.

12.3.3 Managing interoperability

On this question, TOGAF provides a classification consisting of four degrees[aa]:

- Degree 1: Unstructured data exchange, entirely handled by human participants (exchange of documents)
- Degree 2: Structured data exchange, which requires some manual exchange operations (reception, distribution)
- Degree 3: Seamless data sharing, based on a shared exchange format
- Degree 4: Extension of degree 3: A set of cooperating applications based on a reference model

---

[z]An XML schema is used to specify the structure and content of an XML document.
[aa]TOGAF9 29.4 From the Canadian Department of National Defense and NATO.

Phase B: Inter-stakeholder Information Interoperability Requirements (Using degrees of information interoperability)							
Stakeholders	A	B	C	D	E	F	G
A		2	3	2	3	3	3
B	2		3	2	3	2	2
C	3	3		2	2	2	3
D	2	2	2		3	3	3
E	4	4	2	3		3	3
F	4	4	2	3	3		2
G	2	2	3	3	3	3	

FIGURE 12.13

Business information interoperability matrix—TOGAF9. (For color version of this figure, the reader is referred to the online version of this chapter.)

The choice of exchange mode is a key issue, with repercussions on both work organization and implemented applications.

In the context of a transformation project, earlier choices are regularly questioned, for example, to move toward increased automation of exchanges or to better centralize information that is spread across several repositories.

Here again, the choice of solution must take different factors into consideration (organization, IT, cost). Above all, the aim is to justify choices with regard to real business results. For example, is the replacement of a nonstructured document transmission by a structured data exchange really relevant?

It should be pointed out here that this question concerns exchanges in general, and not only exchanges between applications. In phase B notably, the question of exchanges between business actors arises. The following matrix[bb] presents an overview of the type of interaction between different users. Each cell qualifies the type of exchange between users using degrees from the aforementioned list (from 1 to 4) (Figure 12.13).

This type of representation will also be used for gap analysis, between the types of exchange in place and those that are envisaged in the new architecture.

12.4 FUNDAMENTAL CONCEPTS

The following fundamental concepts were introduced in this chapter:

- SOA: Style of architecture based on the concept of service, designed to simplify interactions between architecture blocks while providing the system with significant flexibility.
- Business process: Correlated set of activities that produces tangible added value from an initial request (the trigger event).
- Information types: Information can be classified into structured/nonstructured and persistent/exchanged.

[bb]TOGAF9, Figure 29-1.

Testimonials

CHAPTER OUTLINE

13.1 INTRODUCTION

This chapter contains contributions from two companies concerning their approach to enterprise architecture and TOGAF. These two contributions come from two rather different contexts. The first is provided by Marc Laburte, Enterprise Architecture Manager for Higher Education and Research Establishments. Reporting directly to the French Ministry for Higher Education and Research, this organization coordinates several higher education establishments, while respecting their autonomy with regard to their functioning and diversity. This is one example of the government system architecture work being carried out all over the world to meet new user needs and handle increased user exchanges.

    The second contribution is provided by EDF, one of the global leaders in the field of electric energy. Roland Gueye, Senior Project Officer with the Information Systems Division of the EDF Group, presents the work being carried out within the EDG group to take into account the emergence of new client services. The arrival of Smart Grid-type techniques in particular will have a big impact on systems and collaboration between systems on an international scale (proposals for a reference standard in the field, such as the Smart Grid Architecture Model, reflect the importance of the changes that are underway).

13.2 TOGAF WITHIN THE AMUE

13.2.1 The author

Marc Laburte is senior consultant in enterprise architecture in charge of elaborating and maintaining the architecture of the IT system for the higher education and research establishments within the AMUE.

13.2.2 Presentation of the AMUE

The AMUE[a] is the French university service operator in charge of coordinating the information systems used in higher education establishments. The AMUE organizes mutualization between its members (universities, higher education establishments, the Ministry for Higher Education and Research) and supports common projects with a view to improving the quality of their governance and process.

The main missions of the AMUE are as follows:

- To contribute to the development of its member establishments' information technology system
- To enable its members to use a multifaceted range of software that meets their diverse needs
- To accompany its members in their change and modernization projects with regard to strategy and governance

Some figures: 169 members are represented within the AMUE, including 90 universities and 79 higher education establishments, engineering schools, and institutions.

As an interest group, the AMUE does not manage an organization's system (such as, an IT system), but rather a community of independent systems. This implies a particular type of organization, based on collaboration between different participants and a common range of high-quality services that meet everyone's needs (coaching, methodologies, training, provision of solutions, maintenance, start-up assistance, etc.).

It should be noted that historically each French higher education establishment has had a certain level of autonomy with regard to its budget and decision making. This autonomy has been strengthened over the past year since the application of a recent law in this area.[b] In particular, each university manages its own Information System, its content and architecture.

Naturally, this autonomy, which allows each establishment to closely manage its own mode of functioning, is not contradictory with the existence of similar processes, notably at the heart of the business. These can be translated in information systems through the pooling of components or applications provided by the AMUE. This community must also take into account regulatory evolutions and technological changes, in accordance with international standards. The support that the AMUE provides to higher education establishments also contributes to the implementation of innovations linked to new work modes (dematerialization, mobility, digital) in order to provide its users with optimum services.

---

[a]Agence de mutualisation des universités et établissements d'enseignement supérieur et de recherche.
[b]This law mainly anticipates that by January 1, 2014, all universities will be autonomous with regard to their budgets and the management of their human resources, and that they will be able to become the owners of their real estate properties. This management autonomy has reinforced the need for these operators of the Higher Education Ministry to have their own information systems.

13.2.3 The Government Architecture Reference Model (GARM) of the French state's IS

Since 2011, the French state has been working on a program focused on the modernization of its systems. Continuing the work begun by ministerial and interministerial initiatives already carried out in the digital field, this cross-ministry program will allow a new phase to begin, with work in four main areas:

- Orientation of all those involved in state information and communication systems, through the definition of norms and repositories and the adoption of innovative practices
- Performance steering and risk management by improving the visibility of information system project costs and value
- Conduct of pooling operations between different state departments
- Provision of assistance and advice to ministries, operators, and all those involved in the GARM

These missions therefore apply to universities and higher education and research establishments that depend on the Ministry for Higher Education, for whom they are operators in the same way as the AMUE.

To tackle the complexity of information system change, and to make it simpler, more reactive, and more flexible, the State has adopted an EA approach. This is a long-term legacy change and steering approach, described in the *common State EA Framework*. This reference framework is based notably on TOGAF in terms of its structure and change processes[c] (see Figure 13.1).

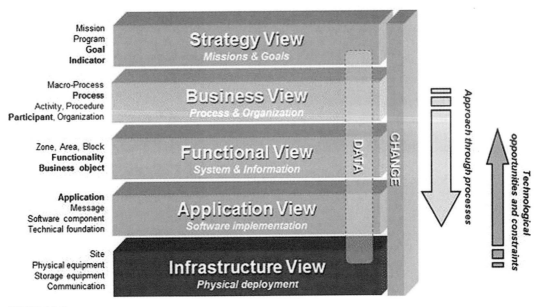

FIGURE 13.1

Overview of the GARM EA framework. (For color version of this figure, the reader is referred to the online version of this chapter.)

---

[c]http://references.modernisation.gouv.fr/sites/default/files/Cadre-Commun-d_Urbanisation-du-SI-de-l_Etat-v1.0.pdf.

The functional view plays a special role in the orientation of change trajectories, notably to increase pooling of cross-organizational functionalities, to organize data sharing, and to refocus the information system on the agent and the user. This functional view, which is more stable over time, enables the reduction of coupling between business and organizational requirements on the one hand, and technical problems and choices on the other hand. Built and maintained independently of technological questions (application and infrastructure view), but also independently of business and organization processes (business view), it facilitates the agility and flexibility of the information system. The functional view thereby constitutes the foundation on which the organization and structuring of the governance necessary to the long-term management of IS change is based.

13.2.4 The AMUE, establishments, and the GARM in the EA approach

The implementation of this common framework has led the AMUE to implement an overall approach with the establishments it supports in order to:

- Respect the GARM as an operator of the Ministry for Higher Education and Research, and therefore the state
- To implement the GARM in a higher education and research context
- To facilitate change in university information systems, in connection with that of the Ministry and the state, by defining trajectories

The work of the AMUE is broken down into three main actions: (1) the elaboration of an inventory of what exists through the application mapping of the different university systems; (2) the development of a common consistency framework with the ministry and the establishments; and (3) the implementation of a first change project concerning reference data and exchange data.

Organization

This work is driven by dual-level governance, with a strategic level and an operational level.

Strategic governance through a Higher Education IS steering committee defines the overall strategy of the IS for all higher education operators by validating change trajectories and arbitrates where necessary. This committee includes participants such as the Ministry of Higher Education and Research, the Conference of University Presidents, the AMUE, and representatives of AMUE members.

Operational governance through a change steering committee monitors the progress of change and its deployment across the different establishments. This operational governance involves participants who are representatives of establishments, the CPU, and the AMUE.

Mapping what already exists

One of the first activities to carry out is the establishment of an inventory of all the applications that make up the IS of the establishments and their integration (exchanges, etc.), since these exchanges can come from numerous sources such as:

- Applications that belong to the establishment (development or purchase)
- Applications from the AMUE range
- Applications from a range developed via interestablishment collaboration through an association
- Applications developed from shared development forges
- Open-source software from organizations such as Apache, Internet 2, moodle, and so on

This inventory enables the subsequent realization through reengineering of a classification plan at the functional level.

Developing consistency frameworks

Alongside this modeling at the functional and application level, a consistency framework implementation approach is used with the Ministry and the establishments across all support domains, such as finance, human resources, and legacy, as well as the core of the business, schooling, student life, and research. For each domain, these consistency frameworks include the modeling of business processes, listings, regulations, and the data dictionary.

Bearing in mind these two approaches, it is therefore necessary to carry out "docking" operations between these business elements and the functional and application definition of the IS.

It should be noted that in this context, the modeling of an IS varies from one establishment to another, potentially with some identical "bricks" being shared, although not necessarily being implemented in the same way. This point highlights the need for shared mapping repositories, developed in a highly collaborative context. Furthermore, certain establishments have processes of their own that are linked to their specific field of teaching or research.

Reference data and shared data

Earlier work has shown that communication and data sharing were a priority in the work to be carried out. This sharing takes several forms: data exchanged within the IS, between universities, communication with departments of the Ministry for Higher Education, local authorities, or different national or international organizations.

In this context, a project has been launched with a view to steering and putting in place shared data processes and management, along with associated tools.

We have chosen to deal with the following points:

- The identification of reference data and its governance
- The definition of pivot exchange data formats, initially concerning the core of the business
- The realization and deployment of exchange and synchronization tools in establishments

In our context, the diversity of systems, both from a technical standpoint and a functional standpoint, constitutes a key point that must be properly managed. Sharing information means that everyone involved must have a common vision in the form of identical data formats, and also means that all systems must take into account any modifications that are made. This has led us to favor MDM-type[d] implementations, which facilitate synchronization and ensure better exchange continuity.

Modeling pivot formats is necessary because it must be possible to use this data in the context of a governance strategy, which pertains to businesses. Similarly, the implementation of tools dedicated to managing these repositories (MDM) and that include their modeling must integrate perfectly with the tool in order to ensure a single, reliable model.

This program is implemented progressively through deployment in a certain number of pilot establishments before generalized deployment.

Findings and thoughts

In the context of our work, it quickly became clear that modeling is an indispensable activity. Given the volumes involved and the assigned timescales, not to mention the diversity of the stakeholders, it is obvious that this work needs to be managed in order to be better mastered. This means using an iterative approach, which avoids the proliferation of heterogeneous models.

---

[d]MDM (Master Data Management).

The first goal is not to dive into modeling work full tilt using detailed graphical diagrams. We have chosen to start with more accessible representations such as matrices or catalogs, which are easier to build and communicate on; for example, the application matrix, which should itself provide the elements necessary to the realization of links between different views of the model (function and process, for example).

This representation foundation constitutes an information base that is progressively added to according to identified needs, for example, in the form of detailed modeling of business processes or reference data by domain.

Today, the GARM does not provide detailed models or tools to realize this modeling and change management. A workgroup has been created by the AMUE and establishments to complete the metamodel through the artifacts necessary to the construction of the IS repositories. This work is based, among other things, on the TOGAF concept of "viewpoints" with regard to the choice of models to use. In this context, the TOGAF approach provides highly pertinent recommendations based on best practices for both the selection of models and their implementation in a tool.

This tooling constitutes an essential part of the enterprise architecture repository. Beyond modeling itself, this tool should provide the elements necessary to the context, such as:

- Teamwork management
- Standard-compliant import and export features (UML, BPMN, XML, XMI, etc.)
- Change management functionalities (scenarios, impacts, etc.)

More generally, we have used the TOGAF framework for two points. First, in the context of the French state system architectures, which partially use TOGAF structures and recommendations with regard to modeling (architecture content framework). This aspect introduces a first layer of international normalization that meets the need to exchange and share common terminology. Second, in the steering and implementation of change projects, which are similar to an "ADM cycle"-type path and associated TOGAF practices.

13.2.5 Useful links

See the following references for the common government architecture framework:

- Australian Government Architecture Reference Models: http://agict.gov.au/policy-guides-procurement/australian-government-architecture-aga/aga-rm
- Federal enterprise architecture (United States): http://en.wikipedia.org/wiki/Federal_enterprise_architecture

13.3 TOGAF WITHIN THE EDF GROUP

13.3.1 The author

Roland Gueye is senior project manager in the EDF Group Information Systems Department, where he is in charge of the Enterprise Architecture capabilities. Roland assists lines of business in the realization of strategic change through the use of enterprise architecture. He is currently working on Smart Grid applications and related information and communication technologies. He is TOGAF 9 certified.

13.3.2 EDF Group[e]

The EDF Group is a leading electricity player, active in all major electricity businesses: generation, transport, distribution, marketing, and energy trading. It has a turnover of €72.7 billion, an installed capacity of 139.5 GW, 39.3 million customers, an R&D budget of €523 million, and 159,740 employees worldwide. The EDF Group is mostly present in France, the United Kingdom, and Italy. It is also present in many other countries around the world such as Poland, Belgium, Hungary, Slovakia, Austria, Russia, Brazil, the United States, and China.

13.3.3 Choice of TOGAF and awareness campaign undertaken

Since 2012, the EDF Group has expanded governance of its information systems to its main subsidiaries. In this context, the EDF Group CIO office is pursuing alignment of all its internal practices (governance, enterprise architecture, security, project management, etc.) with international best practices (COBIT, PRINCE2, ISO/IEC 27000, etc.).

In regard to the practice of enterprise architecture, the TOGAF framework has been chosen to serve as a template for the creation of a reference framework specific to the EDF Group and the context of the gas and electricity sector to support the EDF Group in its various change projects.

Several dimensions are dealt with:

- The reference framework (approach, methods, etc.)
- Human and organizational factors (skills, responsibilities, governance)
- The content repository (rules, use cases, IS knowledge, reusable components, etc.) in order to encourage capitalization and reuse
- The tools necessary to modeling activities and the creation of a content repository

In terms of human and organizational factors, several awareness campaigns have been undertaken to facilitate the development of a new TOGAF culture within concerned departments: the inclusion of certified training in the training catalog, the organization of events on enterprise architecture, the creation of an enterprise architecture community, the participation of EDF enterprise architecture practitioners in operations developed by The Open Group, the strengthening of enterprise architecture governance at group level, the reduction of certain overly localized operations, and so on.

13.3.4 Enterprise architecture work applied to the emergence of Smart Grid applications

Concerning the work on the initialization of a framework and a content repository specific to the EDF Group, transformation projects undertaken by the group due to the emergence of Smart Grid[f] applications were chosen. These transformation projects constitute a life-size experiment facilitating the

---

[e]See the www.edf.com website.
[f]Smart Grid is commonly understood as the modernization of the power system to address known shortcomings of the energy delivery infrastructure, leveraging advancement in IT, communication, operational technology (OT), emerging energy technologies, and consumer technologies. In addition to providing ubiquitous, reliable and reasonably priced energy to consumers, the Smart Grid will help society to address energy sustainability concerns (Gartner, Hype Cycle for Smart Grid Technologies, 2013).

emergence of a reference framework and a content repository, which can then be adapted to other business topics of the group. As highlighted by Philippe Desfray and Gilbert Raymond in the first part of this book, it is better to *avoid defining your architecture framework "above ground" and to use a concrete example, based on a real evolution before embarking on your first TOGAF ADM cycle.*

Among the factors favorable to these Smart Grid transformation projects, let us mention the following:

- The high level of momentum in Europe around this issue (see an example of the work of the European M/490 mandate below).
- The innovation dynamic within the EDF Group itself, associating R&D, IT, strategy, marketing, sales, and logistics in collaborative work and experimental projects.
- The number of business domains concerned (from electricity distribution network management operations to the marketing of electricity and related services), both in France and in other countries where the EDF Group operates.
- The naturally central role of information and communication technologies (ICT) in these transformation projects.

The TOGAF repository provides elements (principles, concepts, vocabulary, methods, etc.) that already enable participants in the gas and electricity sector in Europe to gradually develop an enterprise architecture reference framework specific to this move toward Smart Grid applications.

The results of several studies clearly show the progressive implementation of the components of this type of sector-based framework, in accordance with numerous TOGAF principles. All are possible candidates for inclusion in the EDF enterprise continuum.

This is the case, for example, with the SGAM (Smart Grid Architecture Model) framework produced by the Smart Grids Task Force in the context of European mandate M/490.[g]

The SGAM is a model that describes electrical systems from several viewpoints (business, function, information, etc.), and that is adapted to the requirements and particularities of electricity markets in Europe (Figure 13.2).

If we move beyond the strictly European context and take a look at international standards, the Smart Grid standards identification work carried out by the International Electrotechnical Commission is also worth mentioning.[h] As a reminder, the IEC is the international standards organization in charge of electricity electronics and related techniques (Figure 13.3).

On the subject of best practices in methods, we can also mention the work of the Software Engineering Institute (Carnegie Mellon University) on the SGMM (Smart Grid Maturity Model), which is used to assess the maturity of an electricity sector company with regard to Smart Grid transformation based on eight key areas of analysis (see Figure 13.4). This model naturally finds its place in the preliminary phase prior to a TOGAF ADM cycle.

Still on the subject of best practices in methods, we can cite the work of the International Requirements Engineering Board (IREB) in the field of requirements engineering, work that usefully complements TOGAF's recommendations on requirements management and that constitutes the central part of the TOGAF Architecture Development Method (ADM).[i]

---

[g]See http://ec.europa.eu/energy/gas_electricity/smartgrids/smartgrids_en.htm.
[h]See http://smartgridstandardsmap.com.
[i]See http://specief.org/ and http://www.certified-re.de/en/.

The work on introducing an enterprise architecture framework based on TOGAF (analyzing various materials for inclusion in the EDF enterprise continuum, training, etc.) to support Smart Grid transformation projects within the EDF Group continues on the basis of these few examples of international standards and best practices, as well as many other external[j] and internal contributions that are not presented here.

- X: Domain
- Y: Interoperability (Layer)
- Z: Zone

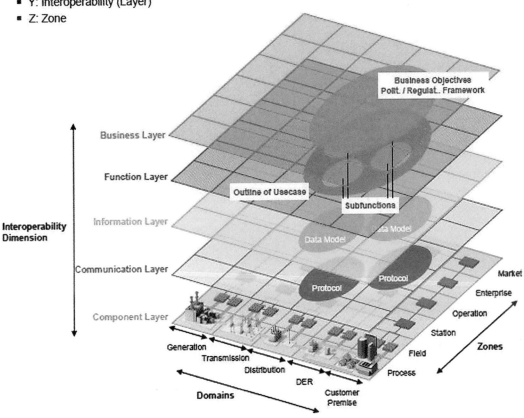

FIGURE 13.2

Smart Grid Architecture Model overview.[k] (For color version of this figure, the reader is referred to the online version of this chapter.)

[j]See also *Standardization in Smart Grids: Introduction to IT-Related Methodologies, Architecture and Standards* (Springer-Verlag, 2013) for an overview of the various building blocks and standards identified by the CEN, CENELEC, and ETSI Smart Grids Coordination Group.
[k]Source: CEN-CENELEC-ETSI Smart Grid Coordination Group.

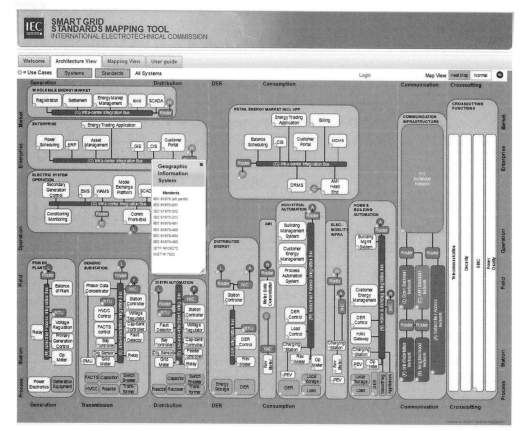

FIGURE 13.3

IEC Smart Grid standards mapping tool (©IEC). (For color version of this figure, the reader is referred to the online version of this chapter.)

FIGURE 13.4

Key areas of analysis of the Smart Grid Maturity Model (SGMM). (For color version of this figure, the reader is referred to the online version of this chapter.)

13.3.5 Useful links

- http://www.edf.com
- http://ec.europa.eu/energy/gas_electricity/smartgrids/smartgrids_en.htm
- http://www.sei.cmu.edu/smartgrid
- http://smartgridstandardsmap.com
- http://specief.org/
- http://www.certified-re.de/en/

ArchiMate

14

ArchiMate is a modeling standard published by The Open Group. ArchiMate has defined a modeling language dedicated to TOGAF from scratch. EAP, on the other hand, has taken the route of reusing and adapting existing standards (UML, BPMN, and UML profiles), both in order to benefit from tools already present in the marketplace and to address a wide community of practitioners already familiar with UML and BPMN.

This chapter briefly presents the ArchiMate standard and shows how ArchiMate and EAP are mapped.

14.1 THE ARCHIMATE STANDARD

The *ArchiMate*[a] modeling language is dedicated to enterprise architecture modeling. Originally initiated outside of The Open Group and TOGAF, it then joined The Open Group and introduced mappings to TOGAF. ArchiMate often refers to TOGAF when specifying specific terms. ArchiMate is now linked to the evolution of TOGAF and is currently evolving to fit TOGAF more closely.

ArchiMate has a core modeling language, and extensions, such as the "Motivation" extension (goals, objectives, etc.) and the "Implementation and Migration" extensions. ArchiMate, like EAP, proposes predefined viewpoints. These viewpoints, as specified by TOGAF, can be adapted to the context of the enterprise and the focus of the enterprise architecture activity.

---

[a]http://www.archimate.nl/. ArchiMate® is a modeling language dedicated to enterprise architecture and is one of the standards published by The Open Group.

ArchiMate structures a model according to the following principles:

- A "Business Architecture" level, which is broken down into the following sublevels:
  - Information
  - Product
  - Process
  - Organization
- An "Application Architecture" level, which is broken down into the following sublevels:
  - Data
  - Application
- A "Technology Architecture" level

ArchiMate therefore uses three top-level TOGAF architecture domains, with data architecture being split between business architecture (Information) and application architecture (Data). The business level handles business information, enterprise organization, business processes, and products. The organization of the model in this book uses the same principle (Figure 14.1).

This structuring is by no means mandatory. The definition of enterprise-specific viewpoints can notably lead to different meanings. For example, we can imagine an additional viewpoint dedicated to system security.

The core language of ArchiMate consists of three main types of elements: active structure elements (business actors, application components, devices, etc.), behavior elements (processes, interactions, use cases, etc.), and passive structure elements (business entities, etc.).

- Active structure elements are entities capable of performing behavior.
- Behavior elements are units of activity performed by one or several active structure elements.
- Passive structure elements are objects on which behavior is performed, such as data.

ArchiMate is strongly focused on the concept of "service," which is a unit of functionality that a system exposes to its environment.

Besides the core aspects of ArchiMate, there are aspects not explicitly covered by ArchiMate, such as goals, principles and requirements, risk and security, governance, policies and business rules, costs, performance, timing, planning, and evolution.

FIGURE 14.1

TOGAF model default structure with EAP. (For color version of this figure, the reader is referred to the online version of this chapter.)

The "Motivation" extension adds "motivational" concepts such as goals, objectives, principles, requirements, stakeholders, drivers, and assessments.

The "Motivation" extension enables the support of requirements management, the preliminary phase and phase A of TOGAF.

ArchiMate's "Implementation and Motivation" extension adds concepts to support the later ADM phases, related to the implementation and migration of architecture: phase E (Opportunities and Solutions), phase F (Migration Planning), and phase G (Implementation Governance). The main concepts are "work package," "deliverable," and "gap."

14.2 ARCHIMATE TO EAP CORRESPONDENCE EXAMPLES

We are now going to present several model examples, taken from the ArchiMate standard, and show how they translate in EAP.

14.2.1 Business layer

EAP distinguishes organization units as a specific kind of actor (Figures 14.2 and 14.3).

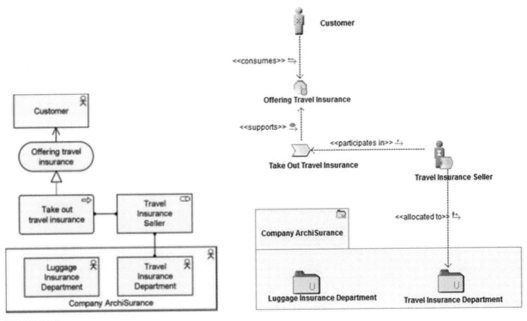

FIGURE 14.2

Business Actor model using ArchiMate and EAP. (For color version of this figure, the reader is referred to the online version of this chapter.)

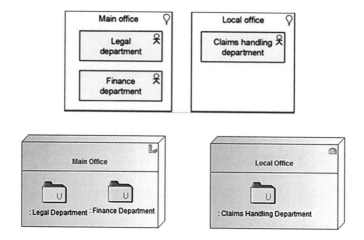

FIGURE 14.3

Modeling locations using ArchiMate and EAP. (For color version of this figure, the reader is referred to the online version of this chapter.)

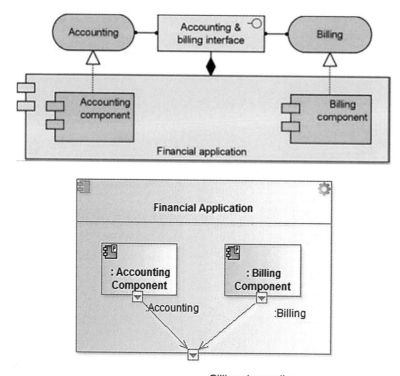

FIGURE 14.4

Modeling application components using ArchiMate and EAP. (For color version of this figure, the reader is referred to the online version of this chapter.)

By reusing UML, EAP takes advantage of its complete and detailed metamodel. In this example, the deployed occurrences are specific entities within EAP, thus enabling specific properties and values to be allocated to them.

14.2.2 Application layer

Many ArchiMate concepts are inspired by the UML2 standard. EAP directly reused the UML2 definition. As in TOGAF and EAP, the main concept is "Application Component."

As shown in Figure 14.4, we see in this example that EAP takes advantage of the UML2 deployment facility. EAP benefits from UML assembly mechanisms through ports and connectors.

14.2.3 Technology layer

UML2's deployment mechanism is very useful at this stage to express, for example, how application components are distributed on execution hardware. ArchiMate reuses the UML2 "Node" concept, but in a simpler, more restricted context (Figures 14.5 and 14.6).

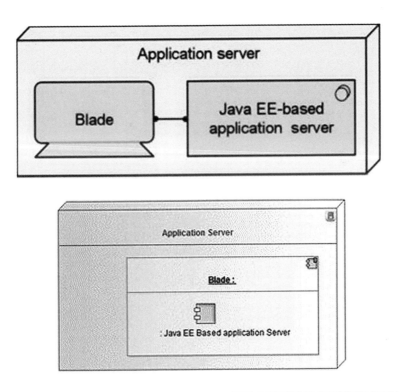

FIGURE 14.5

Modeling an application server node using ArchiMate and EAP. (For color version of this figure, the reader is referred to the online version of this chapter.)

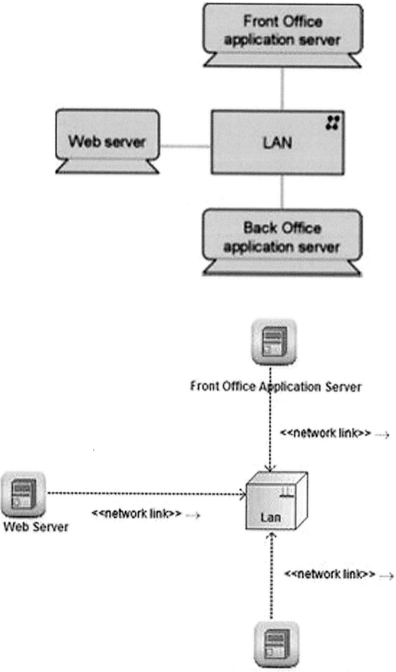

FIGURE 14.6

Modeling connected servers using ArchiMate and EAP. (For color version of this figure, the reader is referred to the online version of this chapter.)

14.3 **DETAILED MAPPING**

The following table presents Modeliosoft Enterprise Architect Solution's support of the ArchiMate standard.

Please note that wherever there is a discrepancy between names, TOGAF terms have been chosen over ArchiMate terms.

Notations are primarily based on the UML and BPMN standards.

From the examples and this table, we can see that there are many similarities. EAP can be considered as a way to implement ArchiMate by reusing UML and BPMN, or in short as a UML profile for ArchiMate.

ArchiMate Concept	EAP/TOGAF Concept	Comments	Notation
Business Layer			
Business actor	Actor	Internal actor and external actor are explained by EAP	
Business role	Role		
Business collaboration	Business collaboration		
Business interface		No real usage identified	
Location	Location	Headquarters and sites	
Business object	Business entity		
Business process	Business process		
Business function	Function		
Business interaction	Business interaction	UML interaction	
Business event	Event		

Continued

ArchiMate Concept	EAP/TOGAF Concept	Comments	Notation
Business service	Business service		
Representation		No real usage identified	
Meaning	Term	This concept is little developed in ArchiMate, but extensively developed in the Modelio "dictionary"	
Value	Value factor on Function		
Product	Product		
Contract	Service contract	Preconditions, postconditions, invariants	
Application Layer			
Application component	Application component	Enterprise Architect Solution breaks components down using component typology to facilitate sound SOA structuring	
Application collaboration	Application collaboration		
Application interface	Required or provided services		
Data object	Entity or business entity		
Application function		No real usage identified. The notion of "Function" does not seem to be relevant to "Application Architecture," and does not fit an SOA-oriented approach	
Application interaction		UML interaction on collaboration	
Application service	Information service		

ArchiMate Concept	EAP/TOGAF Concept	Comments	Notation
Technical Layer			
Node	Node	Generic element	
Device	Server, workstation, etc.	More detailed list on EAP	
Network	Bus		
Communication path	Network link		<<network link>>
Infrastructure interface	Port		
System software	Utility component		
Infrastructure function		No real usage identified	
Infrastructure service	IS service		
Artifact	Technology artifact		
Relationships			
Association	Association		
Access	Flow		<<flow>>
Use by	Consumes	"Consumes" is reserved for actors. For other elements, backward "supports" links	«consumes»
Realization	Component realization	Specialized in Enterprise Architect Solution on components	«realizes
Assignment	Initiator of; participates in; owner of	Enterprise Architect Solution provides more specialized links	«participates in»
Aggregation	Aggregation		
Composition	Composition		

Continued

ArchiMate Concept	EAP/TOGAF Concept	Comments	Notation
Flow	Flow		
Triggering	Flow		
Grouping		Packages and embedding	
Junction		BPMN junction	
Specialization	Generalization		
Extensions			
Language extension mechanisms	Profiles, MDA		
Driver, Goal	Goals	Detailed by specific properties and diagrams in Modelio. The distinction between Driver and Goal can be made through different "containers" or by using specific properties	
Requirement	Requirement	Detailed by specific properties and diagrams in Modelio	
Aggregation	Part		
Realization	Satisfies	OMG SysML norm	«satisfy»
Influence	Positive influence; negative influence		<<+ influence>> <<- influence>>
Aggregation	Aggregation		
Deployment		Modeliosoft Enterprise Architect Solution enables application components to be directly deployed on nodes	

14.4 FUNDAMENTAL CONCEPTS

The following fundamental concepts were introduced in this chapter:

- ArchiMate: Modeling language dedicated to enterprise architecture modeling; related to TOGAF.

The EAP Profile

15

CHAPTER OUTLINE

A UML profile is a mechanism used to adapt and extend the UML standard to specific purposes. The EAP profile defines a UML adaptation for enterprise architecture modeling using TOGAF. The EAP profile enables any UML modeling tool (that also implements BPMN) to support TOGAF enterprise architecture modeling. This chapter presents concept mapping and shows how UML is extended to support TOGAF.

15.1 MAPPING UML AND BPMN TO TOGAF

15.1.1 How UML and BPMN are used to support TOGAF modeling

UML and BPMN are widely adopted standards for business, software, and system modeling. UML in particular has gathered the most popular modeling techniques, thereby providing a very complete set of modeling concepts (metaclasses) on which most TOGAF concepts can be mapped. BPMN is the modeling language of choice for business process modeling. It can be used as such (without dedicated extensions) for TOGAF enterprise architecture. Although UML and BPMN are standards from the same organization (OMG), they are separate entities, and some redundancies exist between them. Since there exist a very large number of modeling tools that support both UML and BPMN, this is not an issue in practice. The coverage of TOGAF modeling is therefore obtained by extending UML through the EAP profile and using BPMN (Figure 15.1).

UML is perceived as a technical modeling language that may not be presented to some enterprise architecture stakeholders. Therefore the EAP profile "hides" UML, and only notions defined in the profile are accessible to architects, with a specific notation dedicated to the different kinds of stakeholders.

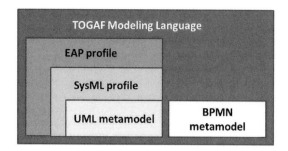

FIGURE 15.1

Architecture of EAP to gather modeling standards for TOGAF. (For color version of this figure, the reader is referred to the online version of this chapter.)

EAP is also based on other standards that complement UML and BPMN: SysML, where a requirement analysis profile is defined, and a business motivation metamodel (BMM) that has been used to define a UML profile.

15.1.2 Conventions for presenting EAP extensions

A profile definition is presented as a specific metamodel that appears as a class diagram presenting concepts from UML (showing the "uml." name prefix) and extensions from EAP (in a profile, extensions are called "stereotypes"). The (BLACK ARROW) link represents an "extension," meaning that the "Component" concept from UML has been extended in the "Application Component" concept from EAP. It provides the mapping (the "Application Component" EAP/TOGAF concept maps to the "Component" UML concept) (Figure 15.2).

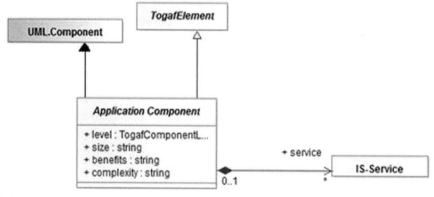

FIGURE 15.2

The EAP/TOGAF "Application Component" concept extends the UML "Component" metaclass. (For color version of this figure, the reader is referred to the online version of this chapter.)

This chapter presents only the essential part of the mapping metamodel. The full metamodel can be downloaded from www.togaf_modeling.org/xxx, and the XMI profile can be obtained at www.togaf_modeling.org/xxx.

15.2 VISION AND REQUIREMENTS

EAP supports the TOGAF vision concepts by implementing the OMG BMM standard. It also reuses the SysML standard profile to support requirement analysis. We see below that there is one extension to SysML in the requirement metaclass to provide the "guarantee" link between requirements and goals.

The concepts related to the "dictionary" (term, dictionary) are also introduced at this stage (Figure 15.3).

TOGAF Element	UML Mapping	Icon	Definition
Goal/ objective	Class		Strategic or operational goal of the enterprise; determines the enterprise's orientations
Requirement	Class		Aptitude required by the enterprise or the IS
Term	Class		Term of the glossary; definition of a concept
Negative influence	Dependency	<<- influence>>	Established between two goals; the origin hinders the realization of the destination
Positive influence	Dependency	<<+ influence>>	Established between two goals; the origin facilitates the realization of the destination
Guarantee	Dependency	«guarantee»	Established from a requirement that, when satisfied, guarantees the realization of the goal
Refine	Dependency	«refine»	Established between two requirements; the origin requirement refines the destination requirement
Satisfy	Dependency	«satisfy»	Established between a model element (for example, an application component or a class) and a requirement; the origin element satisfies the requirement
Verify	Dependency	«verify»	Established between a model element (for example, a use case) and a requirement; the origin element tests the requirement
Decompose	Dependency	<<part>>	Established between goals or between requirements; the origin is a part of the destination
Assigned	Dependency	«assigned»	The origin element (role, process, actor, organizational unit) is assigned to the destination goal

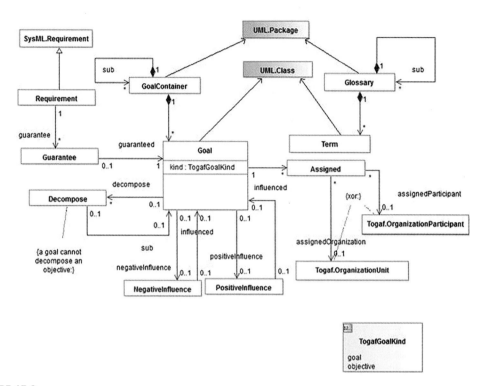

FIGURE 15.3

Profile elements related to Vision and requirement analysis. (For color version of this figure, the reader is referred to the online version of this chapter.)

15.3 GLOBAL STRUCTURE AND ARCHITECTURE DOMAINS

Layers are used to structure an EAP model. The different architecture domains have corresponding layers that can be the root of the associated model (such as the Business Architecture layer). The Business layer, Application layer, and so on are used to further structure their respective domains (Figure 15.4).

TOGAF Element	UML Mapping	Icon	Definition
Layer	Package	(Abstract concept)	Logical grouping, frequently according to TOGAF architecture domains
Business Layer	Package		Groups the business entity (conceptual) model and the business architecture model
Application Layer	Package		Grouping dedicated to application architecture
Business Entities	Package		Grouping dedicated to data architecture at the business architecture level

TOGAF Element	UML Mapping	Icon	Definition
Logical Data Model	Package		Root of the data model, under the application architecture level
Application Architecture	Package		Root of the application architecture model (application components, etc.)
Business Architecture	Package		Root of the business architecture model (processes, etc.)
Technology Architecture	Package		Root of the technology architecture model
Migration	Dependency	-------> «migrates»	Specifies a migration from the origin to the target over two different stages of transition architectures

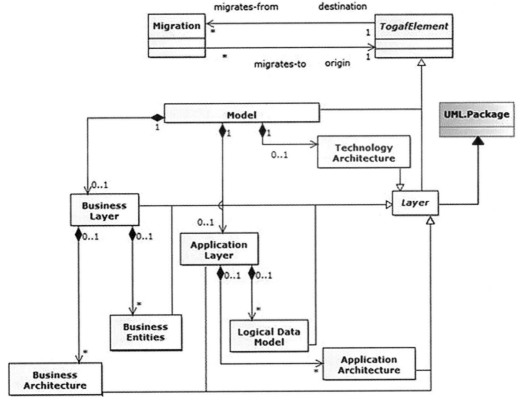

FIGURE 15.4

Generic and structuring part of the EAP profile. (For color version of this figure, the reader is referred to the online version of this chapter.)

15.4 DATA ARCHITECTURE

Business entities are used in business architecture at a conceptual level. A very similar profile model exists for the logical level, with the concepts of Persistent entity, Persistent attribute, Identifier attribute, and Persistent Association (Figure 15.5).

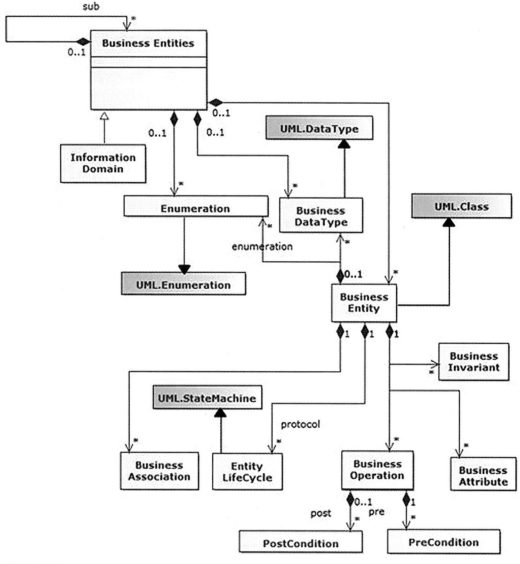

FIGURE 15.5

Profile model of business entities (business architecture level). (For color version of this figure, the reader is referred to the online version of this chapter.)

TOGAF Element	UML Mapping	Icon	Definition
Information Domain	Package		Unit that structures business entities into coherent subdomains
Business Entity	Class	**business entity** attribute : string	Describes the semantics of business entities. (Business class). Can be represented in compact or developed form
Business Association	Association		Association between business entities
Business Operation	Operation		Operation defined on a business entity
Enumeration	Enumeration		Type whose values are predefined literals
Business Data Type	Data Type		Basic type used for business class properties (for example, address)
Pre Condition	Constraint		Condition that must be satisfied before an operation begins
Post Condition	Constraint		Condition that must be satisfied after a business operation is realized
Business Invariant	Constraint		Conditions that must always be true for the occurrences of a business entity
Entity Life Cycle	State Machine		Describes the possible states of an entity and the authorized transitions
Business Attribute	Attribute		Property of a "business entity"
State	State		Represents one stable state of a business entity or a product

Continued

TOGAF Element	UML Mapping	Icon	Definition
Persistent Entity	Class		Entities are taken into consideration at the logical level during phase C; they are represented as persistent entities, used by applications
Persistent Attribute	Attribute		Property of a "Persistent entity"
Identifier Attribute	Attribute		Identifier property of the entity
Persistent Association	Association	$\longrightarrow$	Persistent association between two persistent entities

15.5 BUSINESS ARCHITECTURE (FIGURE 15.6)

OrganizationParticipant is an abstraction that designates roles and actors, as detailed below. Organization Unit and Organization Participant are the main concepts used to model business organization (Figure 15.7).

TOGAF Element	UML Mapping	Icon	Definition
Service Operation	Operation		Operation provided by a business service
Organization Participant	Actor	(Abstract)	Abstraction of TOGAF roles and actors
Actor	Actor	(Abstract)	Actors are broken down into external and internal actors
Event	Signal		Business event (for example, order cancellation, end of marketing season)
External Actor	Actor		Actors who are external to the enterprise but who interact with it (for example, client)
Business Organization Domain	Package		Package that structures the organization (for example, to group processes together)

TOGAF Element	UML Mapping	Icon	Definition
Internal Actor	Actor		Actor who participates in the functioning of the enterprise (for example, the marketing manager)
Communicates	Dependency		Between actors or roles and actors or roles; specifies who communicates with whom within an enterprise
Initiator	Dependency		Between an actor or role and a business process; the origin actor initiates the process
Responsible	Dependency		Between an actor or role and an actor or role or organizational unit; the origin element is responsible
Participates	Dependency		Between actors or roles and functions or business processes; the origin element participates in the process, for example
Organization Unit	Package		Groups the functions and capabilities of the enterprise, which have resources (personnel, material), missions, and a certain degree of autonomy (for example, sales department, administrative department)
Role	Actor	(Abstract)	Usual or expected function of an actor in the context of an activity or business process; a role will always be represented in the form of an internal or external role
Assumes	Dependency		Between an actor and a role; the actor plays the role of destination
Owner	Dependency		Between an actor or a role and a business process; the origin actor is the owner of the process (he or she takes care of monitoring and managing the process)
Use Case	Use Case	Book Trip	Interaction between actors and the system, in the aim of meeting a functional need
Process	Bpmn Behavior		Business process (for example, "Reserve Trip")
External Role	Actor		Role played by a participant who is external to the enterprise
Internal Role	Actor		Role played by a participant who is internal to the enterprise
IO Flow	Dependency		Between data and active elements (for example, between a product and a process (receiver or emitter))
Business Service	Interface		Service provided by the business

Continued

TOGAF Element	UML Mapping	Icon	Definition
Business Operation	Operation		Operation defined at the business level on business entities
Participant Decomposition	Dependency		Between actors or roles; the origin element is made up of the destination elements
Consumes	Dependency		Between a user or an organizational unit and an application component, business interface or operation (for example, a user consumes (uses) an application)
Function	Interface		Produces one of the capabilities of the enterprise (for example, marketing, client contact management)
Service Process Support	Dependency		Between business interfaces, business processes, and functions (for example, a process supports a function)
Product	Signal		Example: Trip, Order
Service Contract	Collaboration		Service contract; the collaboration is used to describe how the contract stakeholders exchange
Business Collaboration	Class		Specific collaboration between business-related elements (actors, entities, services, etc.)
Business Capability	Interface		Capability of an organization or system to provide a given product or service
Function Sequence	Dependency		Sequences between functions
Location	Node		Site of the enterprise including its geographical location
Headquarter Location	Node		Location of the enterprise's headquarters
Part	Dependency		Function decomposition link
Contract Of	Dependency		Between a service and a service contract
Participant Allocation	Dependency		Allocation of an actor to an organizational unit
Localization	Dependency		Between model elements; the source is located in the target (for example, company site)

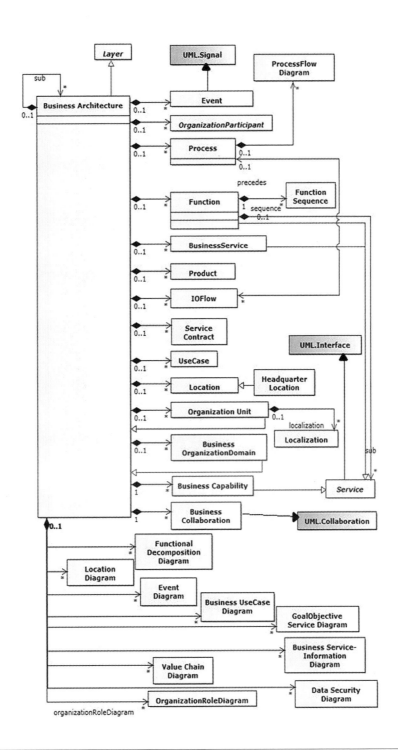

FIGURE 15.6

EAP profile for business architecture. (For color version of this figure, the reader is referred to the online version of this chapter.)

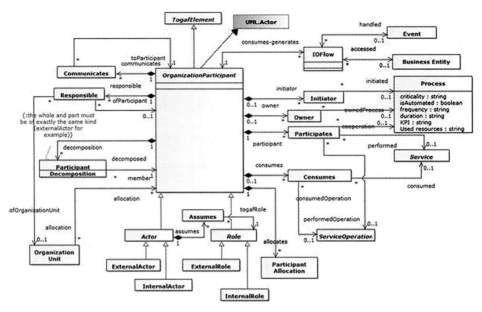

FIGURE 15.7

EAP profile with a focus on the Participant metaclass. (For color version of this figure, the reader is referred to the online version of this chapter.)

15.6 APPLICATION ARCHITECTURE (FIGURE 15.8)

Application Component is a central concept for application architecture. The following view shows this concept in detail (Figure 15.9).

TOGAF Element	UML Mapping	Icon	Definition
Service Access	Port		Point of access to a service required or provided by an application component
Application component	Component		An application component is an autonomous part of the IS, which is configured and deployed. Application components can be physical or logical components
IS Service	Interface		Service provided by the IS
IS Service Operation	Operation		Applies to an IS service
Service Data	Class		Information exchanged between applications, services, or any other information system components
Service Data Fragment	Class		A message can be broken down into several fragments

TOGAF Element	UML Mapping	Icon	Definition
Application Component Attribute	Attribute		Property of an application component
Application Component Operation	Operation		Operation supported by an application component
Application Architecture Domain	Package		Logical regrouping of application architecture elements (components, messages, etc.)
System Application Component	Component		Application system (for example, an IS can be a system)
Provided Service Access	Port		Point of access to service components via services defined at this point
Required Service Access	Port		Required services must be connected to provided services (of other components) that have the same interface
DataBase Application Component	Component		Represents a database or repository
Application	Component		The application is a form of application component that designates applications in the traditional sense of the term (for example, existing application)
Enterprise System	Component		Component representing the enterprise
System Federation	Component		Grouping of application systems/components (for example, grouping of the information systems of several cooperating enterprises)
Entity Application Component	Component		Component that manages a "business entity" (for example, order)
Interaction Application Component	Component		Component that manages interactions with the outside world (for example, GUI, website)
Process Application Component	Component		Component which implements a process
Utility Application Component	Component		Cross-organizationally interesting; often bought off the shelf
Public Application Component	Component		Components dedicated to services that can be accessed from outside the IS (B2B, partner relationships)

Continued

TOGAF Element	UML Mapping	Icon	Definition
Component Realization	Dependency		Realization of a model element by another; the origin element (for example, an application component) implements the target (for example, a process)
Application Collaboration	Collaboration		Description of a specific collaboration between application components

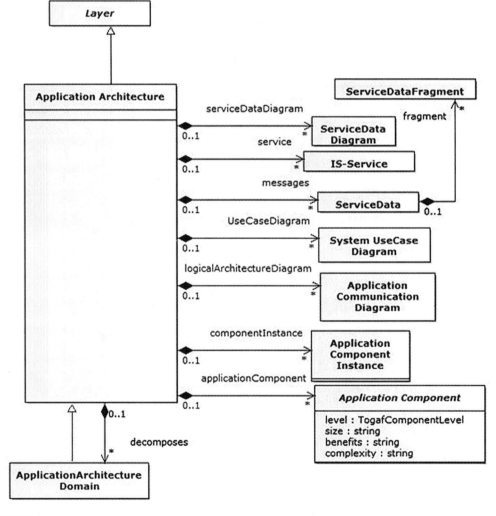

FIGURE 15.8

EAP profile for application architecture. (For color version of this figure, the reader is referred to the online version of this chapter.)

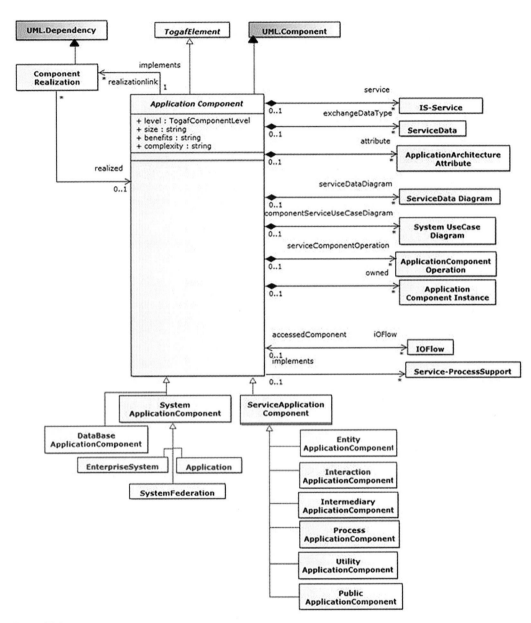

FIGURE 15.9

EAP profile with a focus on the "Application Component" metaclass. (For color version of this figure, the reader is referred to the online version of this chapter.)

15.7　**TECHNOLOGY ARCHITECTURE** (FIGURE 15.10)

Technology architecture deals with the deployment of application components on technology components. A standard set of predefined technology components is provided in order to represent servers, network, workstations, and so on (Figure 15.11).

TOGAF Element	UML Mapping	Icon	Definition
Hardware Technology Component	Node	Abstract element	Hardware element on which application components can be deployed
Technology Architecture Domain	Package		Root of the technology model; package enabling a technology model to be structured
Server	Node		Hardware platform that can be connected to other peripherals and on which application components will be deployed
Work Station	Node		Workstations are linked by network connections to an information system. Application components can also be deployed on workstations
Internet	Node		Internet access node or point
Router	Node		Network router
Switch	Node		Network switch
Network Node	Node		Network node
Connexion	Dependency		Network connection between peripherals or network nodes
Technology Artifact	Artifact		Product resulting from enterprise architecture or IS development work; this can be a file, a technical library, and so on
Application Component Instance	Instance		Occurrences are used to deploy application components; represented under the deployment context (for example, server)
Bus	Node		Communication bus
NetworkLink	Dependency		Network connection

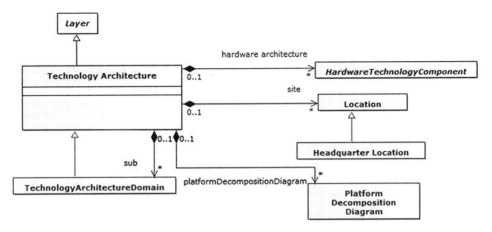

FIGURE 15.10

EAP profile for technology architecture. (For color version of this figure, the reader is referred to the online version of this chapter.)

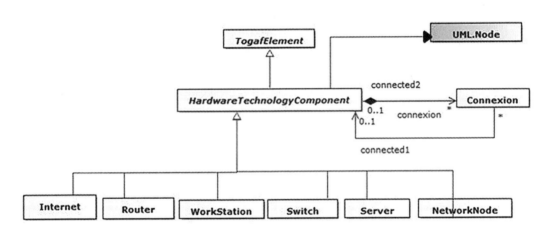

FIGURE 15.11

EAP profile with a focus on the "Hardware Technology Component" metaclass. (For color version of this figure, the reader is referred to the online version of this chapter.)

15.8 FUNDAMENTAL CONCEPTS

The following fundamental concepts were introduced in this chapter:

- Profile: Mechanism that adapts the UML modeling standard to a particular target or purpose.

Glossary

Actor Active agent within the enterprise (a person, a system, or an organization) who participates in the activities of the enterprise. For example, a salesperson who carries out sales operations with clients.

ADM cycle Schema of the sequencing of the phases of the ADM.

Application Operational unit deployed in the information system that handles a set of business functions.

Application architecture Enterprise architecture domain focused on the logical knowledge of applications, their links, and their positioning in the system. By extension, the logical structure of the IS, which can include SOA components, data repositories, or elements to interface with the outside world.

Application component Encapsulation of a set of elementary functionalities of an application, linked to an implementation structure.

Application service set Set made up of the technological components (hardware, software, and processes or programs) used to provide the services necessary to an application.

ArchiMate Modeling language dedicated to enterprise architecture; Open Group standard.

Architecture board Cross-organizational instance of the enterprise responsible for its entire architecture; responsible for controlling architecture, managing the architecture repository, and launching new architecture transformation cycles.

Architecture building block (ABB) Logical description or model of a building block.

Architecture contract Establishes the relationships between the architecture board and all the stakeholders involved in an architecture project; formalizes expectations, constraints, goals to be reached, and appropriate means of measurement.

Architecture development method (ADM) TOGAF method made up of a set of phases dedicated to enterprise architecture work.

Architecture domain Fundamental part of the enterprise architecture; TOGAF defines four architecture domains: Business architecture, data architecture, application architecture, and technology architecture.

Architecture principles Set of stable rules and recommendations concerning the architecture in its entirety.

Architecture repository System that contains and manages all the enterprise information that is useful to enterprise architecture (processes, data, components, deliverables, artifacts, patterns, norms, etc.).

Architecture vision 1. A presentation or overview of the future architecture as it should be. 2. Phase A of the ADM cycle, which explains and presents the future vision of the architecture. 3. A specific deliverable produced by this phase.

Artifact Description of a part of the architecture; generally organized into catalogs (lists of objects), matrices (which include the relationships between objects), and diagrams (graphical representations).

Baseline architecture Architecture (baseline or target) used as a reference; the architecture used as the departure point for an architecture review or redefinition cycle.

BPMN (Business Process Modeling Notation) Language used to model business processes; OMG standard.

Building block A subset or a component of the architecture; technical or functional subset represents a business, IT, or architecture element and can (potentially) be reused and combined with other subsets to form the proposed solution.

Business architecture Architecture domain dedicated to business vision, notably business processes, actors, goals, strategy, functions, and organization units.

Business event Event that can occur during enterprise functioning and that requires management action on the part of the enterprise.

Business function or functionality Produces one of the enterprise's capabilities (e.g., marketing, client contact management, telemarketing).

Business process or process Correlated set of activities that produces tangible added value from an initial request (the trigger event).

Business scenario Prototype or model of a subset of the system, made up of a business process and a set of software components or applications, and of all the technical and organizational elements necessary to attain the desired result; used to validate options and to verify the feasibility of a solution.

Business service Supports the business capabilities explicitly managed by an organization.

Capability Designates the aptitude of an organization or a system to provide a given product or service; materialized by a series of elements (business, organizational, technical) that contribute to the realization of these products or services to the required level of quality.

Catalog Structured list made up of comparable objects, used as a reference.

Common systems Represent highly reusable systems dedicated to very cross-organizational services, such as security, networks, or communication; the III-RM included in TOGAF is an example of a common system.

Concerns Main concerns that are of critical importance for the stakeholders in a system, used to determine the acceptability of the system; can be linked to any aspect of system functioning, development, or use, including considerations such as reliability, security, distribution, and upgradability.

Constraint Condition or rule that an enterprise must respect (e.g., legal constraint).

Data architecture Enterprise architecture domain that includes logical and physical views of data, standards, and data structures used; it also includes the definition of the physical bases of the information system, expected performances, and the geographical distribution of data.

Data entity Encapsulation of data that is recognized by a business domain expert as being an "object." Logical data entities can be associated with applications, storage means, and services.

Deliverable Provided by the architecture and have to be formally reviewed and accepted by stakeholders.

Diagram Graphical view representing a part of a model; it is an artifact.

Driver Internal or external condition that motivates an organizations goals (e.g., regulation modification, new competition).

Enterprise 1. Typically the highest level of description of an organization that covers all missions and functions; often split into several organizations. 2. Any set of organizations that share a set of goals.

Enterprise architecture 1. A formal description, or a detailed plan used as a tool in the implementation of a system. 2. The structure of the system into components, accompanied by the intercomponent relationships, principles, and guides that govern their design and their evolution.

Enterprise architecture framework Coherent set of methods, practices, models, and guides dedicated to enterprise architecture (e.g., TOGAF).

Foundation architecture Generic architecture foundations, in which we find specifications, high-level architecture patterns that apply to all types of enterprises (e.g., TOGAF's TRM (*Technical Reference Model*)).

Gap Observation of the difference between two states; used in the context of "gap analysis," where the difference between "what exists" and "what is aimed for" is identified.

Goal High-level declaration of the intent or direction of an organization; translated into objectives.

Governance Set of measurement, management, and steering processes for a business domain or IS that provides the expected level of result.

Information Any communication on or representation of facts or data in all forms (textual, graphical, audiovisual, digital).

Information domain Logical grouping of information by business domain or according to other criteria (classification, security level, etc.).

Information system (IS) System that supports enterprise activities.

Interface Interconnection and interrelation between, for example, people, systems, devices, applications, and so on.

Interoperability Capability of sharing information and services.

Key performance indicator (KPI) Quantitative and measurable statement used to judge whether or not a goal has been reached; linked to a measurement and to the means of evaluation.

Landscape Architectural representation of components deployed in an operational environment of the enterprise at a given time (e.g., application mapping of the IS).

Logical application component Encapsulation of functionalities of an application that are independent of any particular implementation.

Logical data component Encapsulation of data relative to a business entity.

Logical technology component Logical description of an infrastructure component, which can correspond to a family of similar physical components.

Matrix Representation format that shows the relationship between two (or more) architecture elements in the form of a table.

Message Flow of information exchanged between applications, services, or any information system components.

Metamodel Model that describes how and with what the architecture will be described in a structural way (model of the model).

Method Defined and repetitive approach used to broach particular types of problems.

Model Representation of a subject of interest; provides an abstract representation of the object for a given purpose. In the context of enterprise architecture, the object is all or a part of the enterprise, and the purpose provides the capability of building ''views'' that correspond to stakeholder concerns.

Objective Step in time used to demonstrate the progress made toward reaching a goal (e.g., "increase capability usage by 30% by the end of 2014 in order to support the expected increase in market share").

Organization or organization unit Autonomous resource unit including a line of managers, with goals, objectives, and measurements; can also include external components and/or partner organizations.

Phase Work unit that structures an ADM cycle, made up of a set of stages and practices, input and output. TOGAF defines eight sequential phases (from A to H) and two cross-organizational phases: the preliminary phase and the requirements management phase.

Physical application component Application, application module, application service, or any other "deployable" component linked to a functionality.

Physical data component Physical location grouping storage or deployment of data.

Physical technology component Specific technology infrastructure component (e.g., a particular version of an "off-the-shelf" product or a specific brand and version of a server).

Portfolio Complete set of elements of systems that exists within the organization (e.g., application portfolio, project portfolio).

Profile Defines extensions to a reference metamodel, such as the one frequently encountered when using the UML standard. The models presented in this book are mainly built using a UML profile dedicated to TOGAF and named "EAP (*Enterprise Architecture Profile*)." The TOGAF support in this book is defined by a profile.

Program Coordinated set of change projects that provide business benefits to the organization.

Project Unitary change project that provides a business benefit to the enterprise.

Reference library classification plan "Reference library" part of the architecture repository.

Requirement Statement of a business need that must be managed by one or several architecture elements or by a given work package.

Roadmap High-level action plan for change that will involve several facets of the enterprise (business, organization, technical).

Role Usual or expected functionality of an actor in the context of an activity or a business process; an actor can have one or several roles.

Service Logical representation of a repeatable activity that provides a specified result. A service is auto-contained, and can be made up of other services; presents a usage interface for consumers, who can only use it through this interface.

Service-level agreement (SLA) Usage contract between a consumer and a service provider.

Service-oriented architecture (SOA) Style of architecture based on the concept of service, designed to simplify interactions between architecture blocks while providing the system with significant flexibility.

SMART Acronym for specific, measurable, attainable, realistic, and time-bound, to ensure that objectives are defined in an achievable and verifiable way.

Solution building block (SBB) Physical solution that may become an architecture building block (ABB) (e.g., "off-the-shelf" software, which is a component of the architectural view of the buyer).

Stakeholder Individual, team, or organization that has an interest in or is affected by the result of architectural change.

Standards information base (SIB) Provides a database of standards that can be used in the context of architecture specific to an organization; part of the TOGAF architecture repository.

State or capability increment Result of a change (business and architectural) that provides a performance evolution with regard to a particular capability.

Target architecture Description of the future state of the architecture whose aim is to reach the enterprise's goals.

Technology architecture Enterprise architecture domain; software and hardware capabilities required for the deployment of application architecture.

Traceability Capability of linking artifacts produced by enterprise architecture or realization activities to other artifacts from which they originate or to which they refer.

Transition architecture Transitional architecture between existing architecture and target architecture.

UML (Unified Modeling Language) Standard (OMG) used to model software systems or applications.

View Representation of a part of the architecture from a particular point of view.

Viewpoint Designates the most appropriate perspective for an actor or family of actors; materialized through a certain number of views on the architecture, in the form of diagrams, documents, or other types of representation. A view is "what we see"; a viewpoint is "where we look from" (e.g., business viewpoint, IT viewpoint, steering viewpoint).

Work package Set of tasks identified in order to reach one or several goals for business lines. A work package can be part of a project or a program.

Bibliography

Paul Allen, Realizing eBusiness with Components. 2000; Addison-Wesley.

Bernhard Borges, Kerrie Holley, and Ali Arsanjani. Service Oriented Architecture, IBM, September 15, 2004, SearchWebServices.com.

Yves Casaud, Urbanisation, SOA et BPM—Le point de vue du DSI. 2008; Dunod.

Henri Chelli, Urbaniser l'entreprise et son système d'information. 2003; Vuibert.

Henk De Man, Case Management: A Review of Modeling Approaches. 2009; BPTrends.

Peter Herzum, Oliver Sims, Business Component Factory. 2000; Wiley Computer Publishing.

ITIL. ITIL® Glossary and Abbreviations, www.itil-officialsite.com/InternationalActivities/ITILGlossaries.aspx.

Dirk Krafzig, Karl Banke, and Dirk Slama. Enterprise SOA, The Coad Series, 2005.

Thomas Mattern, Dan Woods, Enterprise SOA: Designing IT for Business Innovation. 2006; O'Reilly.

James McGovern, Oliver Sims, Ashish Jain, Mark Little, Enterprise Service Oriented Architectures: Concepts, Challenges, Recommendations. 2010; Springer.

Joe McKendrick, Seven Areas of Opportunity Around SOA, Circa. 2007; www.thegreylines.net/2006_12_01_archive.html.

Daniel Minoli, Enterprise Architecture A to Z. 2008; Auerbach Publications.

Moin Moinuddin, An Overview of Service-Oriented Architecture in Retail. 2007; Microsoft.

O'Reilly Media, SOA in Practice, The Art of Distributed System Design. 2007; O'Reilly Media.

Chun Ouyang, Wip M.P. van der Aalst, Marlon Dumas, H.M. Arthur, Translating BPMN to BPEL. 2006; http://eprints.qut.edu.au.

Gilbert Raymond. SOA: Architecture Logigue: Principes, structures et bonnes pratiques, Softeam 2007, 2011, www.softeam.fr.

Roger Sessions, A Comparison of the Top Four Enterprise Architecture Methodologies. 2007; ObjectWatch, Inc.

Bruce Silver, BPMN Method and Style: A Levels-Based Methodology for BPM Process Modeling and Improvement Using BPMN 2.0. 2009; Cody-Cassidy Press.

Daniel Simon, Governance of Enterprise Transformation and the Different Faces of Enterprise Architecture Management. 2011; Journal of Enterprise Architecturenot.

The Open Group, SOA Reference Architecture. 2009a; The Open Group.

The Open Group, TOGAF, Pocket Guide. 2009b; The Open Group.

The Open Group, TOGAF Version 9. 2009c; Van Haren.

The Open Group, SOA Reference Architecture. 2009d; www.opengroup.org/projects/soa-ref-arch.

The Open Group, TOGAF Version 9.1. 2011; Van Haren.

Tom van Sante and Jeroen Ermers. TOGAF9 and ITIL V3, Two Frameworks Whitepaper, September 2009.

Mathias Weske, Business Process Management, Concepts, Languages, Architectures. 2007; Springer.

Index

Note: Page numbers followed by *f* indicate figures and *t* indicate tables.